Armies in Revolution

JOHN ELLIS

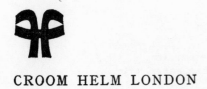

CROOM HELM LONDON

FIRST PUBLISHED 1973
© 1973 BY JOHN ELLIS

CROOM HELM LTD
2–10 ST JOHN'S ROAD, LONDON. SWII

ISBN 0–85664–025–5

PRINTED AND BOUND IN GREAT BRITAIN
BY RICHARD CLAY (THE CHAUCER PRESS) LTD
BUNGAY SUFFOLK

Contents

Acknowledgements

I am above all grateful to Mr Michael Elliott-Bateman and the Department of Military Studies at the University of Manchester for providing an environment in which to pursue this study. Thanks are also due to the Social Science Research Council for providing financial backing during the years 1969–71. Finally I should like to acknowledge the roles of Harry Gilbert whose rigorous criticisms were of the greatest assistance, and of my publisher David Croom whose suggestions have helped to ensure that the narrative retained some degree of fluency.

TO MY MOTHER

Chapter 1   Introduction

This is a study of revolutionary war. The chapters are about different revolutions but the book presents two problems common to them all: how military policy affected the development of a particular revolution and how the social roots of that revolution affected methods of war and military organisation.

Why, for example, should the Chinese Communists have adopted the guerrilla mode of warfare whilst the American colonists or the Bolsheviks in Russia devoted all their efforts to the creation of regular forces? What is the significance of the different social origins of various revolutionary armies: the bourgeois Parisian National Guard of 1789, the proletarian and petty-bourgeois Communard forces, or the rurally based Red Armies of the Russian and Chinese Revolutions? What is the role of a political party such as the Jacobins or the Bolsheviks in the creation of a revolutionary army? What degree of operational autonomy can be allowed to the command personnel of such armies and what is the importance of such agents of the central political authority as the Jacobin *représentants-en-mission* or the Russian and Chinese commissars? Is their central role of an ideological or an administrative nature and to what extent did the chaplains of the New Model Army perform an analogous function? Can an existing regular army be truly revolutionised as was attempted in Prussia or must it be created from scratch as in America and China? Or is the French attempt to amalgamate regulars and revolutionaries the most viable solution? In China the revolutionaries were fighting to seize power whilst in the France of the First Republic and Russia they were fighting to hold on to power. What is the significance of such a distinction for the organisation and tactics of the revolutionary army? And to what extent should the Communards have attempted to seize power in the country rather than trying to hold on to power in the city? How important is it that the armies' organisation and modes of combat reflect the concrete cultural and political preoccupations of the rank-and-file? How far can revolutionary notions of liberty and equality be equated with the maintenance of adequate military discipline? Why in some cases, such as the English Civil War, does revolutionary zeal supplement military discipline whilst in others, the Commune for example, it seems quite inimical to it?

In answering such questions this book will arrive at a comprehensive, historically based definition of what constitutes revolutionary war. This historical perspective is of vital importance. Contrary to the impression given by certain writers and commentators revolutionary warfare does not begin and end with Mao Tse-tung, nor even with guerrilla warfare as a whole. Although, in certain respects, the Chinese Revolution will be put forward as a paradigm, it will be clear by the time that that chapter is reached that Mao was far from being the first to tackle these particular problems, and that others had sometimes solved them, perhaps in different ways, in earlier times. The Maoist political line was a particular response to a particular problem and not a totally innovatory aspect of military practice and theory. It is time that Mao Tse-tung was put in historical context. At present revolutionary warfare is increasingly regarded as a synonym for the Chinese–Vietnamese mode of guerrilla–mobile war. Revolutionaries and counter-revolutionaries alike are in danger of turning guidelines that were specific to a certain situation into dogmas and blindly trying to apply them to circumstances to which they are simply not appropriate. Certainly the Chinese Revolution was of immense significance and that is why it ends this book. But it must not be inferred that Mao is regarded as having said the last word on the subject. The fate of the Hukbalahaps in the Philippines, the Malayan Communists, the Indian guerrillas in Telingana, the Indonesian Communists, Guevara in Bolivia should at least teach us not to think in terms of a unitary 'third world' in which the same set of tactics is always applicable. All revolutions are unique but whatever general rules can be discerned must come from a study of the widest range of historical experience.

As must be clear from the list of questions above this book is primarily concerned with the social and political factors that influence military affairs. Each chapter will concentrate upon the most important social and political factors of the revolution with which it deals in an attempt to show how the actual dynamic of mass revolutionary unrest, in the various situations, affected the military policies of the revolutionary groups. But it would be misleading to claim that these factors alone defined the options open to the revolutionaries. To a greater or lesser extent purely physical or material constraints also limited those options, and it would be best at this stage to clear these aside so as to gain a clearer picture of what actual areas of activity are affected by larger social and political considerations. The book as a whole is trying to take military studies beyond questions of mere technique and static models of the 'rules of war', but it would be foolish to overstate the case and deny that, in certain cases, geographical and material immutables are bound to influence the formulation of military policy.

Geographical factors, for example, are of considerable importance. The larger a country is the more difficult will it be for a counter-revolutionary force to pursue and pin down a group of insurgents. Its communications will become overstretched, it will have to distribute large numbers of men in a piecemeal fashion to guard all places of importance, and it will be more vulnerable itself to a surprise attack by the enemy. Such considerations are basic assumptions of Maoist guerrilla warfare, but they also hold true for more regularised struggles. The sheer vastness of America, even in the days of the thirteen colonies, was one of the main reasons for the British defeat. Even when the Continentals were overcome in open battle, which was more often than not, they were able to retreat beyond the reach of the cumbersome British columns and slowly regroup. In the meantime the British had to disperse their forces to guard against attack from a wide variety of directions. The lightning forays at Trenton and Princeton are perfect examples of British helplessness in the face of a swift, concentrated American assault; whilst Greene's retreat through the Carolinas and Virginia demonstrates how the British were doomed in the face of American willingness to use the space at their disposal to keep their armies intact rather than attempt to decide the issue in a single positional engagement.

Terrain is clearly also of importance in this respect. It was of some limited significance in the American War of Independence. British accounts constantly bemoaned the American habit of lodging their infantrymen behind trees in wooded areas where they could fire upon the British with impunity. Similarly Marion's guerrilla band made its base in the swampy regions of South Carolina where they were almost immune from British or Loyalist attack. Terrain was also a vital component of the Maoist concept of the 'big country'. The sheer vastness of China was of the greatest significance but the task of the counter-insurgency forces, be they Nationalist or Japanese, was made even more difficult by the impenetrability of the Communist base areas, almost always in mountainous regions. Distance is significant in terms of the amount of time it takes to cover it. Thus inhospitable terrain can be just as important a barrier as a no-man's-land of many thousand square miles. Indeed, in certain cases it can be much more of a barrier. Castro's guerrillas were quite safe in the Sierra Maestra area of Cuba, whilst a guerrilla force in Antarctica, for example, would be almost help-less before an enemy equipped with jets, helicopters, or even reliable tracked vehicles.

Thus the existence of a large country, defined in terms of time, is a necessary condition for the waging of a guerrilla rather than a regular war. But even so it does not logically follow that the existence of these conditions will demand a resort to the guerrilla mode. The chapters on the Russian and Chinese Revolutions will show that general social and political considerations are at least of equal importance in deciding whether it is expedient for the revolutionary group to adopt a guerrilla or a regular strategy. Here one is only trying to explain some of the technical parameters within which such a choice is made. Another of these concerns the relative levels of technological expertise. In the American War of Independence, for example, one of the factors that made it possible, though not necessary, for the Americans to adopt the regular form of military organisation that they did, and to be at least able to face up to the British in open battle, even after countless defeats and Pyrrhic victories, was the low level of technological effort required. In the late eighteenth century the essentials of the most advanced type of warfare were the sword, the horse, the musket and the cannon. The nature of the American theatre of operations greatly reduced the importance of the latter. Thus, given that Washington had decided that his army must be made up of regular formations, it was possible, even in view of the parlous financial state of the Continental Congress, to equip such an army; horses, swords and muskets, not to mention rifles, were available in some quantity irrespective of the existence of a formal military organisation. All that was necessary was the manufacture of uniforms, the establishment of a command structure and the inculcation of a suitable spirit of instant obedience. Even when more muskets were needed it required no great technological or organisational breakthrough to supply at least a minimum quantity with the aid of existing gunsmiths.

Much the same is true of the Parliamentary Armies in the English Civil War. The basics of warfare at that time were the horse, the sword, the pike and, to a lesser extent, the arquebus. Because the level of technology was not high the manufacture of such equipment was in the hands of ordinary craftsmen rather than specialised, government supervised production units. Such craftsmen were spread about the country and when the lines of civil war were drawn each side had access to adequate amounts of military material. Thus each side could meet on equal terms in pitched battle and decide the war relatively quickly. Eventually superior Parliamentary organisation and *élan* proved decisive and the reasons for this will be examined in the next chapter. All that is at issue here is why Puritan militancy should have been able to adopt a military posture so quickly.

To a large extent the technological variable alters over time rather than from place to place. Thus throughout history technology has become more and more sophisticated. The more sophisticated it has become the more it has been the preserve of a small group of specialists and the more expensive it has become to produce the various components of an advanced technology. All this has meant that governments have increasingly gained the monopoly of certain aspects of such a technology, particularly the military. Almost by definition a revolutionary group does not have access to either the expertise or the financial reserves to give themselves technological parity in the military field. And the more advanced technology becomes the less likely it is that the revolutionaries will be able to build up a comparable production base of their own. Until they have actually seized power they can only attain parity with the incumbent forces by seizing their weapons and equipment. This is inevitably a very slow process, dependent in the early stages upon the use of ambushes and lightning attacks, and the constant avoidance of undue exposure to the enemy's superior fire-power. The technological differential demands that the revolutionaries adopt protracted, piecemeal, i.e. guerrilla warfare. Clearly this was an important factor in explaining the development of the Maoist theory of guerrilla warfare, particularly in the face of Japanese superiority. And it is a factor that will be of increasing importance in revolutionary struggles of the future.

Nor is the technological factor only of importance in terms of material. It is also of significance as regards the level of expertise. The more sophisticated the actual equipment of an army becomes the more training is required for those who will actually use and co-ordinate it. Even Washington was obliged to use an imported specialist, von Steuben, to teach his Continentals the intricacies of close-order movement. During the Paris Commune it seems likely that one reason why so few of the cannon available to the insurgents were actually used was that few people knew how to load and fire them, or more importantly how to establish the logistical machinery to keep them all in effective action. During the Chinese Civil War yet another reason for the resort to protracted guerrilla warfare was the necessity slowly to train unit commanders at all levels in the actual heat of battle. Even with modern equipment to hand one still needs men able to establish co-ordinated fire-fields and make tactical sense of the deafening chaos of modern combat.

But the technological factor cuts both ways. It can help to explain why certain revolutionary groups might be forced to adopt a protracted mode of armed struggle, but it can also be a factor in helping to explain the success of other groups on the field of open battle. The key distinction here is that between those revolutionary groups fighting to seize power and those fighting to hold on to it in the face of armed counter-revolution. In the former case technology and expertise are likely to be the monopoly of the incumbent regime. But in the latter case, because the revolutionaries have gained control of at least some of the organs of government, they can turn such a monopoly to their own advantage. This will be true in terms of both material and know-how. Thus in the French Revolution the centralised Jacobin state was able to make prodigious efforts in the logistical field. Workers were drafted in, existing armouries were expanded and completely new ones established. During the *ancien régime* the production of muskets had never exceeded one hundred and fifty per day, but by the end of the Year II this figure had reached at least seven hundred. Similar considerations held true in the field of army organisation. Though the bulk of the original noble officer-corps had disappeared by the time of the Jacobin dictatorship, many lower-ranking officers, non-commissioned officers and regular privates remained. Thus the Jacobins were able to build their new formations around a nucleus of experienced regulars who were later officially used to bolster the morale of the new recruits through joint *embrigadement*. The relevance of the Prussian example in this respect is obvious; its particular chapter will be concerned with the social and political weaknesses of the attempt by an incumbent, basically conservative regime to politicise its armed forces. Nevertheless, such an attempt obviously had decided military advantages. The debacle of 1806 had weeded out most of the incompetents of the old army and left a solid base of regulars, particularly the officer-corps, upon which to build a new army. Similarly the Prussian reformers had the enormous advantage of access to the stockpiles and production units of a centralised state that had always made the supplying of its armies a high priority.

The Russian example is also highly significant here. Leaving aside for the moment the reasons for the Bolsheviks' decision to concentrate upon regular rather than guerrilla warfare, it is certainly true that one reason why they were able to adopt such a policy was the very fact that they had taken over state power. Certainly the First World War had occasioned the almost complete collapse of the Tsarist armies. Nevertheless the Communists now had access to the factories that produced the munitions that would be necessary for a new army, as well as such equipment as they were able to salvage from the deserters from the front. Throughout the Civil War war production was a desperately hand-to-mouth business, but it was even so just feasible to think in terms of supplying a large, regular army. More importantly still, it was also possible to think of giving that army an experienced officer-corps. For even after Brest-Litovsk the Tsarist officer-corps still existed, whether in or out of uniform. Because the Bolsheviks were the *de facto* government many of these officers felt it their patriotic duty to rally to the defence of the Soviet regime. Even those who were not so inclined were hauled into the Soviet military machine. Bolshevik state power meant the proliferation of Red terror and the effective threat of reprisals against the families of recalcitrant officers. Trotsky was able from the beginning to think in terms of a regular army because he was always able to supply that army with its nucleus of experienced officers or 'military specialists'.

Clearly then technical factors are of importance in explaining the successes and failures of revolutionary armies. This book is in no way attempting to underestimate that importance. But in periods of revolutionary unrest above all, military affairs are also subject to the general constraints of the social and political configurations of society at large. Much conventional military history seems to have ignored this rather basic point. For this reason there will be little mention in the individual chapters of purely technical considerations. Undue emphasis upon such factors will always underestimate the human element, the very bedrock of history and the molten lava of revolution. Each of the following case-studies throws up questions that are simply not amenable to a purely technical explanation. Given technological parity in the English Civil War why then should the Parliamentary victory have been so decisive? Given Washington was able to create a regular army why should he have been so insistent upon such a mode of organisation? What happened in France during the First Republic such that the revolutionary zeal of the first volunteers degenerated into the militaristic efficiency of the Imperial soldiery? Why was the Prussian reform movement a military success yet a political disaster? How is one to explain Parisian incompetence in 1871 in the face of the shattered armies of the French state? In Russia technical factors help to explain why the Bolsheviks were able to establish a regular military structure, but why should they be so keen to do this and so emphatic in their denunciations of the guerrilla mode? And if Mao Tse-tung were driven for technical reasons to adopt guerrilla tactics, what were the social and political reasons for his actual success in building up such large, efficient and zealous peasant armies? These questions are basic to each of the case-studies and to answer them requires that one examine those most fundamental human aspirations that drive men to revolution in the first place.

Chapter 2   The English Civil War 1642–9

CHRONOLOGY

1642

22 Aug   The outbreak of the Civil War.

23 Oct   The Battle of Edgehill. A Royalist victory.

1643

30 June   The Battle of Adwalton Moor. A Royalist victory.

12 Aug   The passing of a Parliamentary ordinance permitting county committees to raise regiments by impressment.

10 Sept   The Battle of Newbury. A Parliamentary victory.

1644

18 Jan   The Scottish Army enters England on the side of Parliament.

Feb   The Committee of Both Kingdoms is set up to co-ordinate the activities of the Scottish and Parliamentary Armies.

2 July   The Battle of Marston Moor. A Parliamentary victory.

15 Nov   The second Battle of Newbury. A Royalist victory.

19 Dec   The Self-Denying Ordinance is adopted by the Commons.

1645

11 Jan   The plan for the setting up of the New Model Army is adopted by the Commons. Fairfax is made the Commander-in-Chief.

30 April   The organisation of the New Model Army is completed.

14 June   The Battle of Naseby. A Parliamentary victory.

10 July   The Battle of Langport. A Parliamentary victory.

1646

19 Aug   Royalist resistance is finally crushed with the surrender of Raglan Castle.

1647

18 Feb   Parliament resolves to disband the Army without any provision for the payment of arrears of pay.

March   The cavalry regiments elect Agitators. The Infantry soon follow suit.

21 March   A meeting of the army officers and Parliament's representatives at Saffron Walden. The officers present a petition to Parliament.

27 April   The officers present *The Vindication of the Officers* to Parliament in which they uphold their right of petition.

28 April   Eight cavalry regiments draw up the *Apologie* which is presented to Fairfax. This document includes certain political demands.

30 April   The *Apologie* is presented to the Commons. The House decides to vote money for a partial settlement of arrears.

17 May   A meeting of soldiers and officers at Saffron Walden. The sixteen Agitators make a declaration of rank-and-file solidarity.

28 May   The Commons orders Fairfax to disband the infantry by 1 June.

29 May   Fairfax convenes a Council of War at Bury. The soldiers and officers demand an immediate rendezvous of the whole Army.

4–5 June   An Army rendezvous at Newmarket. The officers and soldiers resolve not to disband until their grievances are settled. A General Council of the Army is created, including both officers and Agitators.

4 June   The King is seized by Cornet Joyce at Holdenby.

5 June   The Commons order the infantry to be paid in full on their disbanding.

16 June   The Army issues the names of eleven members of Parliament whom they wish to be purged from the Commons.

26 June   The Commons asks the eleven members to absent themselves.

27 June   In a meeting at Uxbridge the officers issue a conciliatory declaration pledging their confidence in Parliament's ability to resolve the issues.

16 July   The Agitators urge the army leaders to march on London. Cromwell and Ireton urge moderation.

26 July   The appearance of Lilburne's *Jonah's Cry* in which he shows himself extremely suspicious of Cromwell's motives.

1 Aug   The appearance of the *Heads of the Proposals* drawn up by a committee of twelve officers and twelve Agitators.

July   Fifty-seven Commons members, intimidated by the London mob and the Presbyterian MPs, put themselves under Army protection.

6 Aug   The Army enters London and expels the Presbyterian members from Parliament.

18 Aug   In the face of continued Parliamentary intransigence the General Council of the Army meets at Kingston and draws up a *Remonstrance*.

22 Sept   In the Commons Cromwell and Ireton still favour further negotiations with the King.

Sept/Oct   Five cavalry regiments elect new Agitators who assist in the drawing up of *The Case of the Army Truly Stated* and *An Agreement of the People*.

28 Oct   At Putney the General Council debates the *Agreement* and *The Case* with the new Agitators.

8 Nov   Cromwell proposes and carries a motion that the General Council be temporarily suspended and the Agitators sent back to their regiments.

11 Nov   Fairfax and the General Council draw up an alternative manifesto which includes a pledge of loyalty to himself.

15 Nov   In a partial rendezvous of the Army at Corkbush Field, Ware, two regiments openly defy Fairfax and Cromwell. Order is restored after the execution of a leading mutineer.

7 Dec   The General Council meets at Windsor and presents a moderate, non-political petition to Parliament.

1648

8 Jan   The General Council of the Army votes itself out of existence.

24 April   Soldiers of several regiments meet at St Albans to discuss ways of soliciting support for a new radical Army manifesto. The leaders are arrested by certain officers.

29 April   A meeting of the army officers at Windsor to examine their position. They resolve to bring the King to trial.

1 May   The outbreak of the Second Civil War.

15 June   Parliament votes to allow the eleven members excluded by the Army to return to their seats.

17 Aug   The Scots, who are now fighting with the King, are defeated at Preston.

4 Oct   Cromwell enters Edinburgh and the war is effectively ended.

Oct   A series of regimental petitions to Fairfax demanding that those responsible for the war be brought to justice.

8 Nov   A meeting is held between Leveller representatives and Army officers at Whitehall, and an eight-man committee is formed to draw up a new *Agreement of the People*.

16 Nov   The appearance of Ireton's *Army Remonstrance*.

1 Dec   The Army enters the City of London.

6 Dec   Pride's Purge.

10 Dec   The draft of the new *Agreement* is completed.

11 Dec   Ireton submits it to the Army Council of War for their comments.

1649

20 Jan   The *Agreement* is presented to the Rump Parliament where it is quietly forgotten.

27 Jan   Charles Stuart's death-warrant is signed.

14 Feb   An upsurge of Leveller agitation for the election of new Agitators and a new General Council.

22 Feb   The Council of War imposes restrictions upon the Army's right of petition.

26 Feb   The appearance of the first part of the Leveller pamphlet *England's New Chains Discovered*.

1 March   The soldiers protest against the restrictions on petitioning.

25 April   The Levellers appeal again for the election of new Agitators and a new General Council.

2 May   Mutiny breaks out in two regiments.

14 May   About twelve thousand mutineers from various regiments assemble at Burford where they are routed by Cromwell's forces. The ring-leader is executed.

For English history the English Civil War represents the death throes of a certain way of perceiving the world. When war broke out in 1642 men on both sides still defined the struggle in essentially religious terms. Their allegiances and aspirations stemmed from the apocalyptic expectations that had dominated European thought for almost a century and a half. Human society was held to be perfectible if men were willing to solicit divine aid. Moreover it was held that that aid would eventually be forthcoming and the Kingdom of Heaven would be set up on earth. Consequently signs of social conflict and crisis were adduced as evidence of the imminence of such a Godly reign. Of course man had to play his part. It was up to him physically to cast down the walls of Babylon. But once this was done a perfect form of human society would somehow emerge spontaneously.

For many of those on the Parliamentarian side the outbreak of the Civil War was seen as just such an assault on Babylon and the Antichrist within. On the face of it the assault was successful. Pretentions to royal absolutism were beaten down, and eventually the King himself was executed. But the divine Kingdom on Earth failed to materialise of its own accord. Gradually men realised that it would be for them, mere mortals, to conceive and build the social and political environment they desired. The very success of the Puritans in the Civil War brought home to them the inadequacies of their utopian conceptions. They were forced to recognise that the human role in revolution was not merely destructive. Reconstruction too, even within the Temple, was a human task. Thus throughout the Civil War and its immediate aftermath the old faith in the apocalyptic transformation of society gave way to new criteria of rationality and pragmatism by which men themselves sought to shape their own destiny. By 1660 the millenarianism that had provided the ideological underpinnings of the initial resort to arms had become a 'harmless hobby for cranky country parsons'.[1]

This transition was reflected in the history of the Parliamentary armies. But what is important to note at this stage is that both in its apocalyptic and more secular periods that army represented a quite new form of organisation. If the Puritan

Revolution is a crucial watershed in English history, it is also of the greatest significance for military and revolutionary history in general. Between the years 1642 and 1649 the problem was first faced of reconciling the demands of military effectiveness and political revolution. In the English Civil War men had their first prolonged experience of the difficulties inherent in the militarisation of political opposition, and the politicisation of a military machine. The lessons to be drawn from this experience have been a constant theme of subsequent revolutionary history.

THE PRECONDITIONS FOR MILITARY REVOLUTION

The Puritans embarked upon their struggle against royal power in the firm assurance that their actions had a divine sanction. Thus the creation of the armies and many of their subsequent activities are only to be understood in the light of some understanding of religious attitudes at that time. Puritan militarism was interchangeable with widespread notions of religious militancy, and as such engaged with the most basic fears and aspirations of the people at large. Thus it is not so much the religious nature of the struggle that is our essential theme as the extent to which the armies were based upon a genuine popular mobilisation.

The Millenarian Vision

On 1 August 1650 the English Army entered Scotland to suppress the Scots who had joined forces with Charles to overthrow the radicals within the Commons and the Army. When the expedition began the English issued a Declaration justifying their action. This Declaration is a perfect statement of the millenarian expectations that underlay the whole of the Puritan assault on the monarchy. As such it is worth quoting at some length:

> Our souls mourned, and understanding by the manifold gracious promises in the word of God, that a time of deliverance was to be expected to the Church of Christ, and destruction and ruin to Babylon, our hearts together with all the true godly in England, were exceedingly stirred up to pray to the Lord . . . that he would arise to destroy Anti-

Christ, and to save his people . . . Whereupon, after . . .
[the King's] own hard heart had hindered him from yielding
to any overtures that were made to him by Parliament . . .
and a second war . . . being, by the unspeakable power and
mighty goodness of God, waded through, and a second
testimony given from heaven to justify the proceedings of
his poor servants against that bloody Anti-Christian brood,
though with the loss of many precious Saints—we were then
powerfully convinced that the Lord's purpose was to deal
with the late King as a man of blood. And being persuaded
in our conscience that he and his monarchy was one of the
ten horns of the Beast . . . and being witnesses to so much
of the blood of the Saints that he had shed in supporting
the Beast . . . we were extraordinarily carried forth to
desire justice upon the King.[2]

Here is the whole essence of Puritan apocalyptic thought. To
them the world was in a constant state of crisis, as individuals,
and even whole nations, grappled with their overwhelming
sense of sin. This sense of sin represented the spiritual wounds
received in the never-ending battle with the Beast, a battle that
dictated the very nature of human existence and that was
continually being fought at the personal, the national and the
international level. In their own eyes, however, the Puritans
had one important advantage in this struggle. Eventually it
would be resolved and a victor would emerge, and it was
ordained who that victor would be. In numerous references the
Bible foretold that the Beast would be overthrown and Babylon
laid waste. Then men might fully integrate themselves with the
divine purpose and create a true Kingdom of Heaven on Earth.
In the preceding years the exact details of this divine triumph
had been gradually modified: at one point it had been a Godly
Prince who was to carry the Lord's banner, later the assembly of
Godly Bishops and finally a divinely elected group of religious
activists, the Saints.[3] The important point is that, whatever the
precise nature of the leadership, there existed this vision of the
possibility of a perfect world as the ultimate reward for years of
struggle. By basing their appeal on such a view of the world the
Parliamentarians gave their cause an ideological vigour and

popular appeal that was almost without precedent in military history up to that date.

There were of course some cautious Presbyterians who were reluctant to base their essentially parliamentary opposition upon such an all-embracing world view. For who could say but that the destruction of Babylon might not also involve a few of their own fixtures and fittings? Nevertheless, even at the very beginning of the Civil War, there were those who were willing to see the struggle in these millenarian terms. As the war progressed the extent of royal obduracy, and the clear need for the re-vitalisation of the Parliamentary Armies' morale, persuaded others to adopt such a rationale. Even in 1642 Thomas Goodwin was telling the House of Commons that they were presented with an unprecedented opportunity to rebuild the Temple. It was 'an opportunity such as the last hundred years . . . have not afforded the like . . . and if you will not do it, God will do it without you . . . Purge and reform the Temple, though you die for it'.[4] By 1643 it had become clear to another Presbyterian minister that the great battle was being fought. He informed the House that 'when the Kings of the earth hath given their power to the Beast, these choice-soldiers will be so faithful to the King of Kings, as to oppose the Beast, though armed with kinglike powers'.[5] In 1644 the preacher Steven Marshall com-manded the soldiers present in the House to:

> go now and fight the battles of the Lord . . . for so I will not now fear to call them . . . although indeed at the first nothing clearly appeared but only that you were compelled to take up arms for the defence of your liberties . . . do now see that the question in England is whether Christ or Anti-Christ shall be lord or king.[6]

The mobilising potential of such appeals was quite enormous. By describing the struggle in such terms the Puritan spokesmen were meshing with the most basic popular conceptions of the nature of history and human development. At all levels within the Parliamentary Armies men were fired by this apocalyptic vision. A group of Roundheads captured at Shrewsbury told the Anglican Edward Symmons: 'Tis prophesied in the Revelation, that the Whore of Babylon shall be destroyed with fire and sword, and what do you know but this is the time of her ruin, and that we are the men that must help to pull her down?'[7]

The Ethic of Struggle

Millenarian expectations gave the Puritans that vision of impending total change that was vital to the growth of any sort of effective revolutionary consciousness. These expectations were a response to the Puritans' overwhelming sense of sin, and their consciousness of human frailty in a corrupt and largely hostile world. In other words they developed their millenarian visions as a psychological buttress against these feelings of human inadequacy. They allowed themselves to believe that eventually the extent of earthly corruption would necessitate a divine intervention to set men once again on the path of true godliness. To this extent the Puritans put their faith in something above and beyond mere human capabilities.

But the individual Puritan was no mere passive onlooker before the unfolding of actual events. As he was living in an essentially hostile environment his own life had to be one of eternal vigilance and struggle, until such time as God should finally establish his Kingdom on earth. For God worked through human agents, and the worldly manifestation of his will demanded that there exist at least one group of men aware of the ultimate aims of that will. That group must devote itself to the struggle against wordly temptation, such that they at least could provide the leaven of the new society. Thus it was of the utmost importance to the Puritans that they be able to keep alive the group's conception of itself as a divinely elected vanguard body.

It is this factor above all that helps to explain the transition from Church to Army that characterises the Civil War years. For to the Puritans the Church always was an army. Its service demanded exactly those virtues and characteristics that are of the greatest value in active military life. In mid-seventeenth-century England the notion of Christian soldiers was not mere pulpit rhetoric, but rather the statement of a profoundly felt psychological truth. The true Christian was a soldier, and was continually on campaign. Throughout his life he was surrounded by temptation, to succumb to which meant spiritual death. To guard against such a fate he associated with other like-minded godly warriors and submitted himself to a rigid group discipline.

This notion of discipline cannot be stressed too highly. Although the initial association of the brethren was voluntary, once the commitment had been made group discipline became all-important.[8] Respect for the pre-eminence of the group, and the willingness to submerge private identity in the common struggle is obviously a most important feature of any effective military organisation. But such attitudes could be even more important as a mobilising force in their own right. In the event that political developments should begin to indicate the total bankruptcy of the existing regime, as happened in the reign of Charles I, such a conception of religious life would greatly facilitate a transition to organised military opposition. In this respect the implications of the Puritans' everyday attitude to life were never more tellingly described than by Richard Sibbes when he wrote:

> The people of God are beautiful for order is beautiful. Now it is a beautiful thing to see many together submit themselves to the ordinance of God . . . An army is a beautiful thing, because of the order and the well-disposed ranks that are within it. In this regard the Church is beautiful.[9]

This identification of Church and Army continued throughout the War. There was a continuous attempt to perpetuate the identification of military service with the deepest motivations of normal life. Just as the nature of the Puritan Church had facilitated military organisation, so was there an attempt to sustain this original dynamic by nurturing the religiosity of the Army. Puritan leaders tried to ensure that military service never came to be regarded as simply a tedious, if somewhat dangerous chore, but rather always related back to those organisations and modes of thought that were so psychologically basic to large sections of the population. In 1646, for example, the Independent chaplain Hugh Peters laid great stress upon the effect of all this in the Army itself: 'One thing there is most singular in this your army: that whereas soldiers usually spend and make forfeiture even of the civility they bring into other armies; here men grow religious and more spiritual-thriving than in any place of the kingdom.'[10]

Chaplains like Peters were essential in keeping alive the religious rationale of the struggle against the King. Throughout the War preachers were attached to most of the Parliamentary Armies, where they used to conduct prayer meetings and remind the soldiers of the importance of their military service to the cause of God. Before and during the Battle of Edgehill,

> the reverend and renowned Master Marshall, Master Ashe, Master Mourton, Masters Obadiah and John Sedgewick, and Master Wilkins, and diverse others eminently pious and learned pastors rode up and down the army through the thickest dangers, and in much personal hazard, most faithfully and courageously exhorting, and encouraging the soldiers to fight valiantly and not to fly, but now, if ever, to stand to it and fight for their religion and laws.[11]

Speaking of the preachers attached to Essex's headquarters at York, Sergeant Nehemiah Wharton noted: 'These with their sermons have already subdued and satisfied more malignant spirits amongst us than a thousand armed men could have done, so that we have great hopes of a blessed union.'[12] Wharton seems to have been particularly struck by the importance of the chaplains to the Parliamentary forces. In a latter of 1643 he remarked: 'Our men are very courageous, and that they may so continue we desire, according to promise, a supply of faithful able ministers, which we exceedingly want.'[13]

The chaplains retained this important role throughout the War. As late as 1651 the following item was recorded in a newspaper: 'Yesterday marched through this city towards Scotland Colonel Walter Cradocke . . . with two troops of horse attending . . . selected out of their gathered Churches, after their dear brethren Mr Jenkin Jones and Mr Morgan Floyd, to fight the Lord's battle.'[14] It would be fascinating to know how often regiments were gathered in this way, from among the congregations of certain churches. For there is surely no clearer example of the close relationship in the Parliamentary Armies between civil concerns and military service. The identification of Church and Army, life and struggle, becomes complete.

Cromwell, in particular, was anxious to carry this identification to its farthest lengths. For him, only an army imbued with the traditional millenarian notions could vigorously pursue a truly revolutionary war. Particularly after the formation of the New Model Army, he devoted himself to finding those preachers who could adequately convey this union of military duty and religious mission. He began to organise, or at least tacitly condone, a kind of purge amongst the chaplains, dispensing with the services of the less radical Presbyterians in favour of those who inclined towards Independency. This should not be seen so much as an attempt to impose a doctrinaire uniformity upon the Army, as a way of constantly revitalising its spiritual zeal. In fact outward forms were of little consequence to Cromwell. In 1645 he said in the House:

> All that believe have the real unity, which is most glorious because inward and spiritual . . . As for being united in forms, commonly called uniformity, every Christian will for peace sake study and do as far as conscience will permit; and from brethren, in things of the mind, we look for no compulsion but that of light and reason.[15]

In 1650 he went so far as to claim: 'Truly, I think that he that prays best will fight best. I had rather that Mahometanism was permitted amongst us than that one of God's children should be persecuted.'[16] Unfortunately, as the War progressed Cromwell had difficulty in finding the kind of military-religious zeal he wanted. He found it more and more necessary to limit himself to the preachers of certain religious nuances, particularly the Independents. But here he did find just the kind of fervour that he wanted. Increasingly he relied upon that handful of men that he could trust never to neglect the integral connection between military operations and the Lord's purpose. Their sermons all stressed this basic point: 'According to Dell the victories of the New Model Army had not been achieved by pikes and muskets but by the Lord's right hand. Erbury asserted that only the "appearance of God in the Saints" could yield so many strongholds and conquer so many royal armies in so short a time with so few a number.'[17]

An anonymous pamphleteer, in 1649, summed up such attitudes perfectly when he wrote:

> I see none of the power of God left in the Kingdom if it be not to be found in the army; for certainly the power of God did first set them up, and since keep them up, and made its residence among them, and fought their battles, and stormed their cities and strongholds for them; and as the power of God hath produced them, so they again have acted according to God's power.[18]

The Nature of a Just War

Religion, then, gave the Puritans two essential prerequisites for the formation of a revolutionary army. On the one hand millenarianism offered the promise of a better world to come, and gave the soldiers a basic motive for fighting. On the other hand the very nature of the Puritan outlook created men already accustomed to the ideas of struggle, organisation and discipline. By keeping such ideas alive in the Army throughout the War the Puritan leaders were able at all times to maintain a cohesive fighting force with a high morale. But one other aspect of Puritan religiosity remains to be discussed. The expectation of a better world was not necessarily in itself a sufficient reason for actually taking up arms against the King. It was necessary also that the Puritans be able to reconcile themselves to the political implications of an attack on the existing authorities. They needed not only to believe in the possibility of a better future but also that they were obliged to fight for that future, even if that involved the destruction of the existing political order. They needed to doubt not only royal competence but also royal legitimacy.

The ideological foundations for such doubts were gradually evolved in the hundred or so years preceding the Civil War.[19] The fifteenth and early sixteenth centuries had seen the growth and consolidation of the dynastic nation-state. The heterogeneous entourage of largely self-sufficient feudal barons was replaced by a centralised administration to which all were strictly accountable, and for which *raison d'état* became the sole arbiter of policy. The military implications of this development were far-reaching. War began to lose its cataclysmic mystique as those groups within society to whom it had been a self-justifying way of life were gradually forced to identify their own good with that of the state. A new conception of the just war was gradually evolved, in which abstract conceptions of national well-being became of central importance. War was demystified and precisely defined as a policy option, rarely unavoidable, seldom desirable, but always in the last analysis justifiable by reason of state. The survival of the community became to be accepted as the basic criterion. But such a doctrine had the most subversive implications as soon as there was any disagreement as to what constituted the true community. Over the years the Puritans' sense of divine mission, and the intermittent persecution of their Churches, forced them to identify more and more with their own groups and thus to undermine their allegiance to the national community. For many of them the true community came to be that formed of their co-religionists.

For many years the Puritans were able to evade the ultimate implications of this development. They contented themselves with trying to live by a dual allegiance to religious community and nation-state. They tried to reconcile the two by attempting to persuade the state to act in the international interests of the community. This internationalist offensive was never more clearly evident than in England in the years of the reign of James I. The preacher John Preston, in his speeches at court in 1626 and 1627, was a perfect spokesman for the Puritan militants, the 'hawks' of the day. In a sermon of 1627, implicitly urging support for the Huguenots of La Rochelle, he made his point quite clearly:

> When the enemy is assaulting the Churches afar off, he is even then striking at the root of this Church and Commonwealth . . . It is certain that evil is intended against us, and will come upon us, except something be done to prevent it. For there is a Covenant between God and us, and breach of that Covenant causeth a quarrel; the quarrel of God shall not go unrevenged.[20]

But what if the covenant with God should be seen to conflict with the Christian's obligations to his secular ruler? Then the tenuous compromise of the dual allegiance would break down completely. The Christian would have to decide which set of obligations was the most important. The choice could lead to civil disobedience and, in the last extreme, to armed revolution. 'As reason of state justified the King's war, so reason of religion might justify the war of God.'[21] Already, even before the seventeenth century there had come into existence voluntary religious associations, the Huguenot Churches, the Catholic League, the Scottish Covenant, which claimed the right to organise politically and, if necessary, to wage war for the defence of their religion. Such organisations always constituted an implicit threat to state and King. On the one hand they claimed that there existed a political rationale other than that of dynastic security, whilst on the other they posed as a parallel authority to that of the state. In a moment of crisis, already heightened by the avowed imminence of the apocalyptic transformation of society, loyalty to the King would almost inevitably become secondary to the allegiance to God. In this case the religious group might rally beneath the banner of a just war, but a just war that was waged against the King. The aim need not necessarily be his overthrow. But for a time the authority of the ruler would be disputed until he had made sufficient concessions to the pre-eminent demands of those with divine blessing. The demands of religion would be held, temporarily at least, to override the King's claims to political legitimacy.

Clearly such an ideological shift represents an essential step in the transition from mere discontent to armed rebellion. Without such a radical notion of political obligation millenarian expectations and religious discipline alone might never have taken the Puritans past the point of passive faith and social isolationism. As it was, their propaganda campaign, demanding greater English participation in the international struggle against Antichrist, helped to lay the ideological foundations for the eventual rejection of the royal prerogative in favour of the divine mission. If God's purpose could determine what the King should do, it could also, in the face of royal obduracy, demand defiance of the King. In 1640 the Puritan Simeon Ashe perfectly summed up this notion: 'If the Lord please to beat the drum: if the Lord please to bid them arm and come abroad, his call is sufficient.'[22]

THE REALITIES OF MILITARY REVOLUTION

These then were the peculiar conditions that made possible a military revolution in seventeenth-century England. Revolutionary fervour was able to take on a military form because of the organisational and psychological implications of the Puritan *weltanschauung*. The military organism they created was genuinely revolutionary because its existence and purpose reflected the essential ideas of that world outlook. Thus from the beginning the Puritan Armies were a unified, cohesive force feeding off the most basic aspirations of their members. Some attempt was made by the Puritan leaders to keep alive this religious enthusiasm and so perpetuate this cohesiveness. But the resort to armed revolution has its own military and political logic. As the war progressed certain features inherent in the military organisation of Puritan fervour gradually came to the fore and irredeemably changed its character.

The Growth of Religious Libertarianism

The first of these features was a consequence of the very attempt to keep alive religious zeal within the Army. Because the New Model Army represented Puritan militancy at bay its leaders and preachers, in order to sustain its morale, had continually to stress the vanguard role of each of its members. The revolutionary self-consciousness of each soldier had to be raised to the point where he himself felt that he had some part to play in the storming of Babylon. Each soldier had to feel that he was an agent of the divine will. In June 1646 the Independent chaplain Dell preached what may well have been his last sermon to the New Model Army. A year later it was published and Dell attached a short introduction extolling the virtues of the Army. One of the points he isolated was the spirit of prayer:

This the Lord hath poured upon many of them in great

measure; not only upon many of the chief commanders, but
upon very many of the inferior officers and common
troopers; some of whom I have by accident heard praying
with that faith and familiarity with God, that I have stood
wondering at the grace.[23]

In one respect this phenomenon is merely a logical conclusion
of the spiritual hegemony and self-confidence already discussed.
But it would be well to also note its subversive potential. The
situation Dell was describing meant decentralisation of religious
authority. Each soldier was putting his trust in his own communion with the Holy Spirit. In so doing he was placing his
trust in his own interpretation of the divine revelation; and to
the Puritans one of the most important details of this revelation
concerned the nature of post-millenarian society. Thus any
attempt to heighten the religious self-confidence of the soldiers
necessarily meant that they be invited to work out in their own
minds their vision of God's Kingdom on earth. Thus the creation
of religious self-confidence implied the emergence of political
consciousness.

The Independent chaplains in particular actively encouraged
this trend. Not only did they encourage a belief that each man
was entitled to his own interpretation of God's message but also
that every man who so wished should be allowed to preach his
version to his fellows. By 1645 such unauthorised preaching had
reached a level which frightened Parliament into passing an
ordinance forbidding anyone not an ordained minister to preach.
Their fears were admirably summed up by the Presbyterian
John Ley who warned that if such anti-authoritarian behaviour
were allowed to continue the Army would simply split up into
self-governing congregations.:

If so, the army would not be an army, that is an entire and
well-compacted system, or body of soldiers united and
regulated by prudence and authority in a gradual series of
martial command and government, but would break in
pieces into petty parties . . . and so would be of little use
or force, either for conflict or conquest, much less would it
be terrible as an army with banners should be.[24]

Of course what Ley meant was that the Army would not be sufficiently awe-inspiring to the enemies of Parliament. To the prosperous members of the House of Commons such an anarchic organisation, rejecting the central political authority of Parliament, would be as terrible an army as could be conceived.

In actual fact this disintegration of military hierarchy never occurred. But it had certainly been a possibility. For the Independents' brand of religious libertarianism, even though based upon the same millenarian visions that inspired classical Presbyterianism, certainly served to undermine the original concept of disciplined unity—the very concept that had so greatly facilitated the creation of the Parliamentary Armies. Not only did the soldiers of the New Model Army largely ignore the Commons' ordinance on lay-preaching, they were also actively encouraged in this by the chaplains. Perhaps, as Solt has indicated: 'Most of the army preachers made it quite clear that they did not wish to make religion a stalking-horse for political ends. Collier, Denne and Webster all insisted that religious liberty should in no way derogate from the just power of the magistrate in preserving the civil peace and liberty of the kingdom.'[25] But it would be foolish to deny that the effects of what men say are not always what they intend. By encouraging the individual to believe in his own communion with God, and by severely criticising all those who claimed that sainthood was the prerequisite of those with secular position or learning, the chaplains were preaching a doctrine with the most subversive implications. It would be difficult to overestimate the effect of such a new conception of authority on regiments of basically untutored men. The chaplains may have intended to draw a firm line between the religious and the secular, but it would be rash to assume that their audiences accepted the division too.

The Revolt against Military Hierarchy

For the most part discipline in the Parliamentary Armies was firm. Serious infringements of the Articles of War were rare and were severely punished when they did occur.[26] The general feeling was that the whole was greater than its parts; what mattered to the individual was to find himself a place within the whole so that he might offset his own sense of insecurity by regarding the organised ranks around him. One of the key features of such a well-disciplined army was the obedience accorded to those of higher rank. Without it the Army could not function properly and this point was generally understood and respected by all ranks.

Their respect for discipline was also a consequence of the criteria by which officers were chosen. Albeit the Parliamentary soldiers might be very conscious of the need for discipline, it would be hard to expect a revolutionary army to respect officers chosen according to the criteria of birth and privilege of the *ancien régime*. Discipline was tolerable if it was seen to contribute to the achievement of certain political goals; but it would be quite unacceptable if merely the expression of an outmoded hierarchy, the very hierarchy against which the bulk of the Parliamentarians were fighting.

Cromwell in particular was quick to see this point. To him the important thing was that officers must be efficient military men. All other considerations were quite secondary. At first he did seem to have equated efficiency with some degree of breeding. After the debacle of Edgehill he wrote to his cousin John Hampden:

> Your troopers are most of them old decayed serving-men and tapsters and such kind of fellows . . . Their troopers are gentlemen's sons . . . persons of quality. Do you think that the spirit of such base and mean fellows will ever be able to encounter gentlemen that have honour, courage, and resolution in them?

His solution to the problem, however, was not particularly helpful: 'You must get men of spirit, that is likely to go as far as a gentleman will go, or else I am sure you will be beaten still.'[27] But if Cromwell were not quite sure where his men of spirit were to come from, he was quite clear that in the final analysis questions of birth and social position should never stand in the way of selecting efficient officers. In 1643, regarding the promotion of a soldier of an insignificant family, he wrote:

> It may be it provokes some spirits to see such plain men made captains of horse. It had been well that men of

honour and birth had entered into these employments, but
why do they not appear? Who would have hindered them?
But since it was necessary that the work must go on, better
plain men than none.[28]

For the first years of the Civil War this emphasis upon purely
military capabilities was enough to weld the Army together into
an extremely efficient fighting unit. For a time discipline was
kept politically acceptable through the choice of officers,
functional through the need for exceptional military efficiency,
and ideologically necessary in terms of the general desire for
group solidarity. But by the end of August 1645 the Civil War
seemed to be over, and from that date the functional justification
for strict discipline gradually evaporated. As was seen in the
preceding section the religious rationale of the Army also under-
went a distinct change of emphasis. Religious libertarianism and
the stress upon the importance of personal experience brought
about a profound change in the individual's relationship to the
community of believers.

As a corollary to this the individual's conception of his status
within the community also suffered a marked change. The
individual's new autonomy in terms of divine revelation was
carried over into the field of military responsibility and obligation. The soldiers still admitted that officers were necessary, but
they felt that these officers should be aware of their responsibilities to the more self-conscious rank-and-file. Their superior
rank carried privileges certainly, but it was now also felt to
carry certain obligations. The Leveller, John Lilburne, in
December 1648, pointed out that the Army must find 'what is
the most proper way for the advance of officers, so as to preserve
them entire to the interests of the people'.[29] John Wildman,
another Leveller, expressed this idea of mutual obligation in a
pamphlet of October 1647, when he asked the soldiers jealously
to preserve their interests against any threat of coercion from
the officers: 'Ye are no strangers to the way; ye have already
made a good beginning wherein we rejoice. Ye have men amongst
you as fit to govern as others to be removed. And with a word
ye can create new officers . . . The safety of the people is above
all law.'[30]

The Politicisation of the Army

The Parliamentary Armies came into being on the crest of a wave of millenarian expectations. This millenarianism was couched in religious terms, and the exact details of the new society that it looked to were by and large left in the hands of providence. Yet, even before the War broke out, it was realised that the nature of the apocalypse had far-reaching implications for civil society. Prior to the opening of hostilities one preacher had described the Parliamentary task in the following terms:

> Reformation must be universal . . . Reform all places, all persons and callings. Reform the benches of judgement, the inferior magistrates . . . Reform the universities, reform the cities, reform the counties, reform inferior schools of learning. Reform the Sabbath, reform the ordinances, the worship of God . . . You have more work to do than I can speak . . . Every plant which my heavenly father hath not planted shall be rooted up.[31]

This was a new element in millenarian thought. As described at the beginning of this chapter it was an essentially negative doctrine that emphasised the destruction of the old without paying much attention to what would be put in its place. As long as millenarianism was nothing but an individual response to the Puritan's sense of constant crisis and spiritual struggle the doctrine could retain this prescriptive vacuity and still remain a valuable personal shield against the fear of chaos. But the political crisis that provoked the Civil War, and the subsequent formation of the Parliamentary Armies brought these millenarian expectations to be a head. The struggle against Antichrist had actually become a tangible political struggle whose resolution was to be expected in the lifetime of those fighting. Final victory was felt to be imminent and men started seriously to ponder what they expected to be built upon the rubble of Babylon. The real prospect of the pulling down encouraged speculation upon the exact nature of what was to be put in its place.

There were those Puritans who throughout the revolutionary period continued to stress the transcendental, personal nature of the millennium, at the cost of any precise description of its institutional structure. Thus, speaking on a text from Isaiah, 'Behold I create new heavens and a new earth', the chaplain Thomas Collier said in 1647:

> The nature and glory of it lieth in that renovation or re-newing of the mind: an internal and spiritual change, a transformation out of the nature of the first into the nature of the second, Adam . . . For I do not understand by the new heavens, a thing contrary to what hath been formerly, but a higher measure or manifestation of one and the same glory.[32]

But there were many others who did envisage something quite different from 'what hath been formerly'. Both within the Army and outside it there were those who had some fairly clear ideas about the political and economic features of any new society. Theirs was a vision of a perfect society made up of individuals liberated not only through God's grace but also through a more equitable human restructuring of the Commonwealth. It had become clear during the Civil War and its immediate aftermath that a new world would not simply appear from nowhere, but would have to be built on earth by men according to their own criteria of rationality and reasonableness. This introductory paragraph to a pamphlet of January 1649, by the Leveller Richard Overton, demonstrates the new appeal to human capabilities:

> Having seriously considered how many large and fair op-portunities this honourable House [of Commons] hath had within these eight years last past to have made this nation absolute free and happy: and yet . . . until this time, every one of these opportunities have (after some short space of hope) faded, and but altered, if not increased our bondage.[33]

Nor was this new faith in human desires and capabilities limited to the members of one extreme political sect. What is at issue here is a very widespread shift in the conception of the nature of socio-political change. Thus it applied equally well to the arguments of the Levellers' opponents. Decrying their radical visions in 1647 Cromwell pointed out: 'It is not enough to propose things that are good in the end, but suppose this model were an excellent model, and fit for England and the Kingdom to receive, it is our duty as Christians and men to consider consequences, and to consider the way.'[34] Having reached the stage where the visions of millenarianism, the ends, had become political possibilities, it was suddenly realised that the human role in the shaping of the means towards these ends was of paramount importance. In the trauma of political revolution the Puritans began to appreciate the boundless opportunities for human will, but it was a realisation bought at the expense of the primacy of divine will. The more the demand for reform was made and the more the Army was able, through its victorious progress, to see the actual possibility of reform, the more the soldiers had to examine its exact implications. Religion always remained important as a frame of reference but as the War developed so also did rank-and-file ideas about the nature of society as it was and as it might be.

In May 1647 the ordinary soldiers were able to address the officers in these terms:

> Sirs, we your soldiers . . . have served under your commands, with all readiness, to free this our native land and nation from all tyranny and oppressions whatsoever, and that by virtue and power derived from this present Parliament . . . we, even the whole soldiery, have served both the state and you both faithfully and diligently, by which means God hath been pleased to crown us with victory . . . so that we hoped to put an end to all tyrannies and oppressions, so that justice and equity . . . should have been done to the people, and that the meanest subject should fully enjoy his rights, liberty, and properties, in all things . . . Upon this ground of hope we have gone through all difficulties and dangers, that we might purchase to the people of this land, with ourselves, a plentiful crop and harvest of liberty and peace.[35]

Such language hardly represents a precise description of any optimum future arrangement of society, but for the mid-seventeenth century it represents a massive leap forward. Gone is the appeal to a higher Authority for intervention in irrevocably sordid human affairs. Instead men are beginning to trust in their own ability to create the heaven on earth, by reference to their own criteria of what is just and equitable. Having relied for so long upon the supposedly divine sanction for their sense of perpetual struggle they were forced, in the moment of extreme crisis, to ask exactly what they were struggling for.

The clearest indication of the Army's self-awareness was its spokesmen's continual stress upon the difference between themselves and the soldiers of the old mercenary armies. Time and time again speakers and pamphleteers emphasised that theirs was a new kind of army, created for political purposes. As such its members were quite different from the conventional type of soldier who fought only for their sustenance and their pay. To the soldiers of the Parliamentary Armies the difference must have been particularly marked for the notion of mercenary service was not simply a matter of political self-consciousness. In most other armies of the day, even the famous Swedish armies of Gustavus Adolphus, a large proportion of the real fighting troops were taken from amongst the free-roving mercenaries of a dozen other European countries.[36] But in the English Civil War, however unwillingly some of the soldiers might have gone to the colours, they were members of a national army. There is no particular contradiction here. On the surface civil wars might seem to be divisive affairs. But this is only really true of wars of secession, a particular category of civil war. In many others, particularly the English, both sides were fighting for the imposition of their conception of what ought to be the system of government for the whole country. In this sense each army is a national army.

Examples of this new conception of the national army abound. One of its most succinct expositions came from Edward Sexby during the Putney Debates of 1647. At one point he noted: 'If we had not a right to the kingdom, we were mere mercenary soldiers.'[37] The whole case of the more politicised soldiers is contained in this simple pronouncement. The Parliamentary

Armies were held to be a national fighting force, struggling on behalf of their notions of the new society and their place within it. 'They were not a mercenary army, hired to serve the arbitrary power of a state, but continued in arms in judgement and conscience for the defence of their own peoples' just rights and liberties.'[38] Thus spoke John Lilburne in a pamphlet of 1648. In March of that year a letter signed by five soldiers of the New Model Army was sent to Fairfax. In it the signatories observed that they were: 'English soldiers, engaged for the freedom of England; and not outlandish mercenaries, to butcher the people for pay, to serve the pernicious ends of ambition and will in any person under heaven.'[39] A year earlier the Independent chaplain William Sedgewick plainly showed that he too appreciated the difference between the old and new types of warfare. Indeed, so highly did he value the sense of national mission that united the New Model Army, he was opposed to what he regarded as the excessive political debate that was tearing the Army in two. He felt that the Army was irredeemably riddled with faction:

> So your cause is lost, and you only fight because you are an army; because fighting is your business . . . Now you are the last, and heaviest of the nation's burdens; that promised to save and deliver, and turn the greatest tyrants; lose all the good you have done; set up a forcible government; turn war into a trade, England into a camp, perpetuate destruction, and provoke new commotions.[40]

The communistic radical Gerrard Winstanley went even further and attempted some kind of theoretical explanation of the differences between the old and new types of army. His remarks are worth quoting at some length, if only because this was probably the first such theoretical discussion of what constitutes a genuinely revolutionary army. One is here at the beginning of the long historical trail that eventually leads to the masterly, thoroughgoing analysis of Mao Tse-tung. In his blueprint for the new type of state, written in 1651, Winstanley distinguished between 'kingly' and 'commonwealth' armies. The wars fought by the former were merely, 'to destroy the laws of common freedom; and to enslave both the land and the people . . . And this war is called a plague, because that cursed enmity of covetousness, pride and vainglory and envy in the heart of mankind did occasion the rise of it.' But eventually, he held, a new kind of army would rise up:

> If a land be conquered and so enslaved as England was under the kings and conquering laws, then an army is to be raised with as much secrecy as may be, to restore the land again and set it free; that the earth may become a common treasury to all her children without respecting persons . . . This . . . is called civil wars, and this is the wars of commoners against King Charles, now cast out.

In this new type of army the soldier will be:

> of true noble spirits [who] will help the weak, and set the oppressed free, and delight to see the Commonwealth flourish in freedom . . . There is none of this true nobility in the monarchal army, for they are all self-lovers . . . A monarchal army lifts up mountains and makes valleys viz. advances tyrants and treads the oppressed in the barren lanes of poverty. But a commonwealth army is like John the Baptist, who levels the mountains to the valleys, pulls down the tyrants, and lifts up the oppressed; and so makes way for the spirit of peace and freedom to come in and inherit the earth.[41]

All these writers are talking of an entire army united by a common sense of political mission. But in actual fact it was this very feeling of political responsibility that led to the destruction of this first manifestation of a new type of armed force. Though all its members participated in the progression already described from apocalyptic zeal to substantive considerations of political possibilities, it did not necessarily follow that all groups within the Army would have a common notion of what was possible. The process of politicisation gradually revealed what a diversity of religious, political and economic grievances had been temporarily subsumed into the struggle with the Beast. It was realised that though he might have been slain his ten horns seemed to have lived on as divisive issues of radical policy. In other words, once the vague spiritual unease which had so greatly facilitated the initial Puritan mobilisation had been secularised in terms of concrete political ends, the unity of the battlefield gradually dissolved into bitter disagreement. Here the Putney Debates represented a decisive turning point for Cromwell and other Puritan leaders:

> In battle Cromwell had identified the Saints: those who had fought, and died, alongside him against Antichrist were those with the 'root of the matter' in them. The identification became fuzzy at Putney: those whom he had thought to be Saints were denouncing property! Worse, they were as confident as he that they were interpreting God's will correctly.[42]

But this disunity did not immediately become apparent. The first actual manifestations of the Army's political consciousness appeared in early 1647, and were the result of a united stand against Parliament by both the rank-and-file and the officers. The issue was Parliament's threat to disband the Army without settling the arrears of pay that were owed both to the infantry and the cavalry. Determined not to allow this to happen, both officers and ordinary soldiers came together and reached agreement on certain minimum demands that must be met by Parliament before the Army would disband. The *Humble Representation* and *Solemn Engagement* of 4–5 June 1647 represented the high-point of this solidarity between the ranks. All were temporarily united in the struggle against Parliament's arbitrary attempt to hasten the demobilisation. To this extent all were agreed on one point:

> The liberty of address by way of petition to this honourable House, [is] a prime and most essential part of freedom, and of right belonging to the meanest member of the Commonwealth . . . We humbly conceive our being soldiers to be so far from depriving us of our share of this freedom, as it ought rather to be a confirmation thereof to us; we having with our utmost hazard of our lives been instrumental in preserving the same.[43]

For the rank-and-file, however, the question of arrears was only one small part of their expectations from Parliament. Because they had fought Parliament's battles they felt that they should therefore have some stake in the resettling of the kingdom. But their notions of what was involved in such a settlement went far beyond the visions of the more prosperous superior officers, or Grandees as they became to be known. This became quite apparent as the ordinary soldiers began to try and make the Army as much a reflection of their new political aspirations as it had been of their religious fears and hopes. Thus they began to extend the notion of a soldier's political privileges to the internal functioning of the Army. To the rank-and-file this was but a logical extension of the ideas contained in the *Humble Representation* and the *Solemn Engagement*. But to the Grandees any such attempt to tamper with the mechanics of military hierarchy was an implicit attack upon their pre-eminent position within civil society. As has been seen the seeds of this internal upheaval had already been sown by the growth of religious libertarianism. The new political ideas merely accentuated the crisis of authority within the Army. As each soldier felt he had a stake in the kingdom many of them began to wonder whether the officers had any right to act for or to command the soldiers in any but their purely military capacity. The petition just cited went on to elaborate upon this point. To the minds of its signatories: 'The power of the officers doth only extend to the marshalling and disciplining of the army, for the better management and execution of martial affairs and . . . we submitting thereunto, do perform the utmost of obedience that can be required of us as soldiers.' Next comes the crucial distinction:

All which notwithstanding, as we are in the capacity of Commonwealth's men, we judge ourselves to be free as any other of the people, or as our officers themselves, to air either our grievances, informations or whatsoever else may tend either to the right of ourselves, or to the benefit of the Commonwealth . . . [In other words] the officers in matters of that concernment are not (without a free election or consent) the representers of the soldiers, as commoners; but are only their conductors in military affairs.[44]

The soldiers did not simply limit themselves to a tacit acceptance of such theoretical points. Only two or three weeks after

Parliament had resolved to disband the Army, the rank-and-file, fearful of the attitude of their officers, elected Agitators (agents or representatives) to speak on their behalf. As one of them said to Ireton at Putney: 'It was the soldiers did put the Agents on these meetings. It was the dissatisfactions that were in the army which . . . occasioned these meetings . . . and the reasons of such dissatisfactions are because those whom they had to trust to act for them were not true to them.'[45] For a time the Grandees made the best they could of these manifestations of rank-and-file democracy, and the Agitators were co-opted on to the General Council of the Army, a new body set up to represent the interests of the whole Army. 'Now this council was wholly new, and in a way diverse and different from all martial courts or councils of war, that ever the sun beheld in a mercenary army, and as different from the Council by which this army was formely governed.'[46] Thus did Lilburne characterise what was regarded by many soldiers as a final vindication of themselves as a quite different type of army.

Because the officers had agreed to admit the Agitators to their counsels, and had in conjunction with them issued a pronouncement of army solidarity, the soldiers therefore held that a political contract had been entered into. Furthermore they held that this contract was binding on both parties, and each had an equal right to determine future policy. Describing the Army at this time, Lilburne wrote: 'It is . . . clear, as they continued an army at that time not by the state's will, power or command but their mutual agreement, they could be under no other government as an army but such as they did constitute or appoint for themselves by mutual agreement.'[47] Here was the final culmination of the overt politicisation of the Army. Not only did it embrace the political demands and world outlook of those fighting for it, but it was also seen to be an actual microcosm of the real political world. As such it was to be governed by just those precepts that it was held should guide ordinary political life. As long as the whole Army was in substantial agreement as to who was the common enemy—the King until 1645, the King and/or Parliament until 1647—then it could remain sufficiently united to be a powerful arbiter of the nation's affairs. But the emergence of radical demands among

the rank-and-file began to threaten this unity. When the
Grandees resisted these demands the logic of the soldiers' new
conception of themselves as a democratic political entity forced
them to question the validity of the officers' powers. As Overton
put it:

> If the equity of the law be superior . . . to the letter, and if
> the letter should control and overthrow the equity, it is to
> be controlled and overthrown itself, and the equity to be
> preserved, then the rule of the same reason doth tell them,
> that the officer is but the form or letter of the army; and
> therefore inferior to the equitable or essential part, the
> soldiery, and to be controlled and overthrown themselves,
> when they control and overthrow the soldiery in the
> essentials of their being.

Overton cites certain historical examples of opposition to
tyranny and goes on to point out that: 'Thus may the soldiery
renew and revive the same, and even oppose, contradict, dispute
and overrule the commands of their officers themselves to the
contrary, and be equally justifiable with the foregoing precedents.'[48]

But such analogous reasoning was utterly unacceptable to
the Grandees. Particularly when the soldiers actually went so
far as to try to put it into effect. The election of the Agitators in
March 1647 has already been mentioned. In October of that
year certain cavalry regiments lost their faith in these representatives, who seemed to have been consorting too closely and
too long with the Grandees, and they began to elect new ones.
In September a certain Major White was expelled from the
General Council for suggesting, among other things, that the
pay of the officers be reduced whilst that of the ordinary
soldiers be raised. At a general rendezvous of a part of the Army
at Ware in November 1647, two regiments turned up in defiance
of their officers with copies of a Leveller manifesto stuck in their
hats. On the way to the rendezvous Lilburne's regiment drove
away all but one of their commissioned officers. Discipline was
restored but discontent continued. At St Albans in April 1648
several officers of Colonel Rich's regiment had to break up a

meeting of newly elected Agitators from each troop in the regiment. In February 1649 Fairfax imposed some restrictions on the Army's right of petition, and this eventually led to a mutiny of some three thousand soldiers, who gathered at Burford in Oxfordshire. It was easily suppressed, and a cornet, a corporal and a private were shot by a firing-squad.

By that astonishingly limited gesture the Grandees crushed overt radical feeling within the Army. The Army's religious zeal had been strong enough to overthrow a king. But the shift from apocalyptic faith to political aspiration seems not only to have robbed the Army of unity between the ranks, but also to have deprived its radical elements of a great deal of their self-confidence. The new political ideas simply did not possess the ideological coherence to sustain an assault upon social and political privilege. It is clear now, in historical retrospect, that millenarianism was played out as a mobilising force, but this was not so clear to the soldiers themselves. Memories of the unity of the Saints were still too fresh in their minds for them to embark with any confidence on an attack on those who had once been their most prominent leaders. Thus, for the moment, a 'whiff of grapeshot' sufficed.

In terms of a general theory of military revolution the English Civil War can be divided into two distinct stages. For a time, in the struggle against the King, Puritan millenarianism had united the Army in a rather vaguely defined, in social terms, struggle against godlessness and tyranny. In this period the Army had been a perfect revolutionary tool. Indeed the harnessing of the Puritans' fear of chaos and need for group discipline that underlay the formation of the Parliamentary regiments in some ways offers a paradigm of the fusion of social concerns and military service. And it is only through such a fusion that an army can be given the resilience and internal unity necessary for a sustained assault against the power of the incumbent authorities. But in this case the very success of the assault forced the soldiers to examine the concrete implications of their visions of the millennium. This forced them to think in pragmatic terms of means and ends, which not only robbed their visions of their religious connotations but also deprived them of the possibility of total change. In revolutionary terms

the end of apocalyptic faith represented an ideological emascu-
lation. It opened the way for those theories of constitutional
gradualism that have characterised English political thought to
this day. But this did not come to pass immediately. For a short
while the ordinary soldiers did try to make the internal organisation of the Army compatible with their new notions of democratic rights. To this extent they tried to make the Army as
genuinely revolutionary in politics as it had been in religion.
But in so doing they stripped away the façade of unity between
the officers and the rank-and-file, and came up against the fears
of the Grandees for their social pre-eminence. It would be
appropriate to return to the Leveller Sexby at Putney for a
fitting epitaph to this experiment in military revolution:

We have engaged in this kingdom and ventured our lives,
and it was all for this; to recover our birthrights and
privileges as Englishmen, and by the arguments urged
there is none. There are many thousands of us soldiers that
have ventured our lives; we have had little propriety in the
kingdom as to our estates, yet we have had a birthright.
But it seems now except a man hath a fixed estate in this
kingdom, he hath no right in this kingdom. I wonder we
were so much deceived.[49]

Chapter 3   The American War of Independence 1775–83

CHRONOLOGY

1774

27 May   Eighty-nine burgesses from Virginia and Massachusetts call for a colonial congress to support the stand of
Boston against the British.

17 June   The Massachusetts House endorses a call for a
Continental Congress in Philadelphia in September. General
Gage dissolves the House.

2–7 Sept   Four thousand Massachusetts militiamen assemble
in Boston to resist Gage and the British forces.

17 Sept   Congress endorses the Suffolk Resolves calling on the
colonists to prepare for armed resistance.

1775

19 April   Skirmishes at Lexington and Concord (Mass.).

22 April   Massachusetts, Rhode Island, Connecticut and New
Hampshire decide to raise an army of 13,600 men.

10 May   The second Continental Congress convenes at Philadelphia.

15 June   Congress adopts the forces of the four north-eastern
states and names Washington as Commander-in-Chief.

17 June   The Battle of Bunker Hill (Mass.). The Americans are
driven back.

2 July   Washington joins the Army around Boston.

July   The departure of an American force intending to drive
the British out of Quebec.

10 Oct   Congress agrees to raise a Continental army of 21,000
men.

1776

18 Feb   Congress authorises the use of privateers against
British shipping.

26 Feb   Congress places an embargo on all exports to Britain.

3 March   Congress dispatches Silas Deane to Paris to solicit French diplomatic and military aid.

14 March   Congress urges the disarming of the Loyalists.

17 March   Howe evacuates Boston and moves to New York.

15 May   Congress instructs the states to form their own independent governments.

mid-June   The return of the defeated remnants of the expedition against Quebec.

29 June   A British attack on Charleston (South Carolina) is repulsed.

4 July   The Declaration of Independence is adopted by all the colonies.

27 Aug   The Battle of Long Island (New York). An American defeat.

28 Aug   Washington withdraws into New York.

13 Sept   Washington evacuates New York.

16 Nov   Fort Washington (New York) and 2,600 men are captured by the British.

21 Nov   Washington retreats to Newark (New Jersey).

14 Dec   Howe goes into winter quarters.

26 Dec   The Battle of Trenton (New Jersey). A minor but resounding American victory.

1777

3 Jan   The Battle of Princeton (New Jersey). Another resounding American victory.

June–July   Howe evacuates New Jersey.

20 June   Burgoyne opens his campaign, moving south from Quebec.

4 July   Burgoyne captures Fort Ticonderoga (New Hampshire).

7 July   Howe begins embarking his forces from Staten Island.

16 Aug   Burgoyne is defeated at the Battle of Bennington (New Hampshire).

18 Aug   Howe disembarks in the Chesapeake Bay.

11 Sept   The Battle of Brandywine (Penn.). A victory for Howe.

26 Sept   Howe occupies Philadelphia.

4 Oct   Howe again defeats the Americans at the Battle of Germantown (Penn.).

17 Oct   Burgoyne surrenders to Gates at Saratoga (New Hampshire).

15 Nov   Congress adopts the Articles of Confederation.

11 Dec   Washington moves into winter quarters at Valley Forge (Penn.).

1778

6 Feb   Signature of Franco-American treaty.

23 Feb   Arrival of Baron von Steuben at Valley Forge.

28 June   The Battle of Monmouth (New Jersey). An American victory over Sir Henry Clinton, Howe's replacement.

1779

15 June   The Battle of Stone Point (New York). An American victory.

1 Dec   Washington goes into winter quarters at Morristown (Penn.).

1780

12 May   The British capture Charlestown (South Carolina).

25 May   A mutiny over conditions of service amongst several regiments of Pennsylvania Continentals.

10 July   The French disembark 6,000 troops at Newport (Delaware).

16 Aug   Gates resoundingly defeated by Cornwallis at the Battle of Camden (South Carolina).

7 Oct   Loyalist militia defeated at the Battle of King's Mountain (North Carolina).

10 Nov   Nathanael Greene replaces Gates as commander of the southern forces.

1781

1 Jan   Another mutiny amongst the Pennsylvania Continentals.

16 Jan   Decisive American victory against Cornwallis at the Battle of the Cowpens (South Carolina).

7 Feb   The creation of the American War Department.

1 March   Congress ratifies the Articles of Confederation.

15 March   The Battle of Guildford Court House (North Carolina) Another severe check to Cornwallis.

8 Sept   The Battle of Eutaw Springs (South Carolina). A technical but bloody British victory.

18 Oct   Cornwallis surrenders at Yorktown (Virginia).

1782

23 May   The British Parliament authorises the initiation of peace talks.

15 July   The British evacuate Savannah (Georgia).

14 Dec   The British evacuate Charleston.

1783

27 Jan   A committee of American officers lays before Congress a memorial demanding the payment of certain arrears.

15 March   Washington meets the officers' delegates and persuades them to repudiate the Newburgh Addresses, inflammatory denunciations of Congress's attitude towards the Army.

15 April   Congress ratifies the Treaty of Paris, which terminated the hostilities.

10 May   Members of the Society of Cincinnatus endorse its constitution.

18 Oct   Congress decrees the disbandment of almost the entire American Army.

3 Nov   All troops enlisted for the duration are demobilised.

25 Nov   The British formally relinquish control of New York.

Because of its particular bearing on the problems of military mobilisation, religion was the essential theme of the previous chapter. But there were other traditional currents of thought that were of importance in explaining the lead up to the crisis. One of these was a kind of nationalistic pride in England's Anglo-Saxon heritage. In fact, by the time of the outbreak of the Civil War there existed a strong, traditional belief that the ills of English society could be traced back to the Norman Conquest of 1066. Before that date, it was held, the original inhabitants of England had lived as free and equal citizens enjoying a representative mode of government. The Norman Conquest was thought to have destroyed these institutions and imposed alien and despotic rulers. The Anglo-Saxon heritage represented democracy, liberty and the universal right to property; the Norman Conquest had meant the loss of all these precious features:

> If the King owed his title to conquest, and consequently owned all property in the realm, then he also had a right to arbitrary taxation. But if the sanctity of property and representative institutions were part of our inheritance, then we must struggle to preserve them. Liberty, property and patriotism were inseparable.[1]

If nationalism was of such importance in an essentially civil war, one might be entitled to assume that it provided the most basic of motivations for the Americans in the War of Independence. Was it not their whole aim to drive out what they increasingly saw as the agents of a foreign power? Surely, in what was on the face of it a war of national liberation, one can take the existence of a strong, cohesive sense of national solidarity for granted? In fact the essential military features of the War of Independence derive from the fact that such feelings of nationalism were most significant by their absence. Group loyalties in America at this time were founded on purely parochial notions of family and district, and not on any particular sense of being American. Only in the Army were such parochial loyalties transcended; the Army was the only effective symbol of supra-state loyalty. Thus only the continued existence of the Army, as a physical entity, could assure the survival of the colonists' will to resist.

Of course, this is not to deny the importance of widespread anti-British feeling amongst the colonists. Whether they were in fact unduly oppressed by British rule is not at issue here. What is certain is that they felt that they were.[2] But xenophobia, by itself, does not constitute the common sense of national identity necessary for a militarily effective war of national liberation.

Such a war demands the existence of developed feelings of group identity and solidarity. Without such a sense of collective responsibility the war of liberation will never rise above the level of petty ambuscades and an unconnected series of skirmishes. In a genuine war of national liberation those struggling against 'oppression' must not only have characterised the 'oppressors', the 'them', but they must also have some conception of what defines the 'us'. In the War of Independence the first half of the problem was quite straightforward: the 'them' were the British. Their administrators often made only temporary sojourn in the country; they extracted taxes, goods and raw materials which flowed back to England; their red-coated soldiery were often in evidence. As the war itself progressed the identification was made even easier by the British recourse to the use of German mercenaries with their alien language and military habits. The employment of such troops had a great impact upon many Americans and was of great propaganda value if one wished to call the war a struggle against foreign oppression.[3]

But this antipathy towards the British and their allies did not of itself produce an identification of interests amongst the colonists. Though many of them were convinced that they were not British, very few of them went beyond this to regard themselves as Americans. Though the enemy had been identified, an essential first step in the progress towards national liberation, there was no cohesive sense of solidarity amongst the colonists that could create an effective organisational base. Because the colonists had little conception of a collectivity beyond that of town or county, there was no chance of creating an effective political *apparat* to co-ordinate resistance. And in the absence of such political machinery there was no way in which the more enthusiastic patriots could begin to remedy the deficiencies in national feeling. They found themselves caught in a vicious circle: regional diversities and divisions fed upon themselves to create an atmosphere of political apathy and helplessness.

Nationalism and Parochialism

The most immediate and desperate result of this lack of genuine nationalism among the Americans was the widespread neglect of the Army by almost all of the state legislatures and local assemblies. On the face of it the Americans had moved quickly to create a national army. The second Continental Congress had met in Philadelphia on 10 May 1775 and only a few days later it moved to adopt those regiments of militia that had spontaneously heeded the call of the states of Massachusetts, Connecticut, New Hampshire and Rhode Island. But the significance of many if not all of the Congressional initiatives was largely rhetorical, and this particular case was no exception. Throughout the war the various regional assemblies never fully acknowledged that their main responsibilities were to the creation of a supra-state military establishment. The politicians of the state legislatures and the vast proportion of ordinary people in these states limited their military horizons to the state boundaries, and in many cases to the confines of their own county or town. Within such circumscribed areas both legislators and ordinary people were most zealous in assembling hastily mustered bodies of militia to fight against the British. During the whole course of the war, from New Hampshire to South Carolina, there were countless examples of such scratch units performing sterling service in the short-term defence of their own localities.[4] But once the British had left the immediate vicinity of the militiaman's home and hearth these regiments would quickly break up and return to their everyday tasks. Until the British should threaten again they remained resolutely heedless of calls for assistance, either from other states or from the leaders of the supposedly national regular Continental Army.

Congress made persistent efforts to remedy this state of affairs. In October 1775 it authorised Washington to raise an army of 20,000 men, with him as Commander-in-Chief. It drew up a list of the quota of troops which every state was expected to contribute. From the very beginning the states never filled these quotas and the Continental Army always remained lamentably below its paper strength. In September 1776 Congress agreed to higher scales of pay for the Continentals; it also for the first time authorised enlistment for a three-year period and the payment of a twenty dollar bounty, plus a grant of a hundred acres of land, to all who enlisted. In May 1778 Congress decreed that all Continental officers should receive half-pay for seven years after the cessation of hostilities. But none of these measures had much effect. Between 1779 and 1781 Congress was forced to make repeated appeals to the state assemblies to make more effort to fill their quotas of troops. In 1781 it even went so far as to reduce substantially the antici- pated size of the Army to fifty-eight regiments. But despite all these measures, throughout the period of the war, the quotas were not filled and the states showed little enthusiasm for the well-being of their supposedly American Army. In November 1776 the Army had a paper strength of 42,500 men but only about 20,000 were actually in service. Two Congressional resolutions of December 1776 allowed for a Continental strength of 76,000 men, but in March of the following year Washington had a mere 3,000 men under his command, and even by the start of the campaigning season the number had hardly risen above 9,000. As late as 1780, when Congress called for 42,000 Continentals, no more than 20,000 ever assembled for duty. The problem was that the states were never able to take too much interest in the fortunes of a mobile national army that only occasionally fought within their own territory. They preferred to conserve their manpower within their own boundaries and wait until their own lives and property were threatened. In this eventuality the states were remarkably efficient at raising large bodies of troops at very short notice. The parochial enthusiasm of the militia units has already been noted, but there were also examples of large-scale state mobilisations on a more permanent level. In the opening days of the war the states of Massachusetts, Connecticut, New Hampshire and Rhode Island mustered some 20,000 troops around Boston, eighty per cent of whom came from Massachusetts itself. By the time of Burgoyne's surrender in October 1777, the northern states under General Gates had managed to put some 20,000 men into the field to parry the British offensive, creating in the space of a few months a second army considerably larger than Washington's own.

Not only did parochial loyalties hinder the recruitment of the Continental Army but they also had a divisive effect within the Army itself. This was particularly evident in the first months of the war, before and after Bunker Hill. As a contemporary observer wrote of the army around Boston:

Another reason why the army can never be well-united and regulated is the disagreements and jealousies between the different troops from the different colonies, which must never fail to create disaffection and uneasiness among them. The Massachusetts forces already complain very loudly of the partiality of the General to the Virginians and have even gone so far as to tax him with taking pleasure in bringing their officers to court martials [sic] and having them cashiered that he might fill their places with his friends from that quarter. The gentlemen from the southern colonies, in their turn, complain of the enormous proportion of New England officers in the army.[5]

At about the same time Washington himself was moved to complain to Congress: 'I have been in consultation with the generals of this army . . . endeavouring to establish a new corps of officers . . . I cannot say when they are to end . . . as there appears to be such an unwillingness in the officers of one government mixing in the same regiment as those of another.'[6]

The passing of time seemed to do little to ease the problem. In August 1776 Washington's General Orders pointed out: 'It is with great concern, the General understands, that jealousies, etc., are arisen among the troops from the different provinces, of reflections frequently thrown out, which can only tend to irritate each other, and injure the noble cause in which we are engaged.'[7] Major-General Wayne of Pennsylvania was equally aware of such interstate rivalries when he wrote the following remarks to the Speaker of the Pennsylvania Assembly in May 1778. He was complaining bitterly about the quality of uniforms received:

I can only say that your consequence as a state in a great degree depends upon your making a respectable appearance in the field—more especially as the enemy are in possession of your capital—in which case any supineness gives ground for censure which . . . some states are very liberal in bestowing—calling us a dead weight on their hands.[8]

It was typical of the American war effort that not only should the state lines vie with each other to be better dressed, but also that the state that was the cockpit of the war in the north should be regarded by other states as a dead weight.

Sometimes sectional rivalry within the Army reached such a peak that individual commanders actually refused to submit their troops to the authority of Congress or Washington. Such was the case when Brigadier-General John Stark raised a brigade for the New Hampshire legislature in July 1777. On accepting command he made one firm proviso: he and his men must at all time be completely independent of Washington and the Continental Army. The New Hampshire General Court was only too willing to give Stark a *carte blanche* in this respect. Similarly during General Nathanael Greene's campaign in the south in 1780 and 1781 the commander had some difficulty in obtaining the wholehearted co-operation of the various guerrilla commanders operating in that area. Thomas Sumter in particular nearly withdrew his support entirely when Greene's forces moved into Catawba County, a region that Sumter regarded as his personal domain. Certainly Sumter's objections had considerable force in view of the immense difficulties in obtaining sufficient supplies and forage. Nevertheless his sulky behaviour over the next weeks was hardly calculated to increase military efficiency.

It also fell to Greene to be the victim of one of the most exaggerated instances of the states' jealousy of their independence. In early 1781 Greene's army was pursued across North Carolina by the British and was eventually compelled to retreat across the River Dan to take refuge in Virginia. Upon his arrival the Virginia militia, fearing British pursuit, spontaneously assembled all across the state. Upon which the county sheriffs pronounced that as the muster had not been ordered by the correct authorities the whole exercise was illegal, and they promptly sent the militia home again. Even when Governor Jefferson's attention had been drawn to this ludicrous state of affairs he grudgingly allowed only a quarter of the militia to be called up.

In this particular example the attitude of the ordinary people contrasts favourably with that of the state bureaucracies. But one should be careful of inferring that such a contrast was generally characteristic. Throughout the war one of the gravest problems facing the American forces was that of supply, and in this respect the attitude of the people at large was as self-centered as that of the most obstructive bureacracy. The basic cause of the Continentals' supply problem was the chronic financial instability of the colonies. Shortly after the opening of hostilities Congress had been forced to issue its own currency, but the uncertainty of the war years and the perennial shortage of many basic commodities created golden opportunities for speculators and monopolists. As the war progressed rampant inflation made it more and more difficult for the regiments of the Continental Army to obtain goods at prices compatible with their funds from state and Congressional sources. In the bitter winter of 1778-9, when Washington and the rump of his army were in winter quarters at Valley Forge, they found it almost impossible to procure provisions from the Pennsylvania farmers living in the immediate vicinity. For by this time the Continental dollar was almost worthless and the solid yeomanry of Pennsylvania found it more attractive to sell their produce to the English in and around Philadelphia for good English pounds. 'The enemy lived well enough, while twenty miles distant the American army . . . dwindled away through death, desertion and disgust.'[9]

Such activities were prevalent throughout the thirteen states. Everywhere all kinds of speculators and money-grabbing merchants devoted themselves to the exploitation of scarcity, where necessary creating a seller's market through ruinous monopolistic practices. Eventually, in October 1776, Congress was forced to decree that:

> Whereas it has been represented to Congress that sundry inhabitants of the United States, to keep supplies from the army, or promote their own interests, have purchased considerable quantities of clothing, and refuse to dispose of the same, unless upon extravagant or unreasonable terms . . . Congress recommends to the assemblies . . . that laws be provided in each of the states for effectually preventing monopolies of necessities for the army . . .[10]

Following this decree several of the north-eastern states did in fact try to fix a maximum limit on prices and wages. But other states declined to follow suit with the result that speculators simply brought up goods at the regulated prices and exported them to other states where they could obtain the 'free market' price.

On the whole then one has a fairly depressing picture of the level of national solidarity within the colonies at this time. Everywhere in the military, political and commercial sectors loyalties rarely transcended the defence of home and hearth, and in some cases were totally subordinated to the demands of a good profit. Most of the patriot leaders found little comfort in any honest appraisal of the motives of their country-men. In 1779 Alexander Hamilton, an *aide-de-camp* of Washing-ton, wrote to Gouverneur Morris: 'The rapid decay of our currency, the extinction of public spirit, the increasing rapacity of the times, the want of harmony in our councils, the declining zeal of the people, the distresses of the officers of the army . . . are symptoms . . . of a most alarming nature.'[11] In the autumn of 1780 Lieutenant-Colonel Ebenezer Huntington of Connecticut was even more emphatic about the implications of all this for the Army. In a letter to his brother he said:

I despise my countrymen. I wish I could say I was not born in America . . . The insults and neglects which the army have met with from the country beggars all description . . . [He goes on to condemn] my cowardly countrymen who flinch at the very time when their exertions are wanted and hold their purse-strings as though they would damn the world rather than part with a dollar for their army.[12]

Such judgements are perhaps a little harsh. After all the Americans did manage in the end to keep sufficient troops in the field to wage a successful war of national liberation. But it is important to qualify the word 'national'. Perhaps a fairer picture of the mood in the colonies during the war was given by James Collins of South Carolina. Speaking of the Whigs, or those opposed to British rule, he delineated:

At least three classes of [them] . . . The first were those who determined to fight it out to the last . . . The second were

those who would fight a little when the wind was favourable,
but as soon it shifted to some unfavourable point, would
draw back and give up all for lost. The third class were those
who were favourable to the Cause, provided it prospered
and they could enjoy the benefit, but would not risk one
hair of their heads to obtain it.[13]

Even here the analysis is presented in rather emotive terms.
Understandably the writers have let their disgust at the apathy
of their countrymen obtrude too much into their description of
its causes. To the colonists America did not exist as a national
entity and thus they saw no need to exert themselves in the
defence of such a concept. America was full of those who had
fled the pressures of relatively more collectivised societies in
Europe, or people who wanted nothing more than the chance to
lose themselves in the vastness of the American continent and
make their own way free of all those legalistic and political
obligations that characterised the old world. They looked to an
ideal society of tiny self-sufficient units, and were only willing
to gird themselves in the defence of their own family nucleus.
Even in the seaboard areas, where society was somewhat more
developed, the network of interdependent commercial, legal and
political obligations had rarely extended itself beyond the
confines of a particular state. So even here there was little
conception of the potential value of nationhood and thus little
inclination to fight on behalf of it. Thus the vast proportion of
Americans were totally lacking in any sense of responsibility to
a body politic or to any of its institutions. Their loyalties
changed with the ebb and flow of the military struggle.

In the absence of any binding notion of mutual interests it
was inevitable that individuals must test the value of their
allegiances in terms of short-term, parochial gains and losses.
And when such considerations of the narrowest self-interest
failed to mobilise sufficient support for the struggle, the patriot
leaders had no alternative but to try and stimulate resistance
through the example of their own exertions. In the absence of
ideological cohesion there was little the war leaders could do but
fall back on personal charisma. Such indeed was the opinion of
Nathanael Greene after a journey through Virginia in late 1780:

It has been my opinion for a long time that personal influence must supply the defects of a civil constitution, but I have never been so fully convinced of it as upon this journey. I believe the views and wishes of the great body of the people are entirely with us. But remove the personal influence of the few and they are a lifeless inanimate mass, without direction or spirit to employ the means they possess for their own security.[14]

The Search for Authority

If national feeling was at such a low ebb in the colonies at this time it seems legitimate to ask what was the ideological basis of the resistance to the British? Bearing in mind the wholesale transfer of Puritan militants to America it might seem that the same kind of religious factors discussed in the previous chapter were again of importance. Certainly it has recently been convincingly demonstrated that religious forms and beliefs played an important role in the mobilisation of the American people for prolonged resistance.[15] Some of the central notions in the colonial religious outlook are already familiar to us from the previous chapter. Above all the colonists subscribed to the view that the mundane world was in a state of moral chaos in which man was continually struggling for the possibility of divine forgiveness. All men were overwhelmed by a sense of perpetual guilt which they could never truly hope to expiate. This sense of guilt was of great importance in helping to explain to the colonists why they should have to suffer such hardships in the struggle for independence. For how could hopelessly corrupt mortals expect an easy passage in their search for salvation? Even more importantly, such ideas justified further efforts in the hope of an eventual divine intervention. The activities of Congress mirror this attitude perfectly. As early as 20 June 1775 they set aside a day of prayer in which the delegates could confess their sins and raise hopes for intercession. On 20 March 1779 they proclaimed: 'Too few have been sufficiently awakened to a sense of their guilt, or warmed with gratitude, or taught to amend their lives or turn from their sins so He might turn from his wrath.'[16] They called for a day of fasting that Americans might begin to be aware of their guilt. In April 1780 they called for yet another day of fasting: 'To make us sincerely penitent for our transgressions; to prepare us for deliverance, and to remove the evil with which He hath been pleased to visit us; to banish vice and irreligion from among us and establish virtue and piety by His divine grace.'[17] This notion of salvation through suffering was so deeply held that in 1777 Benjamin Rush went to far as to hope that the war would not end too soon because, 'a peace at this time would be the greatest curse that could befall us . . . Liberty without virtue would be no blessing to us'.[18] Such notions were clearly of immense help in sustaining the Americans through the years of war. In Miller's apt words:

> Out of the years between the Stamp Act and the Treaty of Paris emerged a formidable exhaustive . . . re-enunciation of the necessity for America to win her way by reiterated acts of repentance. The jeremiad, which in origin had been an engine of Jehovah, thus became temporarily a service department of the Continental Army.[19]

So far the parallels with the religious spirit within Cromwell's army are remarkably close. In both cases the combatants were able to take heart from the belief that the period of struggle and self-abnegation was merely the necessary prelude to the eternity of bliss and the integration of human happiness and the divine scheme of things. But in one very important respect the outlook of the colonists differed from that of the English Puritans. Whilst the Americans were prepared to acknowledge that their sufferings were an unavoidable consequence of human culpability, and to take some grim-faced comfort from this fact, their religious outlook seems by and large to have lacked the positive dynamic of English Puritanism. American religiosity did not put nearly as much stress upon the importance of self-discipline and the primacy of the dedicated, cohesive group of believers. In other words, whilst religion provided an explanation for the wearying exigencies of internecine strife, economic collapse and protracted warfare, it did not provide the Americans with any guidelines on how best to overcome the terrible inertia that bedevilled the best efforts of the leading patriots. American Protestantism preached the inevitability of being forced to suffer and of involuntary self-denial. But it largely failed to go beyond this. It did not stress the necessity for voluntary self-abnegation, for a wholehearted commitment to an ordered, disciplined group of like-believers immersing their individuality in the collective effort, as a prerequisite of victory over the forces of chaos. Consequently the Americans never went beyond a stage of pessimistic passivity, and throughout the war at least never succeeded in building any organisational structures that could effectively harness their religious sentiments. They never had their equivalent of the Ironsides.

So far the argument has concentrated on the organisational weaknesses of the American war effort. But surely, it might be argued, the existence of the second Continental Congress was a clear indication that there was some unity and some will to fight on the American side? But even here a closer examination of the facts reveals that at best Congress was only a makeshift façade whose activities say more about American disunity than they evidence its unity. Certainly Congress was in theory the body to give some centralised impetus to American military activities and such an impetus was clearly needed. As Thomas Paine perceived as early as 1775: 'By referring the matter from argument to arms, a new era for politics is struck, a new method of thinking hath arisen.'[20] Ironically, however applicable this remark is to our general concept of genuine military revolution, it is perhaps least applicable to the actual course of the American War of Independence. Certainly a new method of thinking was called for to overcome the parochialism and apathy of the colonists. There was indeed much social discontent in the colonies which might have been effectively harnessed in a genuinely revolutionary war. But the war leaders did not attempt that integration of political and social aspirations that was of crucial importance in the English Civil War. Indeed, far from appealing to grass-roots discontent the military activities of the war seem rather to have been a source of embarrassment to the elite, who were eager to make some adjustment in their relationship with England, but who were not at all ready for the pretentions to independence, mass political mobilisation and centralised administration that were of necessity implicit in a resort to arms. From this point of view the bulk of the work of the Continental Congress represents the desperate attempt of politics to catch up with the requirements of a war of liberation.

It is interesting to note that the much-vaunted Declaration of Independence, the only adequate rhetorical and conceptual justification for the war, was not unanimously adopted until July 1776, a full sixteen months after the skirmishes at Lexington and Concord. Even when the Declaration was adopted, after a great deal of acrimonious debate, there never arose the kind of centralised executive machinery that could direct the war effort efficiently. In theory Congress was the body to do this. It had been in existence since 1774 yet even when the states' delegates drew up the Articles of Confederation in 1777 it still remained remarkably weak. It was given the power to declare war, make treaties, control and issue currency and borrow money. Yet it was never endowed with the authority to levy taxes or regulate commerce, nor even raise an army or enforce its own laws. And even these unsatisfactory Articles were not ratified until 1781 after five years of wrangling and bickering.

Naturally the actual direction of the war effort suffered enormously under such handicaps. Not until the end of 1781 was Congress able to set up a Department of War with a permanent secretariat and some executive power. In the intervening six years central direction came from a series of Congressional committees. Their members spent most of their time serving on other committees but even that little time they had in common was largely taken up with disputes about the rights of their respective states. In the winter of 1776 Congress as good as admitted its own impotence when it endowed Washington with almost dictatorial powers in matters of recruitment and the requisitioning of supplies. This should not be regarded as much as a dangerous penchant for military dictatorship as a gloomy recognition of the sad lack of authority at the political centre. In 1778 owing to its inability to raise taxes and thus revenue for the support of its army Congress was forced to direct the individual states to supply their own lines.

The results were notoriously unsatisfactory. By the winter of 1779–80 things had become so desperate that the army in quarters at Morristown almost faded away completely. Lafayette reported to Joseph Reed that on arriving he had found, 'an army that is reduced to nothing, that wants provisions, that has not one of the necessary means to make war, such is the situation wherein I find our troops'.[21] On that very day Washington wrote to Joseph Jones, a Virginian delegate in Congress: 'Certain I am, that unless Congress speaks in a more decisive tone; unless they are vested with powers by the several states competent to the great purposes of war, or assume them as a matter of right; and they and the states respectively act with more energy than they hitherto have done, that our cause is lost.'[22]

Even after the creation of the Department of War central authority was not appreciably strengthened. The Secretary of War, General Benjamin Lincoln, 'only reluctantly exercised authority over areas he believed came under state jurisdiction'.[23] When officers came to his Department for authorisation in various matters he frequently referred them back to the Governors of their respective states. At one point, in the face of mounting pressure from the officers for the settlement of back pay and increases in the rates of pay, Lincoln went so far as to urge them to avoid any settlement in Continental securities and throw themselves upon the mercies of the various states.

Social Revolution and Political Stability

In broad terms the American War of Independence involved no far-reaching changes in the socio-economic structure of the country. On the evidence of its actual results it was in no sense a social revolution. The liberty the American leaders were fighting for was the freedom to develop the financial and commercial interests of their own narrow elite free from any outside interference. At the end of the day the old firm simply had new management. The war saw no kind of dramatic social or, once British authority had been rejected, political upheaval. On the whole there was no great change in the extent of the franchise. There was some displacement of political personnel as Loyalists were replaced by Patriots, but this is in no way to be explained in terms of economic interest or the rise of a new class. The lack of profound social significance is further underlined by the fact that at the end of the war many former Tories returned from exile or political obscurity to resume their old place in society. The old colonialist aristocracy in fact emerged almost unscathed from eight years of war. A few Loyalist landowners were dispossessed and driven from the country for good. But the land was simply resold to wealthy Whigs and was hardly ever split up and redistributed among the poorer sections of American society. Practically all the state governors took an enthusiastic interest in such matters of real estate whilst revolutionary leaders like the Livingstons, the van Rensselaers and the Washingtons all added substantially to their holdings. 'The prices and terms of sale were in fact less favourable to "little men" than the British had been.'[24]

The lack of genuine social revolution, however, should not necessarily lead one to assume an equal lack of social discontent and popular resentment at the activities of the ruling elite. Such discontent undoubtedly did exist and many of the Patriot leaders were only too fully aware of it. There was, for example, an important line of social demarcation between the ruling groups of the old coastal towns and the poorer inhabitants of the backwoods areas. In Massachusetts and New Hampshire there was much discontent among such backwoods colonists over the domination of the revolutionary congresses by the coastal leaders. In Pennsylvania and Maryland in 1776 the inland militia regiments known as the Associators were dominated by democrats fighting against their state assemblies' lack of enthusiasm for outright independence. In Arundel County (Maryland) in June 1776 delegates from the militia battalions came together to draw up a constitution to be submitted to a plebiscite of the whole adult population of the state. Similar rivalries were of immense importance in North and South Carolina. Here the back country, the so-called Piedmont, was inhabited by poor whites driven to seek new opportunities by their inability to compete with slave labour. In neither state were they able to escape the administrative tentacles of the coastal bureaucracies. In the South they were regularly forced to travel great distances to the coast to pay their taxes or to seek legal aid, whilst in the North they were plagued by a host of minor officials demanding exorbitant taxes and illegal fees for non-existent services. In the Carolinas resentment reached such a peak that an organisation was formed known as the Regulators, which endeavoured to sever many of these oppressive links with the coast. They were defeated in 1771 at the Battle of Alamance, and in the next five years some thousand families left the region in disgust seeking refuge in parts of what is now Tennessee.

Such antagonisms were prevalent throughout the colonies as a whole; so also was the awareness of many American leaders of their existence. In April 1776 the aged Joseph Hawley, a member of the Massachusetts Council, wrote to Samuel Adams beseeching him to do something to avert the threat of social chaos. It was quite possible, for:

> The great mob made up partly of your own army and partly of others to drive down on you and disperse you and appoint others . . . to take your place and dictate for the whole continent . . . The people are now ahead of you . . . [Their] blood is so hot as not to admit of delays . . . For God's sake make the best . . . Constitution you can and give it out or the Lord only knows who we shall have for our leaders.[25]

Such fears were obviously exacerbated by the unavoidable fact that thousands of colonists, many of whom were thought to share these antagonisms towards the new American authorities, had been gathered together under arms and as such seemed a standing threat to these same authorities. Certainly their ostensible purpose was the expulsion of the British but who could be sure that they would not wish to complete the task and replace the existing leaders? Consequently the letters and reports of the time abound with references to the unruly attitude of the Army, and with impassioned calls for the rigid imposition of hierarchies of command and obedience.

As early as September 1774 John Adams was remarking that delegates to the Continental Congress, 'were intimidated lest the levelling spirit of the New England colonies should propagate itself into New York'.[26] Once the New England army began to assemble outside Boston in 1775 such fears were voiced more and more, particularly among such pseudo-aristocrats as Washington, who devoted much time and energy to ensure deference to rank and discipline. But he was by no means alone in his fears. In November 1775 Benjamin Thompson was quite explicit about the dangerous revolutionary potential of the New England soldiery:

> The doctrines of independence and levelling have been so effectually sown throughout the country, and so universally imbibed by all ranks of men, that I apprehend that it will be with the greatest difficulty that the inferior officers and soldiers will be ever brought to any tolerable degree of subjection to the commands of their superiors. Many of their leading men are not insensible of this, and I have often heard them lament the existence of that very spirit which induced the common people to take up arms and resist the authority of Great Britain should induce them to resist the authority of their own officers, and by that means effectually prevent them ever making good soldiers.[27]

Here a parallel with the state of the Parliamentary Army in the latter years of the English Civil War begins to appear. In both cases we see the effect of democratic political ideas within the framework of an essentially hierarchical organisation. Similarly, in both armies those with an advantageous position within the hierarchy reacted with horror to the threat of an erosion of their authority. For if they could not maintain their position within the traditionally stratified military organism, what chance had they of maintaining it within society at large, a society in a most manifest state of unrest? There was no shortage of those able to make the relevant historical comparison. A letter from a British surgeon written in May 1775 pointed out: 'Their preachers are Congregationalists, divided and subdivided into a variety of distinctions, the descendants of Oliver Cromwell's army, who truly inherit the spirit which was the occasion of so much bloodshed . . . from the year 1642 until the Restoration.'[28] Alexander Graydon who fought in the war was a little more cautious when he came to write his memoirs: 'Had the contest been a religious one, and our people inflamed by a zeal on points of faith like the Crusaders or the army of Cromwell, this might have been the proper method of exciting them . . . But . . . in Pennsylvania . . . the puritanical spirit was unknown amongst us.' Nevertheless he was careful to point out that, 'it might, however, have been wholly different in New England'.[29]

It is important not to overestimate these similarities. On at least two basic counts the Parliamentary and Continental Armies were quite dissimilar. On the one hand the religiosity of the New Model Army was of much more importance to their military efficiency than was the desperate fatalism of the Americans to their own military efforts. In this respect Graydon was quite correct. The 'puritanical spirit' was unknown among them in so far as the religious beliefs of the Americans lacked that positive dynamic that so boosted the cohesion and faith in the future of the Puritans. Secondly, even though in both armies there developed a rift between the ordinary soldiers and their officers, and even though in both cases this rift was the result of the officers' fear of social upheaval, it was some time before it actually became evident in the ranks of the New Model Army. For a time at least both officers and men shared a common loathing of royal authority and a common belief in the possibility of social and political regeneration. Certainly as the war developed, and as each group was forced to crystallise its ideas, the divergent nature of their visions became apparent. But for a while at least the varied hopes and aspirations of a whole generation of Englishmen had been successfully subsumed in apocalyptic millenarianism. And it was that brief period of unbreakable morale and zealous idealism that had made the Parliamentary Armies such a powerful revolutionary military machine.

But the American Army never passed through such a period. From almost the very beginning its organisation reflected the tensions between those groups that had made up the officer-corps and the rest of society. American society was in a dangerously amorphous state throughout the war years. It lacked national feeling and was corroded by the pernicious effects of sectional self-interest. Religious sentiment could not create a unified military organisation, and neither was there any real authority at the political centre. Furthermore there was already hostility between the different social groups. The net result of all this was that the officers saw it as a prime military task to make the Army at least the repository of deference, natural hierarchy and unquestioning obedience. Perhaps then, they felt, it would be possible to maintain the resilience of such ideas in the culture at large and to go on from there to build up an acceptable political and social structure. It is this that explains Washington's, and others', deep-rooted hostility to the idea of a militia army and their desire to build up regular lines on the European model.

Popular sentiment in general favoured the idea of a people in arms rushing to the defence of their homes and freedoms. In January 1774 a committee of planters in Fairfax County (Virginia) resolved, 'that a well-regulated militia is the only strength and stable security of a free government, and that such a militia will relieve our mother country from any expense in our protection and defence'.[30] The Virginia Declaration of Rights of May 1776 insisted that, 'a well-regulated militia, composed of the body of the people, trained to arms, is the proper, natural and safe defence of a free state'.[31] Whilst the Massachusetts Bill of Rights of 1780 declared: 'The people have a right to bear arms for the common defence. And as, in times of peace, armies are dangerous to liberty, they ought not to be maintained without the consent of the legislature.'[32] In the same year Samuel Adams pointed out to the Marquis de Chastellux that:

> As to the power of commanding armies, it ought neither to be vested in a great nor even in a small number of men: the governor alone can employ the forces by sea and land according to necessity; but the land forces will consist only in the militia, which as it is composed of the people themselves, can never act against the people.[33]

Here, one might have thought, were the vital ingredients for a genuine revolutionary people's war, inspired by the wishes of the mass of the populace. But once war had actually broken out, and the revolutionary leaders had been brought face to face with the unruly attitudes of the rank-and-file, they quickly began to lose some of their faith in a militia army. Washington in particular became exceptionally dubious about the value of such troops. In September 1776 he wrote to John Hancock, the President of the Continental Congress:

> To place any dependence on militia is, assuredly, resting upon a broken staff. Men . . . totally unacquainted with every kind of military skill, which being followed by a want of confidence in themselves, when opposed to troops regularly trained and disciplined, and appointed, superior in knowledge, and superior in arms makes them timid, and ready to fly from their own shadows.[34]

In a letter to his brother written in December 1776 Washington felt himself driven to conclude: 'The unhappy policy of short enlistment and a dependence upon the militia will, I fear, prove the downfall of our cause.'[35]

General Nathanael Greene, the commander of the southern theatre of operations in 1780-81, was equally emphatic about the dubious value of the militia:

> The foolish prejudice of the formidableness of the militia being a sufficient barrier against any attempts of the enemy, prevented the Legislature [in North Carolina] from making any exertions equal to their critical and dangerous situation . . . It is astonishing to me how these people could place such a confidence in a militia scattered over the face of the whole earth, and generally destitute of everything necessary to their own defence. The militia in the back country are formidable, the others are not, and all are very ungovernable and very difficult to keep together. As they come out, twelve thousand might be in motion, and not five hundred in the field.[36]

Washington's answer to the military inadequacies of the militia was quite simple: 'Regular troops are alone equal to the exigencies of modern war, as well as for defence as for offence, and whatever substitute is attempted it must prove illusory and ruinous.'[37] In purely military terms one can see some value in

Washington's insistence. The militia regiments simply did not have the military training or experience to stand up to British and German regulars in an open battle. In such battles, as the late Professor Western has pointed out, 'what was needed above all to break the deadlock on the battlefield was an easy means of concentrating superior force against the enemy's weak points'.[38] To obtain the necessary superior numbers and fire-power it was essential that the American troops receive training in close-order marching and manoeuvring, as well as the disciplined use of the volley. In seeking for such conventional military excellence Washington was no different from many other revolutionary leaders. Even Mao Tse-tung, surely one of the main proponents of a people's war, acknowledged that in the last analysis it is impossible to completely break up the regular forces of the incumbent government without eventually creating mobile regular forces of one's own, and meeting one's enemy in open battle. But in the Maoist scheme of things the stage of regular mobile warfare only comes at the very end of a protracted struggle during most of which the efforts of guerrilla groups and local militia have been tightly integrated into the total military effort. It is these groups which enable the revolution to get off the ground militarily, and thus their political aspirations must form the very bed-rock of the revolution's political programme. If it is to be a genuine social revolution there must be no hint of the contempt for their military abilities that characterised the attitudes of Washington and his generals. And it might have been militarily profitable for Washington to have placed more reliance upon the efforts of the militia, for in its broad terms the American strategy had much in common with more modern guerrilla campaigns, depending as it did upon mobility, terrain and the avoidance of large pitched battles. Alexander Hamilton observed:

It may be asked, if, to avoid general engagements, we give up objects of the first importance, what is to carry the enemy from carrying every important point and ruining us? My answer is, that our hopes are not placed in any particular city or spot of ground, but in . . . [trying to] waste and defeat the enemy by piecemeal.[39]

And Thomas Paine's description of the American War of Independence as a 'war of invasion' offers a concise early definition of guerrilla warfare:

> the conquest of America by arms ... is not within the compass of human practicability, for America is too extensive either to be fully conquered or *passively* defended. But she may be *actively* defended by defeating or making prisoners of the army that invades her. And this is the only system of defence that can be effectual in a large country. There is something in a war carried on by invasion which makes it differ in circumstances from any other mode of war, because he who conducts it cannot tell whether the ground he gains, be for him, or against him, when he first makes it.[40]

But such a mode of warfare demands reliance upon decentralised, fairly independent guerrillas and militiamen. For Washington such a reliance would have been politically dangerous. In the absence of a strong political machine how could a general conscious of his social position and his responsibility to his peers even begin to look kindly upon such units, with their anarchic sense of discipline and dangerous belief in equality?

To show how heavily such considerations did weigh upon Washington's mind one need only return to his fascinating letter to Hancock. So far only the purely military rationalisations of his mistrust of the militia have been extracted. But many of his other remarks are most revealing. He bemoans, for example, the status of the officers in this kind of unit:

> The only merit [such] an officer possesses in his ability to raise men; while those men consider and treat him as an equal; and (in the character of an officer) regard him no more than a broomstick, being mixed together as one common herd; no order nor no discipline can prevail; nor will the officer ever meet with the respect which is so essentially necessary to due subordination.

He goes on:

> Men accustomed to unbounded freedom, and no control, cannot brook the restraint which is so indispensably neces-

sary to the good order and government of an army . . . The
little discipline I have been labouring to establish in the
army under my command, is in a manner done away by
having such a mixture of troops as have been called
together within these few months.[41]

Similar considerations of the pernicious effect of the lack of
discipline in Continental and militia units weighed heavily with
Washington's contemporaries. Even in July 1775 the Reverend
William Emerson was noting the measures taken to forestall
such effects:

There is a great overturning in the camp as to order and
regularity. New lords, new laws. The generals Washington
and Lee are upon the lines every day. New orders from his
excellency are read to the regiments every morning . . .
The strictest government is taking place, and great distinction is made between officers and soldiers. Everyone is made
to know his place and keep it, or be tied up and receive . . .
thirty or forty lashes according to his crime.[42]

In June 1776 General John Sullivan sent back the following
anxious report about the state of the expeditionary force to
Canada:

The regiments here are torn and divided into numerous
parts scattered from one end of the country to another.
This method, besides its being highly impolitic, will ever
prevent the officers from making proper returns of their
men and naturally destroys that subordination which ever
ought to be kept up in an army.[42]

In March of the same year Alexander Graydon bemoaned the
fact that amongst the officers 'so far from aiming at a deport-
ment that would raise them above their privates, and then
prompt them to due respect and obedience to their commands,
the object was, by humility, to preserve the existing blessing of
equality'.[44] In his memoirs he contrasted such behaviour with
that of the New York regiments in 1776: 'They afforded officers

who might have been distinguished without a badge; and who were sufficiently men of the world, to know that the levelling principle was of all others the most incompatible with good soldiership.'[45]

All were agreed that what was lacking in the Continental Army was a good officer-corps willing and able to impose suitable notions of subordination and discipline on the rank-and-file. In September 1776 Major-General Henry Knox wrote thus to his brother:

> There is a radical evil in our army—the lack of officers. We ought to have men of merit in the most extensive and un-limited sense of the word . . . Until Congress forms an establishment to induce men proper for the purpose to leave their usual employments and enter the service, it is ten to one that they will be beat till they are heartily tired of it.[46]

So, too, Washington's revealing letter to Hancock:

> The war must be carried out systematically, and to do it, you must have good officers. There are . . . no other possible means to obtain them but by establishing your army on a permanent footing and giving your officers good pay; this will induce gentlemen and men of character to engage; and till the bulk of your officers are composed of such persons as are actuated by principles of honour . . . you have little to expect from them.[47]

Washington's intense concern about the quality and authority of the officer-corps was shown again in 1780 in the controversy over whether Nathanael Greene should be summarily dismissed from his post of Quartermaster-General. In a letter to Joseph Jones, Washington pointed out that such a move would seriously undermine the confidence of all the officers and, 'There is no set of men in the United States considered as a body that have made the same sacrifices of their interests in support of the common cause, as the officers of the American army.'[48]

These repeated warnings do seem to have had some impact

upon Congress. In September 1776, for example, they drew up a new scale of pay for the Army. Whereas, compared to the pay rates of 1775, sergeants, corporals and privates received exactly the same, all officers received a substantial increase, captains and lieutenants receiving double, and colonels and majors half as much again. By this same decree the officers were accorded various new privileges commensurate with a more elevated social status. Surgeon James Thatcher noted in his journal: 'Each commissioned officer is allowed the privilege of taking a soldier from the ranks as a waiter, and he is exempted from camp and other duty, except in time of action. The officers are also allowed a number of rations in proportion to their rank.'[49] In May 1778 the officers were also promised a half-pay pension for the first seven years after the end of the war; in December 1779 the seven years was extended to life.

The Continental leaders did not merely devote themselves to inculcating habits of discipline into the Army through the creation of an elitist officer-corps. They also tried to impose upon the Army those very military habits which supposedly made British and German privates the helpless slaves of tyranny. John Adams pointed the way in 1777 when the Army was marched through Philadelphia to encourage the civilian population there: 'Much remains to be done. Our soldiers have not quite the air of soldiers. They don't step exactly in time. They don't hold up their heads quite erect, nor turn out their toes so exactly as they ought. They don't all of them cock their hats, and such as do don't all wear them the same way.'[50] Alexander Hamilton drew the logical conclusions in 1779. Referring to a plan of John Laurens to form regiments of freed slaves, he said that he saw nothing amiss in such an idea. Indeed, 'I think their want of cultivation . . . joined to their habit of subordination will enable them sooner to become soldiers than our white inhabitants. Let officers be men of sense and sentiment; and nearer the soldiers approach to machines, perhaps the better.'[51]

Nor was Washington slow in trying to apply this policy to the Army. In the winter of 1777–8 at Valley Forge a Prussian drill-master, General von Steuben, was turned loose upon the soldiery to try and turn them into the automatons of the classic

eighteenth-century battlefield. This account of Major Thomas
Fleury gives a clear enough picture of what was being attempted:

> At six o'clock in the morning the division is ordered to
> general parade, and the soldiers . . . are drilled in ordinary
> marching. An NCO gives the time and the step, and he drills
> them in marching with and without music and drums. This
> drill lasts two hours. At nine o'clock is the parade; the
> soldiers are then taught the few movements in which they
> are to be instructed after the use of arms . . . At three
> o'clock drilling in divisions as in the morning; at six p.m. a
> meeting of the adjutants in my quarters for instructions in
> theoretic manoeuvering and the emphasis to be used in
> giving the word of command.[52]

Once again certain similarities with the New Model Army
emerge; it, too, stressed the importance of discipline. But they
were very different types of discipline, and it is through a
contrast of the two that we can begin to see the basic differences
between the Parliamentary and the Continental Armies. In the
former discipline came from within and was part and parcel of
the soldiers' very conception of revolutionary activity. All ranks
were agreed that discipline and some sort of subordination to
higher rank contributed to the attainment of the common goal.
But this was manifestly not the case in the American Army.
There, discipline was imposed from above by those of a certain
social group who feared the consequences of allowing too much
initiative to the ordinary soldiers. Not only was discipline for
them not a basic component of the revolutionary ideology, it
was used as a counter-revolutionary tool to suppress any
radical tendencies among the rank-and-file.

It is in this light that the whole structure and leadership of
the Continental Army should be examined. The basic point is
that the American 'Revolution' was in no sense a social revolution. But any kind of political upheaval always provokes some
degree of social unrest. All the efforts of the American leadership were devoted to ensuring that this unrest was kept firmly in
check. The war against the British could potentially have been
a genuine people's war. The Americans could, theoretically,

have resorted to full-scale guerrilla warfare, they could have relaxed discipline and allowed elective principles into the government of the Army, they could have attempted to politicise the soldiery with a radical socio-political programme. But in fact they chose to do none of this. American society was dominated by a group of prosperous planters, commercial men and officials whose survival, with or without British rule, depended upon the maintenance of the social *status quo* within the thirteen states. But having chosen to reject British rule in the hope of enhancing their wealth, power and prestige even further, they found themselves caught up in a situation of near anarchy. In the first place there was no sense of nationalism to bind the Americans together. In the second place tensions within American society were not simply on a geographical level; there were also profound social tensions that threatened political stability. In the third place, as a consequence of all this, it proved impossible at first to create a strong central political organisation that could even begin to capture the loyalties of most colonists. The conservatism of the colonial leadership precluded the possibility of a mass-based revolutionary organisation. Thus the Americans had none of the prerequisites for the conduct of a people's war. After a few months of chaos and indecision their military leaders studiously sought to relearn the lessons of European warfare with its total emphasis upon the primacy of hierarchy and unquestioning obedience. Instead of being the vanguard of revolutionary aspirations, the Continentals became the bastion of conservatism and privilege.

Nevertheless, none of this is to deny the paramount importance of the Army in the War of Independence. Whatever form the Army took, the fact remains that in the absence of national solidarity the Army was a vitally important force in giving some semblance of unity to the American war effort. In some ways the American experience represents the most dramatic example of the militarisation of political conflict. For without the Army there was no struggle at all. Nathanael Greene had clearly appreciated this point. In 1781, in a letter to Jefferson, he said: 'The army is all that the states have to depend on for their political existence.' [53] In the absence of strong central political direction the successes of the national army were all that prevented the home front from dissolving into its provincial constituent parts. The victories at Trenton and Princeton, for example, were more important to the maintenance of some semblance of American unity than all the decrees and debates of Congress put together.

Chapter 4   The French Revolution
1789–94

CHRONOLOGY

1789

24 Jan   Preparations begin for the election of the States General.

5 May   The first meeting of the States General at Versailles.

17 June   The Third Estate takes on the title of National Assembly.

13 July   Widespread rioting in Paris and the looting of arms. The decision is taken to form a civil militia for Paris.

14 July   The storming of the Bastille.

18 July   The Parisian National Guard is formally constituted.

July/Aug   Rioting and looting by peasants all over France.

4 Aug   The Assembly abolishes feudalism.

27 Aug   The Declaration of the Rights of Man and Citizen is adopted by the Assembly.

5 Oct   A popular march to Versailles to bring the King back to Paris where it was held he would be safe from counter-revolutionary intrigue.

1790

10 Sept   The troops are forbidden to have deliberating associations within the regiments or to attend political clubs.

1791

1 Jan   The old names of the line regiments are abolished.

29 April   The soldiers are again allowed to attend the clubs.

21 June   The Assembly decrees the formations of battalions of volunteers taken from the ranks of the National Guard.

25 June   The King's attempt to flee Paris fails.

28 Sept   The proclamation of the Constitution. It includes the distinction between active and passive citizens.

1 Oct   The first meeting of the Legislative Assembly.

1792

20 April   France declares war on Austria and Prussia.

11 July   The Assembly declares *la patrie en danger*.

10 Aug   A Jacobin insurrection in Paris.

19 Aug   The National Guard is thrown open to all citizens.

Aug   Forty-two new battalions of volunteers are called up and the stipulation that only active citizens should serve is abolished.

20 Sept   The first meeting of the National Convention. The Prussian army of the Duke of Brunswick is defeated at Valmy.

6 Nov   Dumouriez beats the Austrians at the Battle of Jemappes.

1793

21 Jan   The execution of the King.

1 Feb   England declares war on France.

21 Feb   The Convention decides on a *lévee* of 300,000 men. They also decree the amalgamation of the battalions of volunteers and troops of the line.

25–26 Feb   Serious food riots in Paris.

9 March   The Convention decides to dispatch some of its members as *représentants-en-mission* to every department.

18 March   The French under Dumouriez are defeated at the Battle of Neerwinden.

6 April   The Committee of General Defence is merged into the Committee of Public Safety.

12 May   The Convention passes the 'Maximum' Law imposing controls on food prices.

2 June   Under the direction of the sections' Central Revolutionary Committee the National Convention is purged of the moderate Girondins.

16 June   The adoption of a new constitution.

16 Aug   Carnot formally takes on the direction of military affairs within the Committee of Public Safety.

23 Aug   Carnot issues his decree declaring the *levée en masse*.

4–5 Sept   A popular insurrection in Paris demanding controls on food prices.

29 Sept   The Convention passes the Law of the General Maximum, imposing controls on a whole range of goods and also limits on wages.

15 Oct   Jourdan is victorious at the Battle of Wattignies.

17 Oct   Vendéean insurgents are defeated at the Battle of Cholet.

4 Dec   Full executive powers are given to the Committees of Public Safety and General Security.

21 Dec   The troops are forbidden to issue collective petitions.

23 Dec   A further defeat for the rebels in the Vendée at the Battle of Savenay.

1794

1 Feb   A Ministry of Munitions is set up under the direct control of the Committee of Public Safety.

25 March   The execution of the left-wing radicals Hébert, Vincent and Ronsin.

5 April   The execution of Danton.

26 June   Jourdan defeats Coburg at the Battle of Fleurus.

28 July   The execution of Robespierre and twenty-one other Jacobins by the more moderate Thermidorians.

10 July   The French Army enters Brussels.

The French Revolution differs somewhat from the other social upheavals discussed so far. Both the English Civil War and the American War of Independence can be classed as military revolutions proper. In other words, military activity was an inseparable component of the basic conflict of interests. In England the whole tenor of Puritan thought tended towards an outlook on the world that assumed perpetual struggle and the consequent need for organisation and discipline. Modes of political violence are largely determined by the social, political and cultural characteristics of the time; the Ironsides and the New Model Army were an inevitable consequence of those that underlay Puritan discontent, in its widest political and spiritual sense. In America religious attitudes were not so important in forming the colonial response to British oppression, imagined or otherwise. Nevertheless military operations were an indis-

pensable part of American resistance. For it was only through
the creation of a supra-state military organism that the conflict
was prevented from dissolving into a disconnected agglomeration of local disturbances. In fact, the War of Independence
offers substantial corroboration of the Debray thesis that,
in certain historical circumstances, the development of viable
armed forces under centralised direction is a vital prerequisite of the development of both revolutionary consciousness
and the very process of revolutionary struggle itself.[1] Whereas military struggle in England was ideologically inevitable, in America it was politically indispensable. In either case
warfare and politics went hand in hand.

The French Revolution, however, was not conducted as a
series of military operations. It cannot really be regarded as
either a civil war or a war of national liberation. Indeed most
histories of the Revolution devote only a small amount of space
to what is regarded as its military side. Similarly, in proportion
to the whole body of literature on the Revolution, that devoted
exclusively to military matters is very small. Nevertheless, the
fact that the actual chronology of the Revolution cannot be
drawn up purely in terms of battles and campaigns should not
lead to the assumption that military affairs remained isolated
from the social and political upheavals of 'civilian' life. The
period as a whole still offers fascinating insights into the integral
connection between political revolution and military organisation.

The National Guard: a Class in Arms

It seems fairly clear that there is at least some heuristic value
in discussing the French Revolution in terms of a struggle of the
bourgeois commercial classes against their exclusion from full
economic and political participation in the nation's affairs. Their
principal opponents in this struggle were the monarchy and the
feudalistic aristocracy. The political emancipation of the bourgeoisie could only follow upon the destruction of royal and
aristocratic control of the legislative process and the machinery
of political control. Similarly, economic emancipation depended
upon the elimination of the old feudal land relationships between lord and peasant. But the bourgeoisie were not alone in

their struggle against the incumbent power elite. Other social groups in France were equally dissatisfied with their lot. The peasantry were as eager as the bourgeoisie for the destruction of aristocratic power and the abolition of feudal obligations. The urban poor yearned for far-reaching reform that would guarantee them economic self-sufficiency in the seeming anarchy of wage relationships, with its attendant chronic unemployment and perennial shortages.

In the first years of the Revolution the middle classes, peasants and urban poor presented a loosely united political front. In August 1789 many feudal obligations were abolished by the middle-class delegates of the National Assembly. By August 1792 the power of the monarchy, already severely limited, was destroyed completely. This proved sufficient to satisfy the demands of the peasantry, particularly when in 1793 whatever outstanding obligations there were to aristocratic landowners were declared null and void. Some peasants received land, whilst the vast percentage of them achieved some kind of material advantage. But the requisition of political and economic power by the bourgeoisie was of little benefit to the poor in Paris and the other towns of France. Bad harvests, a crisis of commercial and financial confidence and the basic unwillingness of the middle-class legislators to countenance any erosion of their supremacy over the labouring classes, all meant that they were condemned to remain in abject poverty. Throughout the Revolution the urban poor were victims of what Babeuf described as, 'the gnawing canker of anxiety, general and particular, that is with each of us always, regarding the next day, the next month, the next year, our old age, our children and their children'.[2]

Thus, in their consolidation of power, the middle classes felt themselves menaced on two fronts. They feared both a royalist attempt to seize power again, and some sort of popular movement from below intent on demanding retribution for the hardships of the poor. In these circumstances the bourgeoisie proceeded to arm themselves and set up a class militia to protect their newly gained political pre-eminence. In both the English Civil War and the American War of Independence similar considerations of political power and the threat of popular unrest forced certain groups within the armies to protect their positions through an emphasis upon hierarchy and the tightening of discipline. This was also to become a feature of the regular armies of the Republic. But initially a new phenomenon emerged: a revolutionary armed force specifically designed to protect the interests of one social group at the expense of others, with membership confined to those within the group.[1]

The Parisian National Guard was one of the consequences of the great popular insurrection of 11-14 July 1789, when support for the Third Estate precipitated a direct challenge to royal authority. Every day of the insurrection was marked by widespread searches for arms and powder. Gunsmiths' shops, private houses, the Hotel des Invalides and the Bastille were all pillaged by bands of insurgents seeking weapons. In the eyes of the bourgeoisie these bands contained a terrifyingly high proportion of poor workmen, unemployed labourers and people without fixed abode. The *canaille* was in revolt and what was worse it was successfully arming itself. Thus, as early as 13 July the middle-class leaders began organising a civil militia with which to protect themselves and their property. From the beginning eligibility to serve in the militia depended upon social background, and from the beginning the National Guard made it one of its key tasks to effect the disarmament of the poorer sections of the Parisian population.

On the day of its formation only householders—a singularly select group in eighteenth-century Paris—were summoned to the meetings in the sixty electoral districts. About 13,000 citizens subsequently enlisted, but all vagrants and homeless persons were excluded from its ranks, as were 'even a large part of the settled wage-earners'.[3] In the words of a prominent member of the Third Estate, Pierre-Joseph Barnave, the National Guard was going to be *bonne bourgeoise*. This was re-emphasised on 31 July when the Military Committee of the Parisian Assembly of Electors presented its conclusions on the organisation of the National Guard. Amongst their recommendations was one that no transients or domestics be allowed to join and that even workers and artisans be excluded on the ground that they ought to be left to their work. To achieve this it was stipulated that all members had to pay for their own

uniforms themselves. This stipulation was of particular significance. For not only did it keep the lower orders out of the
Guard, it also heightened the group solidarity of those that
could afford to dress up. The term *sans-culotte* had already
acquired some meaning as a mark of social differentiation;
sans uniforme merely buttressed the barriers of privilege. The
Constituent Assembly gave legal sanction to this social demarcation when it divided the adult male population into 'active'
and 'passive' citizens. To qualify as an 'active' citizen one had
to be above twenty-five years of age, have been domiciled for a
year, not be engaged in domestic service and be paying a direct
tax equivalent to the value of three days unskilled labour. In
May 1790 the Assembly decreed that only such citizens were
eligible for service in the National Guard.

If the bourgeoisie were to feel totally secure they had to
ensure that they not only had the monopoly of organised force
but also that there were no arms available to those outside the
ranks of the National Guard. Such was one of their main aims
from the very beginning. On 14 July 1789 the Parisian deputies
in the Assembly reported that:

> The establishment of the citizens' militia and the measures
> taken yesterday . . . assured the city a peaceful night,
> such as it had not hoped for, bearing in mind the consider-
> able number of individuals who had procured arms on the
> Sunday and Monday before the establishment of the said
> militia; . . . according to the reports of the various districts
> it is certain that a number of these individuals have been
> disarmed and brought back to order by the citizens'
> militia.[4]

On 19 July the Assembly of Electors asked the National
Guard to disarm all those citizens who were not enrolled in the
registers of the district battalions. On 25 July the municipality
announced that manufacturers, dealers and owners of arms had
three days in which to hand them in to the authorities; otherwise they would be confiscated. Lafayette, the commander of
the National Guard, added a letter of his own in which he
assured private owners that those in regular domicile would

have their arms returned once a detailed inventory had been drawn up. This was a most necessary rider without which the Parisian authorities would have effectively disarmed their own Guard. On 10 August the Assembly requested the Guard to give all assistance in disarming those without fixed abode who had still managed to hang on to their weapons.

But the National Guard was not merely a force of organised repression. It is also of the greatest relevance to our basic theme of what constitutes a genuine revolutionary mass army. Certainly the Guard only represented one section of the French population, but within these circumscribed social boundaries it was a paramount example of a politicised armed force. It included only 'active' citizens; but the qualification 'active' was not merely a definition of eligibility to serve in the Guard. It was also the criterion by which eligibility to vote in the primary electoral assemblies was decided. In other words, all those with a 'stake' in the country were allowed to take up arms if necessary to defend that stake. Military service became a function of political responsibility. But this was not all, and here one comes to the most important point. 'Active' citizens were not only eligible to serve in the National Guard, they were also obliged to. Military service became an indispensable corollary of full political participation. This obligation was made quite specific in the Assembly's decree of 1 June 1790, but it had been foremost in many minds from the very beginning. On 26 August 1789, for example, the Assembly of Representatives in Paris declared that registers should be established in which were to be written the names of all those liable for service. It was further decreed that all those who failed their obligations in this respect would automatically be debarred from holding any civic post. In a series of decrees of 21 June, 22 July and 4 August 1791 the Assembly asked for volunteers from the ranks of the Guard to create new battalions of line troops to serve alongside the regulars. Included in one of these acts was the stipulation: 'All active citizens above the age of eighteen are to be entered in the registers of the National Guard . . . If they do not they will lose all civic rights and will be declared unworthy of bearing arms.'[5]

Another way in which the National Guard was made to

reflect the political issues of the time was by the introduction of the elective principle. According to the Military Committee's draft proposals of 1789 divisional chiefs were elected by representatives chosen for that purpose by the ten divisional districts; battalion commanders were chosen by their own district, as were the bulk of the company officers. Such a system almost exactly mirrored that by which the delegates to the National Assembly were chosen—election to the primary assemblies was on universal 'active' suffrage, whilst the election of the legislators themselves was confined to the much smaller primary assemblies. Such procedures are a vital feature of a genuine revolutionary people's army. If an organised military force is to harness the basic political aspirations of the people, its organisation must reflect the principles that underlie them, and, if possible, the procedures that are their expression. The 'active' citizenry of France in the early years of the Revolution felt themselves to be living in a new world. They could only be expected to take up arms in defence of that world if the organisations in which they were to enlist also reflected this break with the past and the new political liberties and opportunities. Whatever legislation was passed obliging them to serve in the National Guard, they would only do so consistently if they felt obliged. They would only feel obliged if their status as soldier was commensurate with that as citizen.

Perhaps this might seem to be a somewhat over-romanticised picture of the citizen-soldier. By and large the 'active' citizens did serve, and often enthusiastically, when called upon to do so. But there was some shirking. Most Guardsmen probably missed some of their duties, some probably never enlisted at all, whilst others certainly tried to engage *remplacements*, less fortunate citizens whom they could equip and pay to take their place. The Assembly itself was not unaware of the limits on the 'active' citizens' capacity regularly to fulfil a rather tedious duty. From the beginning the delegates tried to hedge their bets. In 1789 when the Guard was constituted each of the sixty battalions was given one company (out of five) of paid Guardsmen whose equipment was provided by the municipality. These were to form the nucleus of the force and to be on permanent duty. The bulk of the recruits for these companies were not 'active' citizens but volunteers from the elite regular regiments of Paris, particularly the *Gardes-Françaises*. Many sergeants of the *Gardes* were patriotic volunteers for such duties, but one cannot escape the conclusion that in this instance the Assembly was sacrificing political principle to military efficiency of the old sort. Nevertheless, human fallibility or the fear of a complete break with the ways of the *ancien régime* must not be allowed to obscure the revolutionary nature of the principles that underlay this experiment with a civic militia. Whatever the day-to-day deficiencies in the organisation and the administration of the National Guard one may discern in it a bold attempt to impart to military service the political dynamic that alone can hold men together in times of revolutionary unrest.

So far described, the National Guard was no more than a civic militia. Yet it has a proper place in any discussion of military organisms, particularly given the place that it was originally hoped the Guard would have within the military establishment as a whole. Indeed, at one time it rather looked as though the Assembly was endeavouring to offer the Guard as a substitute for the regular army in the event of the latter's complete disintegration. In December 1789 one delegate, Edmond Dubois-Crancé, offered the blueprint of just such a scheme. His starting-point was simple: 'It is now a right of all Frenchmen to serve their country; it is an honour to be a soldier when this means being a defender of the Constitution and one's country . . . Every citizen should be a soldier, every soldier a citizen.' [6] He went on to envisage an army of three types of soldier. Firstly, there were to be 150,000 full-time regulars drawn from the whole of the male population. But the other two groups were only to be drawn from the 'active' citizens: a provincial militia of all bachelors aged between eighteen and forty, and a reserve, parochial force of some one and a quarter million men ready to defend their home and hearth. What is of particular interest here is the insistence that only 'active' citizens could be allowed the luxury of combining military service and everyday life. As only the 'active' citizens had any sort of political stake in the future of the Revolution at that stage in its development, only they could safely be relied upon not to let everyday contact with their fellow-citizens prejudice them against the forms and

rituals of military service. As they had something to fight for
they would fight more willingly and more effectively. Leverrier
is a little contemptuous of the way in which Dubois-Crancé's
actual blueprint does not square with his rhetoric about the
need for universal military service. But one must beware of
interpreting too freely what he meant by the word 'citizen'.
Both his actual plan and later remarks about the absolute
necessity of only permitting 'active' citizens to join the volunteers of 1791 lead one to assume that he always, in his own
mind, prefixed that word with an implicit 'active'.[7]

In fact his scheme was decisively rejected by the Assembly on
12 December. But the ideas it contained were not lost. Throughout 1790 the Parisian Guard was put through a rigorous programme of military training to turn it into at least a useful
reserve for the regular army. Men of over sixty years of age
were formed into veterans' companies and boys under eighteen
into battalions of so-called *Élèves de la Patrie*.[8] Also in 1790 the
National Guards of certain provincial towns formed a sort of
ad hoc alliance with the line regiments doing garrison duty there.
In April the Guard at Montauban formed just such a *fédération*
with the Languedoc Regiment, and the Guards of Toulouse and
other towns soon followed suit. In the Franche-Comté the Royal
Étranger Regiment was similarly supported by local bodies of
the National Guard, as was the Conti Regiment in Amiens. The
Assembly gave its blessing to such alliances, and on 4 June the
King authorised, 'the coming together of regiments of troops
of the line with the national militias'.[9] On 30 May 1790
de Lameth was prompted to forecast at the Jacobin Club: 'His
majesty was going to order the general fusion of the troops of
the line and the National Guard and that it was the only way to
bring back peace and harmony.'[10]

The most far-reaching attempt to render the Army bourgeois
came in the decrees of summer 1791. These called for just under
100,000 volunteers taken exclusively from the ranks of the
National Guard. They were to assemble in departmental
battalions and go to the frontiers to fight alongside the regiments of the line. The paid, full-time companies in the Guard of
Paris and other cities were dissolved and their members forced
to enlist in the regular army. Here was a clear attempt to create

at least a part of a regular army that would be motivated by the same political commitment as the National Guard. But the attempt was always doomed to failure if only because there were not enough 'active' citizens to fill the massive requirements of French defence. By the time of the next mass mobilisation of 1792, again based upon volunteers, the distinction between 'active' and 'passive' citizens had been abolished. Nevertheless the Assembly's attempt to create a homogeneous army selected on the grounds of common socio-political interest is of the greatest importance. In some respects it represents the hey-day of the search for a military organisation that best suited a nation in the throes of revolutionary transformation. Albeit the National Guard stood for the defence of sectional interests, its organisation represents the closest integration of political self-interest and the need for an effective military establishment. Fully conscious of this, the Assembly fought against its disintegration as a bastion of middle-class privilege to the bitter end. Even after 4 September 1791, when the Assembly was forced to provide the uniforms and equipment of the volunteers and so tacitly to condone the large influx of 'passive' citizens into the battalions, it did not relax its hold on the 'sedentary' companies, those that remained behind to perform the traditional policing role. Here the distinction between 'active' and 'passive' was upheld for as long as possible, as was the obligation to provide one's own uniform. It had proved illusory to hope that external defence could be left to one fraction of the nation. But that fraction could never dare to surrender its monopoly of force in the field of internal disturbance.

The Nation in Arms

Had the French Revolution remained a purely internal affair there seems little doubt that the formation of the bourgeois National Guard, and perhaps its partial amalgamation into the regular army, would have represented the limits of the politicisation of the armed forces. But this was not to be the case. The attack on the traditional ruling groups in France greatly alarmed the monarchs and governments of the other European powers. Eventually they felt themselves driven to resort to armed intervention, and in 1792 France was obliged to declare war on Austria and Prussia. From then on French military policy was somewhat ambivalent. At the root of everything was the need to mobilise vast armies to resist the aggression of Austria, Prussia and, eventually, Great Britain. This necessitated constant and concerted state intervention to co-ordinate and supply these armies. To this extent the French Republic was inevitably driven to centralisation and the suppression of dissent. National self-preservation increasingly precluded the luxuries of democratic debate or a reliance on unchecked revolutionary idealism.

However, it would be a great mistake to assume that the governments of the National Convention were particularly eager to encourage this drift towards centralisation. None of the great personalities of the period, be they Girondin or Jacobin, were aspirant dictators or even compulsive bureaucrats. They all sincerely abhorred the maxims of blind obedience and political isolation that were the very *raison d'être* of the standing armies of the *ancien régime*. The Army, they held, should be the representative of the nation, the armed manifestation of the new democratic ideals that permeated society. As Saint-Just said in 1793: 'All that is not new in a time of innovation is pernicious. The military arts of the monarchy are no longer suitable for us; we are a different type of man with different enemies.'[11] Even in the days of the *ancien régime* there had been those who had wanted some sort of minimal integration of the Army into political life. Hippolyte de Guibert, one of Louis XVI's Ministers of War, had pointed out: 'In most countries of Europe, the interests of the people and those of the government are very separate; patriotism is merely a word; citizens are not soldiers; soldiers are not citizens; wars are not the quarrel of the nation; they are that of the ministry and the sovereign.'[12] In May 1791 the Cordeliers Club re-echoed such sentiments: 'The title "army of the line", the name of any type of military unit which might be kept separate from the nation, should be forever erased from the dictionary of liberty, in which one should only find mention of "the popular forces, uniquely and completely national".'[13]

The formation and organisation of the National Guard was an attempt to put just such a doctrine into effect. But the ascendant bourgeoisie tried to ensure that revolutionary military service remained their prerogative. They defined the nation as only that section of it which had a manifest material and thus political stake in its future. In short, the nation was exclusively defined in terms of its ruling class. Except for the pressure of international events such would have remained the case. But European aggression forced the whole nation-state on to the defensive, and the sheer material demands of an adequate defence and counter-offensive forced the revolutionary leaders to call upon the resources of the whole nation. These resources included manpower, and for this reason alone it became imperative to abandon a narrow interpretation of what constituted the nation and to abolish the distinction between 'active' and 'passive' citizens.

In July and August 1792 this momentous step was taken. In July the Assembly decided to ask for forty-two new battalions of volunteers as well as an additional 50,000 troops for the army of the line. The call was still for volunteers, but this time the Assembly had decided that the pressure of international events rendered it unfeasible to rely upon the fervour of only one section of the nation. On 11 July the Convention declared *la patrie en danger* and called upon the services of all able-bodied men. Lazare Carnot in his report to the Assembly of 1 August explained the reasons for this tactic:

> Everywhere that one section of the people remains constantly under arms, whilst the other is not, these latter necessarily become the slaves of the former, or rather both are reduced to servitude by those who are able to take over the positions of command. It is thus absolutely necessary in a free country that every citizen be a soldier or that none is . . . It is necessary that by the time of peace at the latest all the line battalions should become battalions of the National Guard.[14]

Mention has already been made of this desire to integrate the line with the National Guard and make national defence a political responsibility. But Carnot is here introducing a new element; he is looking to a time when the ranks of the National

Guard will be open to all citizens, irrespective of their social position, and thus to a time when defence of *la patrie* will be the responsibility of the whole nation. In the same speech he made his position quite clear:

> Your Commission proposes to you that all those with the wish and the ability to come to the defence of their country be armed with the same type of muskets. It puts it to you as the only vigorous measure commensurate with the present crisis, as the only policy which could cause to tremble our enemies within and without.[15]

Not only was such an act militarily necessary, but it was also an inevitable political response to the feelings of the people at large. As early as 1791 Robespierre, ever in touch with the aspirations of the *petit peuple*, had posed the question in these terms:

> Are those without certain predefined abilities, and those who do not pay a certain amount in taxes, thus slaves? Are they outsiders to the other citizens? Are they without a commitment to the public interest? . . . Will you alone enjoy the right to defend yourselves and to defend them? Then recognise that all citizens with a fixed abode have the right to be enrolled in the registers of the National Guard.[16]

On 13 August the final step was taken. The General Council ordered all the citizens in the sections to form themselves into companies. All suffrage qualifications were abolished and all were accorded the right to arm themselves. Now both internal and external defence had been taken out of the hands of just one section of the population, and had been handed over to the nation at large. The class in arms had become the nation in arms.

As a corollary of this trend towards the arming of the nation, there had been a continuous campaign to erode the autonomy and exclusiveness of the army of the line. Just as it was held that the bearing of arms could not be the prerogative of a class, so also was it deemed unworthy of a nation in revolution to foist this responsibility upon a group of paid professionals. For this is one of the features of a genuinely revolutionary military policy. Military service is not seen as a trade but as the right of everyone physically able to bear arms. The true social revolution must harness the aspirations of the whole mass of the people, such that they will regard it as a self-imposed obligation to bear arms in defence of that revolution, in defence, in other words, of what they feel to be their own interests. In such circumstances it becomes unthinkable to leave the monopoly of armed power in the hands of a professional elite, particularly when that elite was formed and organised according to the principles of the *ancien régime*.

Carried to its logical conclusion, then, this revolutionary policy towards the old regular army would have involved its total disbandment and replacement by the battalions of national volunteers. There were in fact many requests for just such a decision. But the revolutionary leaders themselves, under the pressures of time and circumstance, never felt they had sufficient scope for such a drastic reorganisation of their military establishment. In the face of international aggression they simply dared not disband the only experienced component of their armed forces, and entrust the fate of the Revolution to the raw volunteers. Nevertheless, they did determine at least to try and make the regular army compatible with the more basic revolutionary tenets.

One of the most important of these was the hatred of aristocratic privilege. In 1789 the officer-corps of the line army was almost completely dominated by the aristocracy. Indeed, since 1781, the social categories within the Army had actually hardened with the introduction of a decree that demanded nobles should produce unassailable proof of four generations of nobility. Although provision was made for what were called 'officers of fortune', those who had risen from the ranks, a further decree of 1788 laid down that such persons should not rise above the rank of lieutenant. In 1789 the aristocracy accounted for at least ninety per cent of the officers-corps. The revolutionaries determined to eradicate this caste. In this case they were greatly aided by the officers themselves, a large number of whom resigned their commission or fled the country in the face of the general attack on aristocratic privilege. The climax came in June 1791 with a new oath of loyalty for officers which made no mention at all of the King. By August of that year 1,500 officers had refused to take the oath. They were all compulsorily retired on quarter pay. The spate of resignations increased. Between 15 September and 1 December 1791, 2,160 officers resigned or emigrated, and between 27 April and 15 July of the following year another 542 left the Army. It has been estimated that in all some 7,000 officers emigrated from France during the revolutionary period.[17] This was not the whole of the noble officer-corps but it is safe to assume that by mid-1792 the Army had rid itself of its potentially most disloyal elements.

Greatly aided though they were by this self-purgation, the revolutionaries took their own steps to eliminate the possibility of the Army being dominated by a reactionary social group. In February 1790 they voted a decree opening all ranks of the Army to commoners, whilst in June of that year the hereditary nobility itself was abolished. Also in February 1790, in an effort to keep the officer-corps at a manageable size, it was fixed at a strength of 9,406 as against the 35,000 of 1788. In the autumn of 1790 the Assembly began to try and regularise the formation of the new officer-corps. It was decreed that three-quarters of its sub-lieutenants were to be chosen by competitive examination and the remaining quarter taken from the senior NCOs. All lieutenants and captains, and two-thirds of the colonels and lieutenant-colonels, were to be chosen on seniority alone. Clearly the Assembly was making a concerted effort to destroy the notion of the corps as a bastion of privilege. On 24 June 1791 it went further and declared that a full half of the sub-lieutenancies should be open to the most senior NCOs. In November the examination system was abolished entirely and the gates fully opened to promotion quite independent of intellectual ability and the implicit reliance on the educated and therefore more elevated social groups. By 1793 the results of this combination of the opting out of the aristocracy and the increased mobility within the military hierarchy had become fairly apparent. By this time:

The former NCOs of the regular army dominated the officer ranks below the grade of lieutenant-colonel. A lieutenant-colonel was high as most of the ex-rankers had reached. Colonel was still a grade dominated by men whose only military service had been in the capacity of officers. However, since many lieutenant-colonels were commanding regiments, there was still a sizeable minority of regimental commanders who had had experience in the ranks.[18]

The attack on the Army of the *ancien régime* was not simply limited to this restructuring of the old officer-corps. On 1 January 1791 the titles of the regiments were abolished and replaced with simple numbers. In July all the foreign regiments in French service, the mercenaries *par excellence*, lost their special appellations and were completely integrated into the national army. The term *bas-officier*, our equivalent of non-commissioned officer, was changed to *sous-officier* to rid it of its invidious social connotations. In the autumn of 1792 twelve regiments were disbanded because of their chronic political unreliability. Most important of all, perhaps, in April 1791 the troops were allowed to frequent political clubs and so to take their full part in the political life of the nation. In the words of Alexandre de Beaumarchais to the Assembly:

> In a free state those who make up the army are citizens; they sacrifice a portion of their liberty the better to subordinate themselves [to military regulations]; but this sacrifice, which they make of their own free will, does not prevent them having, before their enlistment, rights as citizens, which they do not cease to exercise during their period of service; it does not prevent them from still having, as soldiers, rights to exercise.[19]

The State in Arms

It would be unwise, however, to take too one-sided a view of the government's relations with the line army. For the essential point remains that it was never disbanded. Throughout its vicissitudes in the early years of the Revolution those in power seem to have given little serious thought to its actual elimination. Indeed, in 1790, when it began to seem as though the Army might disintegrate of its own accord, the government

took vigorous steps to stamp out the nascent political consciousness which they felt was responsible. In the words of La Tour
du Pin, then Minister of War: 'The major part of the military
forces is breaking the law and forgetting its oath; orders are
ignored, the bonds of discipline are relaxed or broken . . .
almost everywhere officers are insulted or maltreated.'[20] He
felt that the cause of all this was simply the new political
awareness of the soldiers, as evidenced by their informal
councils and discussion groups that had sprung up throughout
the Army. He was in no doubt about the undesirability of such
bodies: 'If [the army] becomes a deliberative body, the government will degenerate into a military democracy. Who is immune
to being frightened by these committees of non-commissioned
officers and soldiers in the regiments, formed without the knowledge and even in defiance of the officers?'[21] This speech was
delivered in June. On 6 August the Assembly produced a
comprehensive law forbidding all such councils within the
Army:

> The deliberate associations established within the army
> under whatever form or title will cease forthwith . . .
> [Those responsible for further violations] will be deprived
> forever of the title of active citizen, and will be declared
> traitors to the country . . . unworthy to bear arms,
> drummed out of their units. They may even be condemned
> to suffer corporal punishment.[22]

Though this law was forgotten some eight months later, it is
instructive to note the lengths to which the Assembly was
prepared to go to keep the line army in being. Indeed, one
might go as far as to say that it seemed unlikely that the
Assembly of eight months later would have been prepared to
make such concessions to political principle had not the more
draconian measures of their predecessors already halted the
drift towards a collapse of discipline. As in the New Model
Army and the Continental Army, when the rank-and-file is
composed of one social group and the political leadership of
another, discipline and at least some deference to higher ranks
will always remain a prime consideration.

The revolutionaries' desire to keep the line army in being remained a constant political factor in the following year or so. Though the state wished, if possible, to recognise the eligibility of even the line regiments to participate in political life, it was not about to allow these regiments to disappear. Two laws of 1792 demonstrate this quite clearly. On 25 January all National Guardsmen not on active duty were required to report to the capital town of their canton, and were there given the chance of enrolling in the line army. Those that did were to be given a cash bounty and allowed to enlist for three years instead of the usual eight. A second law of 22 June maintained this length of service and the payment of a bonus. But it also lowered the minimum age from eighteen years to sixteen and, more importantly, allowed the departmental authorities a bounty of ten livres for each recruit to the line that they were able to enlist. It also set a quota of line troops for each department; the total for the whole country was set at some 50,000. As S. F. Scott has pointed out this decree was tantamount to a form of conscription. As such it is doubly significant. On the one hand it represents the first incursion of the government into this form of recruitment. On the other hand it is of some interest to note that this dangerously non-revolutionary measure was adopted to augment the strength of the regular army.

Proponents of the great revolutionary significance of the military policy of the French at this time make much of the law of 21 February 1793 by which the line regiments and battalions of volunteers were amalgamated into composite units known as *demi-brigades*. These were composed of two battalions of volunteers and one of regulars. Great importance has been attached to the revolutionary rhetoric which surrounded this decree. Certainly, one of the authors of this scheme, Dubois-Crancé, had opposed the suggestion of certain members of the Convention that the *demi-brigades* be formed of two battalions of line and one of volunteers: 'That system, instead of destroying . . . all the vestiges of the *ancien régime*, would fortify them [and] double . . . the dangers . . . One would thus make soldiers of the line out of the volunteers, and not volunteers out of the soldiers of the line.' [23] He went on to point out that if one adopted his scheme it would, 'reforge the ties of comradeship between the line and the volunteers; it will give to one group exemplary displays of civic responsibility and devotion'. His next words are slipped in almost as an afterthought but are none the less of great importance. Such an organisation, he goes on, would also, 'teach discipline to the other groups'.[24] Whilst there was certainly some thought of politicising the regulars through contact with the volunteers, one should not underestimate the extent to which the members of the Convention also hoped to guarantee a tolerable level of subordination among the volunteers. Nor were the reasons for such a step purely political. Orthodox military considerations alone demanded some sort of reorganisation along these lines. In this respect it is worth noting that a similar organisation had already been used in the Republican Armies, but not so much to disseminate political enthusiasm as to stiffen the ranks of the volunteers whose morale under fire lagged far behind their ideological fervour. In 1792 Lafayette had often made use of a tactical unit known as a *brigade* made up of two battalions of mixed line and volunteers. Other examples foreshadowed the *amalgame* even more exactly:

> The 1st battalion of the 17th Infantry Regiment was combined with the 1st battalion of the Meurthe and the 2nd battalion of the Soâne-et-Loire to form the 7th Brigade of the Army of the North in late July 1792. At the same time the 1st battalion of the 45th Infantry Regiment was united with two battalions of volunteers to form the 2nd Brigade at the camp of Mauberge. In the army of Dumouriez . . . the infantry was organised in essentially the same manner.'[25]

Neither Lafayette nor Dumouriez, tepid revolutionaries who both went over to the counter-revolution, could be thought to be particularly concerned with the ideological consequences of such an organisation.

Already there are three important reservations about the genuinely revolutionary nature of French military policy at this time. Firstly, the authorities were desperately anxious to keep the standing army in existence for as long as possible. Secondly, they showed themselves willing to resort to conscription and administrative bribery if their internal political initiative failed to arouse sufficient popular enthusiasm. Thirdly, even when the line army did officially disappear, it was used to dilute the revolutionary fervour of the genuinely popular units and help give an example of the virtues of traditional military discipline. In this latter respect, it is worth recalling that the line army on the eve of the *amalgame* was far from being a demoralised force on the verge of disintegration. The effective strength of each regiment had been steadily climbing since the grim days of 1790, and by 1793 it was under the command of a completely renovated officer-corps, almost all of whom had served in the army for many years.[26]

With these considerations in mind we come to what many writers regard as the key event of the military history of the Revolution, the *lévees en masse* of February and August 1793. After the *levées*, it is often held, France became a genuine nation-in-arms, moulding universal patriotic enthusiasm into a formidable military machine that was then able to repulse the assault of the combined European powers. But by the time of the *levées* France had in fact ceased to be a nation-in-arms, and was starting towards administrative centralisation and the suppression of dissent. For the *levées* relied upon conscription rather than upon the spontaneous desire of the people to fight on behalf of a social movement that they saw as being responsive to their own aspirations. The formation of the National Guard and the calling up of the volunteers in 1791 and 1792 had incorporated this reliance upon popular, or at least sectional, self-interest, and to that extent there were authentic attempts to integrate the political and the military and create a true people's army. With the introduction of conscription the state no longer needed to create a socio-economic environment for which men would deem it worth fighting. The obligation to fight became the thing on which all the other activities of the state were based. In a nation-in-arms the desire to fight originates with the people themselves, on behalf of a genuine collectivity of interests and mutual obligations. In a state-in-arms the desire to fight is not a necessary precondition; military service becomes an obligation decreed by those in power. It becomes not a self-imposed duty to oneself and society, but a legal obligation imposed from above, and not necessarily justified in any other terms than those of the legal penalties for not fulfilling it. Collective and positive self-interest becomes personal and totally negative self-interest.

Of course one could not claim that the *levées en masse* did not to a great extent depend on real popular enthusiasm. Both Danton and Robespierre, in the Convention, had long been spokesmen for such a policy, and neither would be likely to advocate anything that did not have support in the streets and the popular assemblies. In September 1792 Danton said:

> A part of the people is going to betake itself to the frontiers, another is going to dig trenches, and the third, armed with pikes, will defend the interior of our towns. Paris is going to second these great efforts. The commissioners of the Commune are going to proclaim . . . an invitation to the citizens to arm themselves and march to the defence of the nation . . . We demand that whoever refuses to serve in person, or to hand in his arms, be punished by death.[27]

The popular clamour reached a peak in July 1793. On 7 July Aristide Valour demanded 'that the awful mass of the people be armed, that a million muskets be handed out'.[28] On 21 July the Section of Finisterre gave an ultimatum that if all traitors and rebels had not laid down their arms within eight days, all adult males between the ages of sixteen and forty-five would be armed and sent against them. The ultra-left *sans-culotte* newspaper, *Le Père Duchèsne*, was monotonously insistent in its calls for a general arming of the people. On 28 July Sebastien Lacroix, a friend of Danton, told his sectional assembly that a general mobilisation must be proclaimed: 'May the friends of the fatherland arm themselves . . . may those without weapons bring up the ammunition; may the women bring the food and make bread . . . Eight days of enthusiasm can do more for the fatherland than eight years of combat.'[29] On 12 August a deputation of *fédérés* told the Convention that they must, 'make an appeal to the people; let the people rise up *en masse*; it alone can destroy so many enemies.'[30] On the 16th they made yet another appeal: 'The whole nation is more easily inflamed than one section of its citizens. If you ask for a hundred thousand soldiers they will not be forthcoming, but millions of men will respond to a universal appeal.'[31]

Clearly, then, there was much popular support for the idea of a *levée en masse*. By undertaking it the Committee of Public Safety, established on 5 April, did not erode its legitimacy in the eyes of the people. Perhaps even, as Lefebvre says, the call for the *levée* was forced upon the Committee by popular pressure.[32] But the fact still remains that once this measure had been decreed its very logic, the logic of universal conscription, tended to concentrate power in the hands of the state apparatus. The measure owed something of its origins to popular enthusiasm and initiative, but carried to its logical conclusion it sounded the death-knell for the possibility of further such initiatives. In this respect the armies of the Year II are the forerunners not of the people's armies of twentieth-century Asia, for example, but of the horrendous military machines of the two World Wars.[33] They taught not the integrated co-existence of civil participation and military obligation but the complete subordination of one to the other.

Carnot's mobilisation decree of 23 August 1793 gives some idea of the administrative nightmare that the *sans-culottes* had brought down on themselves:

All Frenchmen are in permanent requisition for army service. The young men will go to fight; the married men will forge arms and carry supplies; the women will make tents and uniforms and will serve in the hospitals; the children will shred the old clothes; the old men will be taken to the public squares to excite the courage of the combattants, the hatred of royalty and the unity of the Republic.[34]

By December 1793 France had an army of some 700,000 men organised into 213 battalions of regulars and 725 battalions of volunteers and conscripts. These in turn were organised into 213 front-line *demi-brigades* and just under 100 in reserve.

This whole vast array of men had to be kept supplied with cannon, muskets, ammunition, transport, forage and food. On the whole the relevant commissions of the Committee of Public Safety performed this mammoth task successfully. It was indeed a truly prodigious achievement. But when one comes to an examination of the way in which it was achieved one begins to appreciate the true consequences of conscription. To put into effect the decree of 23 August the Convention had eighty-two of its delegates sent all over France to aid the local authorities with the massive administrative problems. These *représentants-en-mission* were not an innovation brought in by the decree: two representatives had been sent to each department under a law of 9 March 1793. But the massive problems inherent in the *levées* gave them full scope to use their almost absolute powers. They were responsible only to the Convention and the Committee, sending the former a weekly report and the latter a daily one. They could order requisitions, dismiss and replace civil and military personnel on the spot, take any measures that seemed necessary to them to re-establish order wherever it might be threatened, bring before the Revolutionary Tribunal anyone deemed to have obstructed their operations, arrest and even have all suspects deported and take any measures necessary for the well-being of the troops. In effect, 'the *représentants-en-mission* were invested with unlimited powers for the exercise of those functions which were delegated to them'.[35]

It might well be objected that these representatives had two attributes which place them squarely in the best traditions of authentic military revolution. Do they not, for example, represent the perfect integration of civil and military operations? This is certainly true in one sense for the representatives were almost omnipotent in both spheres of activity. But this integration was only intended to operate at the administrative level. In other words, the representatives were given such sweeping powers simply to facilitate the supplying of the armies and generally increase their logistical efficiency. Certainly there were those who took it upon themselves to try and regulate the political and economic affairs generally of their areas. And usually such regulation was made with the interests of the *sans culottes* in mind. Fouché in the Nièvre, Bandot and Taillefer in the south-west, Isoré and Chasles in the north, Saint-Just and Lebas in Alsace all present examples of such policies.[36] But their missions were only individual initiatives. The measures they took were only implicit in their powers, never explicitly asked for by either the Convention or the Committee. This will be an important point in discussing the Russian and Chinese Revolutions, particularly the latter. In both cases we shall come across politico-military personnel who seem to have much in common with the *représentants-en-mission*. At this stage it is only necessary to re-emphasise that the representatives were intended to be super-bureaucrats rather than political commissars. Their guillotines were meant as particularly effective tools to cut through red tape and not as weapons in a class war.

The second attribute of the representatives that merits further clarification is their relationship with the soldiers. At first sight one might see close parallels with the chaplains of the Parliamentary Armies. Certainly they were empowered to deal with the soldiers' grievances about conditions of service, and also to keep them in touch with political events in the country at large. They were responsible for the distribution of 150,000 newspaper subscriptions that Bouchotte, the Minister of War at that time, made between January 1793 and March 1794, and the 400,000 copies of the Declaration of the Rights of Man that he also made available. On 10 October 1793 Saint-Just described the tasks of the representatives in the following way: 'They must be fathers and friends to the soldiers . . . sleep under canvas . . . be present at military exercises . . . not hob-nob with the generals . . . Day or night the soldiers ought to find him ready to listen to them.'[37] On 23 October he gave the following ultimatum: 'All chiefs, officers and agents of the government whatever are commanded to satisfy within three days the just grievances of the soldiers. After this interval we will ourselves hear the grievances, and we will give such examples of justice and severity as the army has not yet seen.'[38]

But the representatives' concern with the welfare of the soldiers was of an essentially paternalistic nature. In other words it was founded on an ultimate respect for the absolute powers of the central executive authority, of which the representatives were merely the agents. They were prepared to listen to the grievances of the soldiers and, if necessary, dismiss unsatisfactory officers, but they also expected that the soldiers only express these grievances to the representative themselves. Their solicitude was in no way an attempt to encourage the soldiers to put their faith in their own analysis of their political rights or expectations. In this way the representatives differ totally from the chaplains of the New Model Army. Both were with the troops to bolster morale, but each group worked from quite different premises. The chaplains believed in the validity of the individual revelation. Their conception of religious knowledge was of an essentially libertarian nature, almost a kind of spiritual anarchism, and thus had the profoundest implications for the soldiers' notions of their own political role. The chaplains encouraged individual speculation and thus helped to keep alive a revolutionary morale based on the soldiers' own assessment of what they were fighting for. They were doomed to disappointment, but the point nevertheless remains that for the duration of the war at least theirs was a genuinely revolutionary army, fired by a positive revolutionary dynamic. The representatives, on the other hand, had no time for individual soul-searching or the subversive freedoms of rank-and-file debate. Their conception of their role was essentially authoritarian. They were prepared to make adjustments to the military system to suit the demands of the troops, but it had to be clearly understood that only they had the right to make such adjustments, and that their decision was final.

In the last analysis one finds that the Republican armies of the Jacobin dictatorship have more in common with the Continental Army of the War of Independence than with more genuinely revolutionary organisms such as the New Model Army. Albeit civil authority was the ultimate arbiter of Republican military policy, this does not necessarily mean that the Army was of a revolutionary nature. It is not of itself important whether authority finds its ultimate sanction in the civil or military sphere. What are important are the ends to which this authority is used. And in the American and French Revolutions it was eventually used to stifle grass-roots debate, the debate that is of those that made up the bulk of the armies. In both cases the existence of authority became its own justification for obedience, rather than it stemming from the soldiers' own decision to fight in an organisation that best answered to their social and political interests. In the absence of a cohesive sense of nationalism the Americans lodged this authority with the military leadership. The officers used the Army to create a microcosm of their vision of an ideal hierarchical civil society, until such time that society could produce a strong central authority of its own. In France such a civil executive did exist, but it too took great care to ensure that deference to its authority counted for more than a reasoned acceptance of its political goals. Freedom, or the lack of it, became the dispensation of authority rather than a reason for its existence.

But in broad terms the French Revolutionary Wars can be discussed in terms of the same basic relationship that underlay the English Civil War and the American War of Independence. The final modes of organisation and discipline in the armies of the Year II were once again a function of the basic conflict between the lower classes and those with more moderate notions of how far society should be reorganised. But in the French Revolution this conflict of interests was explicit throughout. From the very beginning the middle classes felt it necessary to organise their own militia to counter the threat of unduly radical demands from below. As the Revolution developed it provoked foreign hostility whose very scope forced the bourgeoisie to make a temporary alliance with the lower orders to provide themselves with the necessary cannon-fodder. To make this alliance at all workable the middle classes were forced to pander to *sans-culotte* rhetoric. The Jacobins came to power and certain temporary economic controls were introduced, and the revolutionary leaders were forced to tolerate a mushrooming of grass-roots democratic organisations. Such organisations were even allowed in the armies for a while, whilst the middle-class delegates made much of their solicitude for the well-being of the troops under their command. But such solicitude only went so far. The revolutionaries were careful to prevent the total disintegration of the regular, traditionally hierarchical army, and dedicated themselves to extending the writ of absolute central authority at all levels of civil and military life. Gradually the revolutionary class militia became nothing more than an army of the old type; by far the largest ever seen up to that date, certainly, but still essentially an army organised according to traditional concepts of discipline and hierarchy. Without an appreciation of this gradual transition, even in the revolutionary period, it is impossible to explain how the citizen-soldiers of 1791-2 became the *grognards* of Napoleonic imperialism.

Yet even so the French Revolution does offer an example of a genuine revolutionary military force, perhaps one of the best examples to appear in these pages. For until the bourgeoisie were obliged to seek manpower outside their own class they were able to present a truly united armed front. In order to give their political aspirations concrete reality they were forced to create a military body to protect their class from reaction from above and excessive radicalism from below. To harness the political energies of their group effectively they had to be able to present military service as part and parcel of the struggle for political emancipation. This they did both by excluding all those who were not members of the particular social group and by organising the Guard along the same democratic principles that were to regulate the bourgeois conception of civil society. Military service was made a real reflection of political self-interest, and the National Guard became an authentically revolutionary military organism. There was for a while even some attempt to create a line army of volunteers based upon the same group exclusiveness, an army which many hoped would rid them of the necessity for a regular army of the old sort.

All of which brings us to the basic lesson of the French Revolution within the terms of this book. A true people's army is more than one that is open to all. It must also, in organisation and day-to-day conduct, reflect the conscious political interests of its members. Indeed it is not even necessary that the people's army be open to all. The necessary integration of military service with the broader socio-political vision is quite possible, even perhaps facilitated, within the framework of one class or social group. Certainly, on the evidence of the French Revolution, one can fairly claim that the more 'popular' an army becomes, the less is it revolutionary. The army loses that internal authority that comes from a rank-and-file consciousness of

being part of a real revolutionary dynamic. When this happens
the Army either fades away, or is in danger of being rent asunder
by the contradictory interests of the diverse social groups within
it. In either case the authority to hold the Army together must
now come from outside or from one group within it. Revolutionary self-discipline is replaced by the crude fear of punishment. There is no more right to the Kingdom and the soldiers are
again mere mercenaries.

Chapter 5 The Prussian Army Reforms 1806–15

CHRONOLOGY

1806

10 Oct The Prussian advance-guard is defeated by Napoleon at the Battle of Saalfeld.

13–14 Oct The Prussians are again defeated at the Battles of Jena and Auerstadt.

1807

14 June The Russians are defeated by the French at the Battle of Friedland.

9 July Frederick William is compelled to sign the Treaty of Tilsit with Napoleon.

25 July The Military Organisation Commission is set up to examine the shortcomings of the Prussian Army.

4 Oct Baron Stein is recalled by the King to supervise the work of reform.

27 Nov A Commission is set up to examine the behaviour of the Prussian officer-corps in the campaign of 1806 and to discipline those found wanting.

1808

15 March The Military Reorganisation Commission submits a draft plan for a military establishment based around a small standing army and a national militia composed of the propertied members of society.

27 July All Crown-land serfs are given full possession of the land they till.

3 Aug The King decrees the abolition of corporal punishment for minor breaches of military discipline.

6 Aug A decree is enacted abolishing the ban on non-noble recruitment to the officer-corps.

8 Sept Frederick William signs the Treaty of Paris by which the size of the Prussian Army is limited to 42,000 men.

9 Oct   The abolition of serfdom is decreed throughout Prussia.

19 Nov   A decree is issued authorising some measure of self-government in the cities.

24 Nov   Stein is compelled to resign by Napoleon.

1809

31 May   Major Schill is killed in the fighting at Stralsund that marked the end of his abortive nationalist insurrection.

1810

14 Feb   A further decree on the Emancipation of the Serfs is issued.

11 Nov   The abolition of serfdom becomes operable from this day.

1811

11 Sept   Hardenberg issues a modified decree on the abolition of serfdom.

1812

15 March   Frederick William ratifies a treaty with France by which he agrees to supply Napoleon with 20,000 Prussian troops in the event of the outbreak of hostilities between France and Russia.

25 June   Napoleon enters Russia.

14 Sept   Napoleon enters Moscow.

30 Dec   General Yorck signs the Convention of Tauroggen with the Russians by which he agrees to withdraw his troops from the French command.

1813

3 Feb   Volunteer Jäger units are established by the Prussians for the training of future officers.

7 Feb   The East Prussian *Landtag* agrees to the creation of both *Landwehr* and *Landsturm* units.

9 Feb   All cantonal exemptions on liability for military service are abolished throughout Prussia.

27 Feb   Frederick William concludes a military alliance with Russia.

16 March   Frederick William declares war on France.

17 March   A decree is issued establishing the Prussian *Landwehr*.

17 April   The *Landsturm* is created.

4 June   At Pleiswitz an armistice is signed with Napoleon.

28 June   The death of Scharnhorst.

17 July   The King orders the regular military supervision of all *Landsturm* units. That in Berlin is abolished completely.

10 Aug   Austria joins the Allies and hostilities with France are resumed.

14 Oct   Napoleon is defeated by the Allies at the Battle of Leipzig.

1814

30 March   The Allies enter Paris.

3 Sept   Boyen issues his edict on army reorganisation and the recognition of the principle of universal liability to military service.

11 Nov   Boyen issues a detailed decree on the organisation of the *Landwehr*.

1815

20 March   Napoleon arrives in Paris from his exile in Elba.

22 May   Frederick William pledges to give his subjects a constitution.

14–16 June   The Battles of Quatre Bras, Ligny and Waterloo.

The previous chapters have dealt with cases in which military reform was a pragmatic response to an actual state of social and political crisis. Various kinds of revolutionary aspirations, and sometimes the fear of them, forced the emerging political leadership to create military organisms that would effectively either reflect or contain the new political radicalism. In a situation of political turmoil the army, like all other institutions of the state, had to come to terms with the prevailing value-system. This is one of the basic theses of this book. Though armies are conventionally regarded as the most traditionalistic, hidebound component of the state apparatus, one must not therefore assume that they are immune to widespread unrest within society at large. Perhaps it could be argued that the army is a little less responsive to social pressures than other components of the state, both in terms of the shock required to unsettle it and the amount of time needed for it to react, but this does not mean that armies stand outside societies or above the sets of beliefs that are the latters' spiritual scaffolding.

It has been seen how the very successes of the New Model Army were, in part at least, a consequence of the militant, almost para-military nature of the Puritan *weltanschauung*. It has been seen how in the American War of Independence the contradictions between the conservative nationalism of the socio-economic elite and the frustrations of many of the ordinary people forced the elite, which had captured the military leadership of the struggle, to re-emphasise traditional modes of military behaviour and organisation. And it has been seen how in the French Revolution the new bourgeois conceptions of political freedom and elective representation influenced the vision of the nature of military service. In each case the stresses and strains of acute social and political unrest high-lighted the extent to which military organisation was a reflection of the more basic realities of the society itself. But whilst situations of revolutionary unrest offer examples of this relationship in its clearest relief, they are far from being the only occasions on which it can be discerned.

The period under discussion in this chapter is not one of particular social unrest. Neither revolution nor even riot or *jacquerie* were likely developments in early nineteenth-century Prussia. Certainly there was a measure of discontent in both town and countryside, a discontent that embraced those very groups, peasant, artisan and bourgeoisie, whose brief alliance in France had occasioned such dramatic political upheaval. But the history and structure of the Prussian state militated against the possibility of such a volatile alliance being created. All groups were either too ignorant or too afraid of the others for there to be any hope of even a temporary combination of forces. Furthermore, over the years, the habit of subservience, be it to feudal landlord, bureaucrat or absolute monarch, had become firmly implanted at all levels of society. The Prussian state apparatus, then, was not threatened from within. But the latter years of absolutism, as autocracy dozed beneath the laurels of Frederick William I and Frederick the Great, were also years of political apathy. The highly centralised state machinery still functioned, but it gradually lost its sense of direction in both internal and external policy. The original creative dynamic was lost, and both army and bureaucracy gradually succumbed to an intellectual and administrative flabbiness.

If left to its own devices a state could survive, even materially prosper, under such circumstances. One might even argue that such a deeply grooved predictability and the total lack of political curiosity and originality are the very stuff of internal political stability. But all states whose survival depend on such attitudes must beware being caught up in events outside their frontiers. Then their smug introspection can become a liability. The military and the bureaucracy find themselves strait-jacketed by outmoded ideas and a purely domestic orientation. Army and administration find themselves without the techniques or the material for an effective response to external aggression, whilst the nation as a whole is suddenly seen to have degenerated into an agglomeration of parochial units. Certainly the Prussian response to the rise of Napoleon was a particularly inglorious episode in her history. In 1795 she had withdrawn from the first allied coalition against revolutionary France in order to acquire her share in the partition of Poland. She had taken no part at all in the War of the Second Coalition. Even when Austria joined the (third) Anglo-Russian Coalition in August 1805 Frederick William III of Prussia chose to remain neutral. In October, at Potsdam, the Tsar did persuade him to commit himself to an armed mediation on behalf of the Allies, but after Napoleon's crushing victory at Austerlitz he signed an alliance with the French by which he agreed to give up Neuchâtel and Anspach in return for Hanover. But it was all too clear who was the dominant partner in such an alliance. In February of the following year Frederick William was forced to give up the Duchy of Cleves to the French and to close his ports to English vessels. In July the Confederation of the Rhine was formed under French protection thus denying the Prussians any hope of playing the leading role within Germany, or of forming any mid-European counterbalance to French power. At the same time it was even rumoured that Napoleon, in an effort to appease England, was contemplating handing her back Hanover.

At this stage the Prussians felt themselves obliged to make some show of force. They mobilised their army, and in October sent Napoleon an ultimatum demanding that he withdraw his troops across the Rhine. On paper their demands were not reckless. They, like the French, could quite easily put 130,000 men in the field. But parity of numbers was a misleading indication of the real balance of forces. In almost every other respect the Prussian Army was sadly inferior to the *Grande Armée* of Napoleon. For one thing the actual Prussian mobilisation was chaotically organised and incomplete, and no attempt at all was made to call up the forces of East Prussia. The Army was placed under the command of the aged Duke of Brunswick whose vacillating incompetence had already been fully in evidence in the campaign of 1792–5. Even under Brunswick there was little central direction of the military effort, plagued as it was by administrative confusion and the Duke's total disdain for thorough staff work. But the situation became even more intolerable when, in September, the King and his suite of advisers and confidants arrived at headquarters. All their time was spent in profitless discussion and arguments and it became impossible to formulate any coherent plan of action. As a consequence, in the first two weeks of October, Napoleon was able to defeat the Prussian forces piecemeal at the Battles of Saalfeld, Jena and Auerstadt. The suddenness and comprehensiveness of these defeats reduced the remainder. of the Prussian forces to an unco-ordinated rabble. Only Blücher and Scharnhorst managed to keep any units in the field, as they doggedly pushed towards Mecklenberg in an effort to keep the French advance guard out of East Prussia. Elsewhere Prussian generalship reached its nadir. At Magdeberg General von Kleist and twenty-three other generals surrendered their 24,000 men without even attempting to put up a fight. At Prenzlau, Hohenlohe and Massenbach also capitulated without a fight even though they were within a few miles of sanctuary. Similarly the commanders of the fortresses at Erfurt, Hameln, Spandau,

Kustrin and Stettin all laid down their arms without the least attempt to delay the French advance.

Probably the only bright point in the events of the ensuing months was the attitude of Frederick William. Driven with the rump of his forces into East Prussia, he stubbornly resisted Napoleon's attempts to draw him into a separate peace, and he placed his remaining East and South Prussian regiments at the disposal of the Russians who now agreed to assist him against the French. But the leadership of Bennigsen, the Russian commander, left much to be desired and Napoleon was able to maul the Russian Army severely at the Battle of Friedland, in June 1807. The Tsar quickly decided to sue for peace without even consulting Frederick William, who was in turn forced to bow to Napoleon's harsh demands at Tilsit, in early July. To begin with the Prussian state was cut in half. The pre-war lands of 5,570 square miles, with a population of 9,752,731 shrank to 2,877 square miles and 4,938,000 inhabitants. The French also exacted heavy financial contributions in the form of both direct payments to the French treasury and the support of the victor's garrisons west of the Vistula. The Army itself, although not limited in size under the provisions of the Tilsit treaty, was driven into the far eastern corner of the realm. Except for six fortresses in the East all strongpoints were to be garrisoned by the French. A Convention was also signed at Königsberg three days later which made provision for the gradual withdrawal of the French occupation forces, but the stipulation was made that this withdrawal would only take place 'provided that the levies made on the country had been met'. But not a word had been said either in the Convention or the Treaty of Tilsit as to the exact amount of these levies, and so the French were able to maintain their troops there as long as they wished. Thus some 150,000 troops and 50,000 horses were to be maintained at Prussia's sole expense. The states of the kingdom were divided into four departments and France supervised the whole administration of the country, except for justice which remained in the hands of the Prussian courts. All Prussian officials had to take an oath of loyalty to the Emperor, and the entire revenues of the occupied provinces went directly into the Imperial treasury:

Profound misery crushed the entire country. The price
of corn had become exorbitant. Salt had doubled . . . In
certain parts the population was threatened with actual
famine, with only one head of cattle out of twenty and
one horse out of fifty left to it. The thousands of half-pay
officers were allowed a ration of two pounds of bread a day
lest they should die of hunger. The Prussian Minister in
Paris . . . [said] that 'he could furnish a specific list of
towns where two-thirds of the houses are standing empty
and their owners wandering at large. And I could add to it
a much longer list of villages that are entirely deserted . . .
In the city of Berlin itself . . . six hundred houses have
already been abandoned'.[1]

But perhaps even worse, from the point of view of the survival
of the Prussian state, was that there were very few objections
to this sudden change of rulers. The Prussian state was dying
but mourners were few and far between.

Napoleon quickly revealed his intention of transforming
the shattered land into a satellite of his empire, and
important sections of the Prussian people seemed all too
willing to submit to that fate. Among the middle classes
and the aristocracy, the military debacle bred widespread
defeatism and a not inconsiderable degree of opportunism;
and among the intellectuals voices were soon raised to argue
the advantages of adhering to Napoleon's new European
order even if this should involve the reduction of Prussian
sovereignty. Simultaneously, in the great mass of the population, there was little evidence of resentment over
Prussia's humiliation and even less of any popular desire to
avenge it.[2]

Military defeat had finally revealed the extent to which high-
handed centralisation and arbitrary autocracy had undermined
the whole legitimacy of the state.
In France such a moral and political bankruptcy had precipitated violent internal upheavals, and the figureheads and
much of the administrative machinery of the *ancien régime* had

been swept away. In this respect the Prussian monarchy was more fortunate. Its shortcomings were only revealed when it seemed that it had been effectually eliminated as a political force. The full extent of its bureaucratic oppressiveness only became apparent when the reign of the bureaucracy seemed to have been ended for ever. As the tenuous nature of the people's loyalty to the state became manifest the state itself became simply an object of contempt. Those who had lived within its borders simply sighed with relief at its apparent demise, whilst its French conquerers understandably failed to see the harm in allowing a regime that commanded so little respect to survive in a skeletal form. Indeed Napoleon was so confident that he had dealt Prussia its death blow that for a year or so he did not even bother to make any provisions about the size or composition of the Prussian armed forces. It was not until the Treaty of Paris of September 1808 that he forced the King to agree to a ceiling of 42,000 troops for the Prussian Army.

Political Reforms

However, Napoleon's contemptuous dismissal of the possibility of future Prussian resistance was but the first of the political blunders that led to the destruction of his empire. For one should never sit back and expect a state simply to wither away. Even where national feeling is at its lowest possible ebb there are those with a vested interest in underpinning their social and economic positions with the procedures and institutions of central authority. Even when its military component has been demoralised and shattered, even when it has been deprived of half its territory and population, the body politic will, if left to its own devices, gradually heal itself.

Prussia after 1806 was no exception to this rule. Almost as soon as the Treaty of Tilsit was signed a few military and political leaders began to come forward whose sole concern was the regeneration of the state and the eventual end to foreign occupation. Much of their attention was devoted to the creation of a new army, but it is here necessary to attempt to sketch the broader political context of these military reforms. For it is only then possible to gain a true impression of their significance. As has already been seen in the preceding chapters, the response of armies to periods of acute crisis is but a reflection of the most basic political issues. This will be seen to be the case with Prussia. The underlying problem between the years 1806 and 1815 was how to regenerate the state effectively and reassert royal authority throughout the whole nation and Prussian influence throughout Europe. The latter consideration in particular demanded that the state have an effective military arm. But the former forced those with the wit to profit from the recent disasters to speculate about just what had been wrong with the Army before Jena, and with the state that had produced it. Why had the Army been so easily and so thoroughly defeated, and why was that defeat so little lamented by so many Prussians?

To a few more thoughtful and honest men the answer seemed clear. Royal absolutism, archaic social relationships, and bureaucratic rigidity had prevented the bulk of the population from feeling that they had any freedom to express their opinions about how they should run their lives. At every stage, and in every sphere of his life the Prussian citizen was told what to do and what not to do. He had been totally deprived of all individuality and initiative, such that the state merely demanded his obedience rather than earned it. Thus when the state began its precipitous decline its citizens felt no particular commitment to try and arrest it. Gneisenau summed up the situation when he said, in 1807: 'From time immemorial every effort has been made to make men useful to the state machine . . . but far less has been done to make them free and noble and independent so that they believe that they are a part of the whole and that they possess a value in themselves.'[3] Baron von Stein, who headed the Prussian government for a short while after the military collapse, and who was as responsible as anyone for the resurgence of the national will, expressed similar thoughts in a memorandum written at Nassau shortly before he took office in which he expressed a determination 'to reawaken collective spirit, civic sense, devotion to the country, the feeling of national honour and independence, so that a revivifying and creative spirit would replace the petty formalism of a mechanical apparatus'.[4] In a letter to Hardenberg written at about the same time he elaborated a little on this: 'We must destroy . . . this narrow attachment to the machine which is the destructive characteristic of the bureaucracy. The nation must become accustomed to manage its own affairs, we must get out of the state in which it is kept by an administration that is at once servile and fussy.' [5]

Here are the twin themes of the reform movement that followed the collapse of 1806. The reformers were advocating an increase in political liberties so that men might feel more able to develop their moral and physical capabilities. To this extent they were recommending some adjustment in the subject's relationship with the state and, in formal terms at least, a relaxing of the state's authority over the individual; they aroused the suspicions of many of the conservative elements within Prussia who looked on their suggestions as little more than poisonous 'Jacobin' radicalism. Even in terms of the reforms suggested this accusation was a trifle absurd. But when one bears in mind the ultimate aim of the reformers it becomes little short of ludicrous. For the concept of the nation, 'the whole', 'a collective spirit' was what was of central importance to the reformers and not simply change for its own sake, or indeed for any reasons not predicated upon the survival and resurgence of the nation-state. They were not opposed to the social and political relationships that characterised the Prussian *ancien régime* on grounds of abstract principle, but because those relationships had manifestly failed to bind the state together in its hour of crisis. As Stein said after his first audience with Frederick William, in August 1807: 'The chief idea [behind the reforms] was to arouse a moral, religious and patriotic spirit in the nation, to instil into it again courage, confidence, readiness for any sacrifice on behalf of independence from foreigners and for the national honour.' [6]

If the reformers had been able to obtain this new national cohesion through rhetoric and tub-thumping alone they would have gladly limited themselves to that. But they were all too aware of the bankruptcy of the regime seriously to hope that they could make any progress without granting any concrete reforms. If they were to create a new mass commitment to the nation, if they were to make the notion of the 'fatherland' meaningful to its inhabitants, they had to make some effort to create a new constitutional framework which would give the Prussians some vested interest in fighting for its preservation. In an endeavour to create such a framework the reformers concentrated on three broad areas. One of these was the Army and the whole of the next two sections will be devoted to the issues raised by military reform. The other two were the status of the Prussian peasantry and the question of conceding some measure of representative self-government.

Probably the most dramatic example of the total political alienation from the nation was that of the Prussian peasantry. Legally they were mere serfs, they were *erbuntertänig*, that is legally tied to the land they worked and liable to be sold along with it. 'Politically the serfs were in practice the subjects not of the King but of their lord.'[7] But it was the peasantry who provided the bulk of recruits for the Army. And in the Army they had as officers just those men, the Junkers, who were their lords and masters in civil life. Therefore to the ordinary soldier military service was but an extension of the feudal relationship which defined his position in everyday life. He owed his obedience to his officers in just the same way that he owed his landlord the greater part of his crop and of his time. There was thus no sense of loyalty or commitment to the regiment, army or state because the relationship was of no mutual advantage. It was completely one-sided and the peasant soldier was only kept in line by the harshest disciplinarian methods. The catastrophe of 1806 made it quite clear that institutions based upon such a crude manipulation of fear were too brittle to withstand any kind of setbacks. They were devoid of that resilience and flexibility which comes from a widespread recognition of mutual self-interest. For the peasantry the state was an almost meaningless concept, and thus when the authority of the officers was undermined by continued military reverses the individual units lost the one thing, the fear of the knout, that had held them together.

To the reformers there seemed only one effective solution. The serfs must be granted legal and political freedom. Their ultimate loyalties had to be transferred from their lords to their King, and thus to the nation of which he was the head. The theoretical basis of the emancipation of the serfs was perfectly expressed by F. A. Stagemann, one of the officials actually in charge of the implementation of the reforms:

> A new generation is born, a generation that will send its children to the country's service instead of to the cemetery; a generation no longer bowed to the ground by material and spiritual poverty. It will form a people armed with strength and will, a people that will wipe out the country's shame and re-establish the glory of its honoured name.[8]

Thus on 9 October 1807 a decree was published that declared serfdom abolished, the measure to take effect from 11 November 1810.

But from the beginning the actual implementation of this measure was fraught with contradictions. Although the reformers were most keen to bring the peasants into the real political life of the nation, to give it, as it were, a last-minute transfusion of committed citizens, they were also loathe to alienate the landlord class in the process. For though they wanted a revitalised army they were in no way trying to sever the close traditional links between the Junkers and the officer-corps. They did in fact try to expand the social catchment area of this corps, but not to the exclusion of its most faithful bastion.[9] But to try and create a loyal rather than cowed rank-and-file almost inevitably meant alienating the Junkers. For it was quite impossible to attempt to give the serfs their freedom without seeming to be trying to undermine the traditional supremacy of the Junker landlords. The attempt to minimise this impression is clearly revealed in the provisos and qualifications with which the successive decrees on the emancipation were hedged about.

On paper this measure was straightforward and comprehensive. From St Martin's Day 1810 all peasants were free men and they were allowed to participate in untrammelled free trade in land. But even here there were serious problems. For one thing, which of the peasants' duties to their landlord came from their status as serfs, and were thus now abolished, and which came from their tenure of the land itself, and were thus to remain in force? For it should be borne in mind that only the former Crownland serfs, some 47,000 families, were ever given that most precious of gifts, the full possession of their lands. The rest ceased to be serfs, but not to be tenants. Secondly, what would be the actual repercussions of absolutely free trade in land? This seemed desirable to allow the newly liberated peasants the economic room for manoeuvre and 'liberty' to increase their holdings, and thus their stake in the nation. But how were they to accumulate the necessary capital either to buy the land they held as tenants or to extend this land? If such possibilities were effectually denied them the peasants might just as well have remained as serfs. Here the ambivalence of the reformers' attitudes to the peasants and the Junkers is once more in evidence. To some extent at least it is feasible to regard this aspect of the emancipation edict as a long-term concession to the landowners. For only they had the necessary resources to indulge in trade in land, and thus they would now be able substantially to increase their outright holdings at the expense of the peasantry, who would gradually be reduced to the status of landless labourers. In this respect it is worth noting that before Stein's recall to power, Friedrich von Schroetter and Theodor von Schon, both convinced disciples of Adam Smith, had been working on a plan for the abolition of serfdom simply because the feudal system of land tenure was inefficient and inimical to a capitalist exploitation of agriculture. Eric Hobsbawn, with this point in mind, makes the following interesting observations:

The Pomeranian example, where later in the century some two thousand large estates covered sixty-one per cent of the land, some 60,000 middle and small holdings the rest, and the remainder of the population was landless, is doubtless extreme, but it is a fact that a rural labouring class was too unimportant for the word 'labourer' even to be mentioned in Kruniz's *Encyclopaedia of Domestic and Agricultural Economy* of 1773, while in 1849 the number of landless or substantially wage-employed rural labourers in Prussia was estimated at almost two million.[10]

Stein himself, and perhaps others of the more idealistic reformers, was opposed to this inherent tendency towards the aggrandisement of the landlords' estates. According to him, 'one legal limitation on the free conveyance of land must remain, that which restrains the avarice of the rich and prevents the absorption of the land by the seigneurial domain'.[11] But even his attempts to restrain this 'avarice' were hedged with qualifications. By a decree of 14 February 1808, an amount of land equal to that acquired by the landlord had to be leased out in large units on hereditary tenure and free from labour obligations. But the permission for the absorption of peasant lands was left to the decision of the provincial authorities, although their permission could only be granted in those cases where the peasants' tenure was either not hereditary or of recent standing, or both. Nevertheless, this still left the landlords much scope for the expansion of their estates.

After Stein's dismissal, on the orders of Napoleon, in November 1808, the emancipation legislation was further qualified in favour of the landlords. The hereditary, unlimited leaseholders were left out of account altogether, it being rashly assumed that their status was adequately commensurate with the reformers' vision of economic and political freedom. An even more damaging provision was that a large number of peasants who had a non-hereditary lease on their land were required to give up a half of it to the landlord in exchange for freehold ownership of the remainder. Others who had rights, whether hereditary or not, to the produce of the land they tilled were required to surrender one-third of that land. There was also provision made for the payment of compensation, in cash or kind, to the lord for the loss of his peasants' compulsory services. A further law of May 1816 cut down the categories of serfs eligible for emancipation even further, and also decreed that a serf had himself to apply for emancipation, rather than it be enforced automatically. One might equally have had deaf men wait to hear their name called before being issued with a hearing-aid.

Clearly the reformers' concern for the political self-respect of the peasantry was not going to push them into unduly undermining the socio-economic predominance of the incumbent landowning, and military elite. For it was through this elite, with its ancient tradition of loyalty to the King, that much of that monarch's authority was kept alive, although in an unsatisfactorily oblique manner. The reformers were keen to give the masses some stake in the nation but not at the expense of a total rejection of traditional authority structures. The same hesitancy and ambivalence was clearly in evidence in the reformers' attitude towards the creation of some form of representative government. Once again these contradictions were highlighted by the differing attitudes of Stein and his successors.

Stein himself was perhaps more radical in his attitude towards representative government than in his approach to the emancipation of the serfs. Doubtless much of the explanation for this stems from the fact that in the towns, the proposed foci of his new democratic institutions, there was no equivalent of the reactionary yet indispensable Junker class. Before Jena the administration of the towns was entrusted to functionaries nominated by the government. By an order of 19 November 1807 Stein abolished these functionaries and instituted elective municipal councils in all Prussian towns. Of course, even here Stein's measures were only radical in relation to the political norms of his time and place. The right to vote was only given to those of respectable life and morals, and who possessed an annual income of not less than 150 thalers. But their new rights were fairly extensive. They were allowed to elect a municipal council of between twenty-four and one hundred members, which in turn was allowed to elect the executive organs in charge of framing a budget, imposing taxes raising loans and alienating communal property.

But Stein went further than this. He envisaged the municipal councils as a mere beginning, as a school for a politically conscious bourgeoisie who would eventually go on to discuss broader questions in greater regional and national assemblies. His final goal was the creation of an elective, bicameral, national Reichstag. But his successors, particularly the next Chancellor, Hardenberg, were neither willing nor able to push through this latter measure. On the whole subject of a national representative assembly, Hardenberg displayed a degree of equivocation that reveals his reluctance to offend the Prussian vested interests. His attitude to the whole problem is clearly revealed in the following two pronouncements. In a memorandum to the King in November 1808 he said:

One must ensure that popular participation remains compatible with a monarchical constitution and . . . prevent it from degenerating into something revolutionary . . . Manipulation and utilisation of the spirit of national solidarity is, to be sure, of the utmost importance, yet it must, above all, be done prudently and cautiously so that it may not defeat its own purpose by spoiling everything.[12]

In September 1807, at Riga, he had made his position equally clear in a document written in a period of enforced retirement. Reforms were necessary, he admitted, but 'their execution should not be entrusted to large composite assemblies, and only a few government officials should be asked for their opinion . . . A small number of discerning and well-informed individuals should direct the reforms.'[13]

Once again one notices the fatally divisive conflict between a desire for reforms that would create a politically conscious nation-state and the dread of such reforms eroding the power of central authority. Hardenberg's subsequent initiatives amply demonstrate the inherent incompatibility of these two positions. In December 1810 he summoned an Assembly of Notables to approve new fiscal legislation which he was attempting to bring into force. But the selection of its membership was rigged in favour of the nobility (thirty out of fifty-nine) which prevented it from having any particular significance to the people at large. Even then Hardenberg was terrified of establishing any kind of pseudo-representative precedent, and from the very beginning the Assembly's role was of the most limited advisory nature. As he wrote to Stein in December 1810: 'The government alone must have the right to convene, to dismiss, and to propose legislation; great care must be taken to forestall any crystallisation of resistance which might interfere . . . with the government's actions.'[14] In September of the following year the government tried to sidestep the whole issue of a national assembly by adding this title to that of an advisory body already contemplated—a commission for regulating the provincial and national debt arising from the war. The way in which it was hoped that an assembly could simply assume such duties as an ancillary to their main task clearly shows how limited the government expected them to be. Once again the nobility were to be guaranteed an excessive proportion of seats (fifty per cent) and the provincial governments were to be allowed to exclude any member not deemed suitable. Finally, the deputies were forbidden to accept mandates from their constituents. The Assembly did however press for the drawing up of a constitution and this was promised by a royal decree of May 1815.

But this decree contained two crucial provisos: the national assembly that the constitution would create was to be a purely advisory body and it was to be chosen from among the members of the provincial Estates, the traditional bulwarks of aristocratic privilege. The government's implacable resistance to anything but an advisory assembly was re-emphasised by Hardenberg in July 1817 when the constitutional commission was finally convened. In 1819 Hardenberg offered Wilhelm von Humboldt a post in the cabinet with responsibility for constitutional matters, yet he at the same time insisted on drawing up his own version of the draft constitution. But by this time the reactionary 'advice' of Metternich, and some slight political unrest within Prussia itself, had almost convinced Hardenberg that the time was not yet ripe for any kind of constitution. In August 1819 Prussia helped to draw up the notorious Carlsbad Decrees, and on 31 December of that year Hardenberg forced the King to dismiss Humboldt. The incompatibility of rigid central control of national policy-making and the desire for some kind of representative institutions had finally been revealed. The experiment in reform was over and the Prussian state marched squarely down the road of reaction.

The Reform of the Army

The purely political side of the reform movement has been dealt with at some length; the military reforms that form the focal point of this chapter cannot be understood without a clear appreciation of the wider goals and constraints that dictated policy at this time. As will be seen, just the same aspiration for some kind of widespread political participation was the basic motivation of the reformers, whilst just the same fears for the sanctity of the central authority bedevilled their efforts to create

a truly national army. For even the most zealous of the reformers was in no way attempting to tamper with the essential
structure of the state. They were looking outwards rather than
inwards. They wished to restore Prussia's national self-respect,
to rid her soil of the foreign invader and to make her once again
a power to be reckoned with in Europe. To do this it was necessary to make certain adjustments to economic and political
relationships within the state, but the efficacy of such adjustments was measured against the resulting increase in international influence rather than against abstract considerations
of social justice. Gerhard Ritter's assessment of the place of
Clausewitz's life and work is of the utmost relevance here.
Clausewitz was concerned with one main question:

> War as a means of discipline, as the most effective spur
> to the nation's political education, as a method for harden-
> ing its militant power drive . . . Clausewitz was not con-
> cerned with moral questions, let alone cultural or aesthetic,
> but with a specific political problem, how to transform
> what was no more than an area sharing a common culture
> into a determined political entity, a confident and militant
> nation-state jealous of its freedom and its reputation.[15]

It was to this end and this end alone that the military reforms
were to be directed. Thus all reform was to be tightly controlled
from the centre. There was to be no hint of the kind of rank-
and-file democracy that we have observed developing in other
countries at other periods of crisis. The army was to be the
expression of the national will rather than of the particular
socio-economic interests of any group or class. As Scharnhorst,
the leading figure among the military reformers, said: 'The
nation must be imbued with self-reliance, it must have an
opportunity to know itself and to stand by and for itself. Then
and only then will it have self-respect and inspire respect in
others.'[16]

The central demand of the military reformers was that service
be both compulsory and universal. One of the chief reasons for
the disastrous defeats of 1806–7, it was felt, was that the Army
was only recruited from amongst a limited section of the popu-

lation, the peasantry. In theory all adult males were obliged to do military service but in practice, over the years, large groups of able-bodied men had been exempted from it because of the trade they pursued or the area they lived in. Frederick the Great, for example, had gone so far as to claim that: 'In wartime recruits should be levied in one's own country only when the bitterest necessity compels.'[17] So by 1804 not only were those native Prussians in the Army all taken from the most depressed section of the nation but almost fifty per cent of the Army at full strength were in fact mercenaries. It was this heterogeneous character of the Army, claimed Gneisenau, that was at the root of the disaster at Jena. It 'had contributed more than anything else to the enervation and degeneration of peoples, which destroyed the warlike spirit of the nation and its sense of community by relieving the other sections of society from the duty of directly defending the state'.[18]

The theoretical obligation of universal service had been stated yet again in the Canton Law of 1792, but the following qualification was appended to it:

All members of the state are not useful for this purpose; further, other functions are at hand which are not less important for the support of the body politic, so exemptions from this rule exist, dependent upon the decision of the representatives of the state, who consider which classes will serve the defence of the land, and which are qualified for exemption.[19]

In 1804, out of 2,320,122 men theoretically liable for military service, 1,170,000 were freed by territorial privileges and a further 530,000 by reason of estate, profession, religion or property. Even before 1806 there had been some demands for universal military service. Von Behrenhorst had approached the problem obliquely in 1799 when he stressed the importance of moral and spiritual values if one wanted an effective army. Clearly he was trying to draw some conclusions from the *élan* and enthusiasm of the Armies of the First Republic. In 1803 von Knesebeck proposed a universal service army from which there would be practically no exemptions.

But it was not until after Jena that such ideas began to be seriously mooted. On 25 July 1807, a mere fortnight after Tilsit, a Military Reorganisation Commission was set up. Even the vacillating Hardenberg was at this stage in favour of universal service: 'Military conscription should be wholly altered. All previous exemptions, without any exception, should be terminated. Everyone who does not serve the state in some way, should be obliged to perform military service in the regular or reserve troops.'[20] In December 1808 the Reorganisation Commission recommended to the King that he decree the universal obligation to military service, but after much dithering he declined to do so, apparently fearful at the prospect of arming the whole citizenry.

But even here only some of the reformers seemed genuinely anxious to harness the patriotism and idealism of the whole nation. Thus, in March 1808, a plan was drawn up to increase the armed forces of the state by creating provincial militias to supplement the standing army. But this militia was only to be open to members of the propertied classes, and was to have the maintenance of internal security as one of its functions, 'The commission remarked that only a militia which consisted of lower-class elements could arouse apprehension.'[21] Only those who could make a deposit of one hundred thalers and provide their own arms and uniforms were to be eligible. In December 1808 the idea was mooted of a National Watch based around the garrison police forces created under the terms of the Treaty of Paris. Once again the same property qualifications were to be applied to restrict membership. Stein himself was vigorously opposed to these class divisions. He wanted all citizens to be eligible for the line army, those actually serving to be selected by lot. Everyone not called up in this way was to be liable to service in the reserve formations.

But the King himself was not prepared at this stage to agree to the formation of any kind of reserve militia, with or without a class pedigree. Eventually the reformers were forced temporarily to abandon the whole idea, and they fell back on the stratagem of creating some kind of trained reserve by means of detaching every year a small number of troops from the line regiments, holding them ready for instant recall, and replacing them by raw recruits. This was known as the *Krumper* system, but it was far from the dramatic innovation described by more traditional writers. By autumn 1810, for example, only 3,448 men had passed through the ranks as novices, been given some quick training and released again to their homes. Clearly such numbers could do little more than form the bare nucleus of any proposed new formations.

In actual fact the old canton-based system of recruitment, with its large numbers of exempted categories of civilians, remained in force until February 1813. Even when it was abolished it was not because the King had been persuaded to act on a question of political principle alone. He was too committed to the forms and traditions of his predecessors to lend more than half an ear to the abstract advice of the reformers. But in 1812 external events once again precipitated a crisis within the state and forced the King's hand. During 1811 it had become increasingly apparent that there would be an eventual breakdown in Franco-Russian relations. Once again the reformers began to urge the King to sanction a full mobilisation of Prussian manpower. But he remained unconvinced by their faith in the military potential of his people, and in March 1812 a Franco-Prussian Treaty was ratified which assured Napoleon an auxiliary force of 20,000 Prussians in the event of a war with Russia. Three hundred Prussian officers resigned in disgust, and Clausewitz wrote of the treaty: 'I believe . . . that the shameful blot of a cowardly capitulation is never wiped away; that this drop of poison in the blood of a people is transmitted to posterity and will cripple and undermine the energy of later generations.'[22] In July Napoleon advanced into Russia. His fate there is well known, and by December his shattered armies were staggering back across East Prussia. Once again the King's advisers urged action. Once again he ignored such advice and remained sunk in an inactive torpor. But this time the initiative was wrested from him by the unprecedented action of one of his most senior generals. On 20 December Yorck, who had been in command of the Prussian contingent with Napoleon's forces, concluded a treaty with the Russians at Tauroggen in which he asserted the neutrality of his forces.

Before the King had had time to react Stein arrived in East

Prussia and convened a meeting of the *Landtag* there. Before this assembly, as Stein later related, 'General Yorck proposed the formation of a reserve of 130,000 men to keep his corps up to establishment, a militia of 20,000 and an armed population [to serve] whenever the enemy crosses the Vistula, and lastly a corps of 700 volunteers equipped at their own expense to act as a nursery for officers.'[23] The *Landtag* unanimously endorsed these proposals, and on 7 February 1813 they agreed to the creation of a *Landwehr* of all able-bodied men between eighteen and forty-five years of age. Prussia as a whole adopted this plan a mere two days later and all cantonal exemptions were abolished. But this particular decree was only intended to fill the reserve units of the regular army, and it was not until 17 March that a genuine *Landwehr* was created. Duty in it was made compulsory for every man aged from seventeen to forty.

In theory the reformers had now achieved one of their main goals. They had succeeded in having the principle of universal military service decreed in fact, and so had moved nearer to their total vision of a revivified nation in which the extension of political liberty would create a widespread desire to defend that liberty. The reformers did not see the enactment of universal service as a means of forcing men to join the Army, but rather as the abolition of bureaucratic restraints on the subject's own new desire to serve. Political emancipation would create the categorical imperative. The military reforms would merely give that imperative the freedom to express itself. But it is important to note that there were still to be important limitations on such expression. Certainly the Prussians had been given political liberty, relative to what they had known before, but the reformers by no means envisaged the kind of freedoms that inspired the more radical elements encountered in the previous chapters. The essential logic of the Prussian reforms was, however, the same. To create a more authentically popular army it was necessary to make military service contingent upon increased participation in the total socio-political environment. This the reformers clearly discerned. On these grounds they advocated the emancipation of the serfs and the creation of more democratic representative institutions.

But their enthusiasm for any increased participation stopped short of any tendency towards the erosion of the authority of central state power, and thus towards any radical adjustment of the *status quo*. Therefore the whole problem of universal military service had to be solved without unnecessarily upsetting the social balance of power. As Shanahan says it was 'a problem of universal conscription in a class society'. Whilst it was important to introduce the principle of universal military service, it was even more important to ensure that the existing class hierarchy did not break down. It is in this light that one should examine the actual workings of the new mode of recruitment and military organisation. 'In 1813,' to cite Shanahan again, 'the problem . . . was simplified by providing a military organisation for each social group: a national militia (the *Landwehr*) for the landed peasants an the moderately well-to-do, volunteer officer training units [the Jäger Corps] for the upper-class youths, and the regular army for the masses. So it was that in 1813–14 most of the conscripts were still the poor and landless.'[24] Thus, although the reformers wished to promote the notion of military service on behalf of the nation, they were also careful to ensure that such service was given within a stratified system of organisation. At the same time that one served the nation, one was kept equally aware of responsibility to one's class.

But even here the reformers had to grapple with certain contradictions. Certainly it was necessary that the various social groups be kept aware of their true social station; on the other hand it would be dangerous to allow the various auxiliary formations too much independence from the line, the central military apparatus. As has been emphasised above, the necessity for tight central control was a major consideration for almost all the important figures of the period, be they reformers or reactionaries. In their first recommendations to the King in March 1808, the Reorganisation Commission had in fact advised that the line and the militia train separately, 'because the experience [of joint manoeuvres] would endanger the national patriotism of the militiamen. Their spirit would be depressed by enforced association with mercenaries.'[25] But once the creation of a militia had actually been decided upon in 1813, the logic of centralisation asserted itself. From the begin-

ning, the administration of the *Landwehr* organisation was
placed in the hands of the four military governments of
Königsberg, Stargard, Berlin and Breslau. As Shanahan
points out: 'the military governments were intended to serve
the larger interests of statecraft. This organisation dispersed the
troops for the defence of the great rivers and made possible
royal control of the militia, thus safeguarding absolutism from
the interference of the estates.'[26] Furthermore, as the war
progressed, the *Landwehr* came more and more to be regarded
as an adjunct to the line rather than as an independent organisation. Badly depleted line regiments began to draw upon
Landwehr units to fill their complements, and these units were
increasingly treated as reserve depots for the regular army. By
June 1813 *Landwehr* regiments were incorporated wholesale
into regular army brigades. Whilst we noted the ambivalence
of such an *embrigadement* with regard to the armies of the First
Republic, it can be fairly asserted that the Prussian authorities
were eager to inculcate the militia with the attitudes of the line
rather than to inspire the regulars with excessive political zeal.

This fear of any organisational autonomy, and the consequent
suspicion that the traditional links of obedience and deference
might be broken, appeared even more prominently after the
cessation of hostilities. In 1814 and 1815 Hermann von Boyen,
the new Minister of War, had tried to perpetuate the advances
made by the reformers. In the summer of 1814 he introduced a
new law on the line army, by which all male Prussians of twenty
and over were liable for military service. By a new law on the
Landwehr, of November 1815, it was decreed that in peacetime,
Landwehr units should be kept separate from the line, and
individual *Landwehr* units should remain and recruit in their
own localities. Officers were to be elected by their peers, though
only, it must be admitted, from a list drawn up by the provincial authorities. What is more, such candidates had to be
former army officers, former volunteer riflemen with good
records, ex-NCOs who owned some land or possessors of at least
ten thousand thalers capital. But even these modest proposals
were too much for the King and the bulk of his advisers.
Boyen's measures were attacked for their endorsement of the
principle of universal service: 'The University of Breslau

attacked what was referred to as the militarisation of all citizens and especially the equalisation of masters and servants, educated and uneducated, cultured and uncultured, which resulted in destroying individuality and substituting "an indistinct . . . undifferentiated mass".'[27] Such people also attacked the extent of organisational autonomy conferred upon the *Landwehr*. In December 1819 the King felt himself able to demand a closer fusion of the line and the *Landwehr*. He actually disbanded thirty-four *Landwehr* battalions and stipulated that in future all field commands should be given to officers of the line alone. He also insisted that the sixteen *Landwehr* brigades should be incorporated into regular divisions, even in peacetime. Faced with such a broad attack upon his work, Boyen was left with no alternative but to resign, and the very notion of any future reform was completely expunged from Prussian military life.

The Problems of People's War

It is fairly clear by now how Prussian attitudes to her armed forces were bedevilled by certain contradictions inherent in the dual desire for grass-roots political enthusiasm and political stability under a strong centralised administration. No aspect of Prussian policy reveals these contradictions more clearly than the way in which they approached the problem of promoting an authentic people's war.

For certain of the reformers, no matter how rigidly the principle of universal service was applied in the line and the *Landwehr*, the mere existence of these units showed an inadequate response to the problem of fully utilising the military potential of the nation. For the simple constraints of the availability of muskets, uniforms, wagons and horses, etc., meant that only a fraction of the able-bodied male population would ever see service in these organisations. For the more radical of the reformers the solution was the creation of a third force, without uniforms or military firearms, and based around their own towns and villages, in which all those not enrolled in the line or the militia would be obliged to serve. Such units would be of a purely defensive nature, and would aid the more regular formations should hostilities be carried into their locality.

As early as 1808 Gneisenau was fully convinced of the desirability of such a scheme. He believed 'that Prussia's only hope lay in a national insurrection. His elaborate plan for an uprising of fifteen and a half million people in North Germany included an idealistic hope that by saving the state the people could thereby win a constitution and other political reforms.'[28] Such desires for national insurrection were largely inspired by the news that filtered through of the success of the Spanish *guerrilleros* against Napoleon's armies. In late 1808 the Spanish regulars had been shattered by the French, but the people at large refused to submit to Napoleonic rule and almost immediately small bands of partisans, peasants and ex-soldiers, took to the hills and incessantly harried the French forces. By 1813 there were many thousands of such partisans. Don Francisco Espoz y Mina, operating in Navarre, alone had some 13,000 men under his command.

> Everywhere uniforms were secretly made for his soldiers, and the highest mountains, as well as almost impassable defiles, were the seat of arms manufactories, munitions dumps and hospitals. His sick and at times his wounded were cared for in villages and hamlets, and quite a few in the very houses where those who had caused their wounds were lodging.[29]

But this was far from being an isolated case.

> Evasive and indomitable partisans like . . . Julian Sanchez in Old Castille . . . Porlier and Longa in the Cantabrian sierras found it comparatively easy to shift their positions when the pressure on one region was too great for them . . . Although the French armies were very numerous indeed, and remained so until they were milked for the invasion of Russia, no small proportion of them were tied down in garrison duties; they could thus only be concentrated with difficulty, and with certain loss to the patriots of the districts from which they had been withdrawn . . . Of one thing there can surely be little doubt and it is that the *guerrilleros* were of an assistance to Wellesley which it would be impossible to exaggerate.[30]

The news of such activity was not without its impact on certain Prussian leaders. Gneisenau persistently advocated this method of resistance to the French. In 1811 Scharnhorst submitted a plan to the King which advocated the use of widespread guerrilla warfare backed by the existing regular troops fighting in the fortresses. Boyen also advocated such a mode of fighting, although he did acknowledge that its success might be dependent on Russian support. In 1810 and 1811 Clausewitz gave a series of lectures in the War Academy at Berlin in which he outlined the virtues of this type of warfare, 'little wars' as he called them. A distillation of his views is to be found in his *On War*, published posthumously:

> Armed peasants are not to be driven before us in the same way as a body of soldiers who keep together like a herd of cattle . . . Armed peasants . . . when broken disperse in all directions for which no formal plan is required . . . It is on these weak bodies that the fire of a national war usually first properly kindles itself . . . According to our idea of a people's war, it should [be] like a kind of nebulous, vapoury essence [and] never condense into a single body.[31]

In 1812, in the *Bekenntrusse*, he drew up a scheme for a partisan force in which all those aged from eighteen to sixty, who were not with the regular army, would arm themselves with muskets, scythes and pitchforks and, equipped with a bag of supplies, a padded cap and some kind of provincial insignia, they would devote themselves to 'hindering French officials, capturing detachments and attacking convoys, conducting ambushes and lending support to the regular army'.[32] They would use the swampy forests of Prussia as their impenetrable base areas. Stein too had absorbed the significance of the Spanish experience and in December 1812 he wrote to Tsar Alexander advising him what to do in the liberated Prussian territories. Basically he advocated a *levée en masse* in which four out of every hundred able-bodied males would be taken into regular formations, whilst the rest of the male population would serve in a two-tier militia.

But all this theorising and advice lacked a real popular base.

The Spanish waged guerrilla warfare effectively because there had been a genuine popular upsurge against Napoleon. The Spanish leaders were able to harness an authentic nationalistic spirit amongst their subjects, and thus keep alive resistance in the face of French counter-terror. But such feelings did not exist in Prussia at this time and spontaneous resistance was almost non-existent. In Silesia, in 1809, there was a grouping of patriots around Count Gotzen, a friend of Stein, who planned to purchase 20,000 muskets in Austria and establish shooting clubs as the nucleus of a future insurrection. But the plan was simply not rooted in reality and it came to nothing. In the spring of 1809 Major Ferdinand von Schill attempted to provoke a national uprising, but it proved completely abortive and Schill was killed in fighting around Stralsund in May.

So the reformers were driven to the absurdity of trying to create a popular guerrilla army by decree. On 21 April 1813 they enacted the creation of the *Landsturm*. All able-bodied men aged between eighteen and sixty were to serve in it. Its members were to wear no uniform 'as uniform would cause them to be recognised'. At the approach of the enemy the inhabitants were to flee their villages, organise under previously nominated officers and take refuge in the woods from whence they would harass the enemy. As they fled they were to carry off their corn, smash the casks, burn the mills, bridges and boats, and fill in the wells. 'For,' in the words of the decree, 'it takes less to rebuild a village than to feed the enemy.' Gneisenau was even more far-reaching in his conception of people's warfare. According to him every male over the age of seventeen would be armed, local officials of dubious loyalty would be suspended, the property of cowards and traitors would be redistributed to war victims and titles of nobility would lapse unless merited by distinguished war service.

But even the reformers themselves, in the last analysis, were ensnared by the contradictions already noted in this chapter. Indeed one is entitled to ask whether they were not happier having to create a popular revolt by decree, for they hedged it about with such qualifications that one doubts whether they could have regarded a spontaneous uprising with much enthusiasm. From beginning to end the decree reveals its authors' intense concern with the maintenance of the social *status quo* and the pre-eminence of the central authority. From the start the *Landsturm* forces were to be under the command of the provincial authorities, civil and military. Only local units could be mobilised on the initiative of the local commander, and his appointment had to be endorsed by the provincial governors. Gatherings of local units could only be sanctioned by army and corps commanders or provincial military governors. Any assembly of the *Landsturm* without authorisation was to be punished as mutiny. All its members had to swear an oath to abide by the following Article of War:

> Any attack on, robbery or looting of, property in friendly territory, without orders from commanding generals and military governors, any attempt to evade taxes, duties, compulsory labour, or due obedience to local authorities resulting from or aided by, the arming or mobilisation of the *Landsturm*, will be mercilessly punished by death.[33]

After the first three months of its existence the captains of the local units were to be chosen by the troops, but the decree also stated that only landowners, state and local officials and teachers were to be eligible.

Here surely was people's warfare without the people. The cohesion and initiative of the *Landsturm* was undermined by the limits on its choice of leaders; its freedom of action was limited by an almost fanatical respect for property; and what Clausewitz had hoped would be a 'vapoury essence' came into being as little more than a comical marionette totally dependent, at every stage, upon the authorisation of central authority. It was completely subservient to a puppet-master whose potential partial or temporary paralysis was the reason for its existence in the first place! It is small wonder that within three months the whole organisation had almost completely ceased to exist.

But the brief and inglorious history of the *Landsturm* is but an extreme example of the basic incompatibility of the twin goals that motivated the Prussian leaders at the time. They wished to revivify the nation by creating a political environment in which all levels of society would feel a positive commitment to the struggle for national recovery. They wished, in short, to make military service a self-evident political obligation. To this end they liberated the serfs and increased the scope of local political competence. Some even advocated the creation of a national representative assembly and some form of constitutional government. On the other hand, however, these same leaders were determined to maintain the authority of the very central government whose inertia and atrophy had precipitated the original crisis. There is certainly nothing intrinsically non-revolutionary about wishing to assert the authority of a central leadership. But it must be a new leadership, advocating a new system of socio-economic organisation. But this was not the case in Prussia. Even the most radical of the reformers had absolutely no conception of doing away with the monarchy, or of doing any more than merely tinkering with the mechanism by which it asserted its absolute authority. The serfs were liberated, but only because this also allowed a more rational, capitalistic exploitation of agriculture by the incumbent landowners. The principle of universal service was decreed, but great care was taken to ensure that each social group had its own organisation, and thus that class stratification would remain as distinct as ever. Partisans were brought into existence, but it was decreed that they could only remain in existence for as long as they avoided behaving like partisans.

In the last analysis it has to be recognised that the people's army of 1813 was a completely artificial creation. Its mode of organisation was not predicated upon the real social and political aspirations of the people at large, but on the preconceptions of the incumbent political and military leadership. Certainly they had learned something from the armies of the First French Republic, and they were genuinely convinced that the measures they advocated represented a substantial increase in political liberty. But their real goal was not the extension of liberty, as a matter of principle, but the strengthening of the existing state to make it a more formidable opponent in the international arena. Thus all their political concessions were constantly qualified by their ultimate concern for the survival of the state. When forced to follow through the logic of their position,

Scharnhorst and Gneisenau were quite emphatic. 'In the case of a surprise attack by France, a universal army must fight to maintain the King and his family, and in extremity go down honourably with weapons in hand.'[34] And should the nation be strong enough to avoid this heroic fate, Stein was equally emphatic about the uses to which the new national army would be put. He wanted, 'universality of responsibility for service in war, binding upon every class of civil society', but only because 'through this it will be possible to inculcate a proud, warlike national character, to wage wearying distant wars of conquest and to withstand an overwhelming enemy attack with a national war'.[35]

Clearly concern for political liberty could not long coexist with such a respect for the most overtly bellicose *raisons d'état*. If political reform was to be meaningful, the social and political *status quo* would have to be radically altered. The paternalism of the reformers would have to give way to flexibility and a much greater responsiveness to popular demands. But if the existing state was to assert itself internationally, it must have internal stability. Only the maintenance of the existing hierarchies could, it was thought, guarantee that stability. The integration of power politics and domestic reform is, in the end, an impossibility. The contradiction must resolve itself. So it was that by 1820 political reform had become either a fond memory or a scurrilous rumour.

Chapter 6   The Franco-Prussian War and the Paris Commune 1870–71

CHRONOLOGY

1870

19 July   France declares war on Prussia.

4 Aug   The French are defeated at the Battle of Wissembourg.

6 Aug   The French are defeated at the Battles of Firbach and Froeschwiller.

2 Sept   Napoleon III surrenders at Sedan.

4 Sept   The Government of National Defence is formed and the Republic proclaimed.

5 Sept   The Committee of Twenty Arrondissements is formed.

18 Sept   The siege of Paris begins.

2 Oct   Gambetta quits Paris for Tours.

27 Oct   The capitulation of the fortress at Metz.

31 Oct   A revolutionary *journée* in Paris against the Government of National Defence.

2–4 Nov   Negotiations begin between Thiers and Bismark.

1871

19 Jan   A Parisian sortie against the Prussians at Buzenval fails.

28 Jan   A three-week armistice is signed.

29 Jan   The Government of National Defence resigns to make way for elections to a National Assembly.

24 Feb   First meeting of the General Assembly of the (Parisian) National Guard.

1 March   The Assembly ratifies peace preliminaries. The Prussians enter Paris.

3 March   The Republican Federation of the National Guard is constituted.

10 March   The Assembly moves to Versailles.

13 March   The Central Committee of the National Guard is set up.

18 March Blanqui attempts to seize the National Guard cannon. An insurrection follows and he flees Paris.

26 March Elections for the Council of the Commune in Paris.

28 March Proclamation of the Commune of Paris.

1 May Creation of a Committee of Public Safety.

9 May Creation of a new Committee of Public Safety.

18 May The Assembly ratifies the Treaty of Frankfurt.

21 May The Versailles forces enter Paris.

22–28 May Bloody Week. Twenty thousand Communards perish in the suppression of the Commune.

The abiding impression left by the Prussian experiences in the Napoleonic Wars is one of artificiality. Whilst there were those who saw that the experience of the French Revolution indicated the need for greater grass-roots political participation, there was nobody in Prussia willing to make the political and economic sacrifices that would give such participation a realistic base. The French experiences of 1870 and 1871 also reveal such artificiality. In nineteenth-century France, much more than in Prussia, there was a vivid memory of the great achievements of the French Revolution, both on the military and the political fronts. As time passed the memory of what had actually happened became somewhat distorted by mythical interpretations of what might or should have happened. But the mythical aspect of popular memory merely gives a greater resilience. Yet in France too, when these fond recollections were tested against the realities of social and military crisis, no group emerged that was able to put into effective practice the radical dogmas that seemed the logical inference from the activities of the armies of the Year II. Throughout the century, particularly in the twin crises of 1848–51 and 1870–71, there were many who demanded an extensive reform of the Army. In the early years of the Second Republic the pusillanimous middle-class elements who took power managed to keep the demand for reform at a largely rhetorical level. In the social and military crisis that followed the Franco-Prussian War the new leaders found themselves compelled, for military reasons alone, to attempt a thoroughgoing overhaul of the military system. But just as in Prussia,

these men were either unwilling or unable to make the socio-
political reforms that would have effectively underpinned the
adjustments to the military system.

Historical Introduction: 1815–70

In the aftermath of the Napoleonic Wars, due both to revulsion
at home and pressure from the victorious allies, it was decided
that France must rely upon a small army of professional, long-
service regulars. By a law of 1818 the Army was limited to
240,000 men, most of whom would enlist for eight years, a few
for six.[1] In 1832 the strength of the Army was fixed at 500,000
men, sixty per cent of them to serve in the line regiments, the
rest in the reserve. To keep the Army up to strength it was
estimated that 80,000 recruits a year would be needed, to be
taken from the Frenchmen in their twenty-first year. A lottery
system was established to select these unfortunates. All those
eligible drew a number out of an urn, and the 80,000 lowest,
les mauvais numéros, were obliged to serve. The length of service
was fixed at seven years, it being hoped that after such a period
of barrack-room life many of the soldiers would feel incapable of
returning to civil life, and would re-enlist for a further seven
years. The intention was clearly to set the regular soldier apart
from the rest of the nation. Military service was to become a
self-sufficient world to which no alternative seemed possible,
rather than just another facet of full participation in the life
of the country. In short it was simply a piece of ghastly bad
luck. Nor did the burden fall equally on all sections of the
population. All those who drew a bad number were allowed to
offer a replacement in their stead. Clearly, such replacements
had to be bought, either through a payment to themselves or to
their family. Equally clearly, only the more prosperous could
afford such payments, and only the very poor were sufficiently
desperate to accept them. Thus the Army was founded not only
on political alienation but also on social privilege.

By and large, the French were happy to tolerate this state of
affairs. Amongst the middle classes particularly, the ultimate
futility of Napoleonic imperialism and the new opportunities
for self-enrichment at home had bred an atmosphere of smug
pacifism. Military service was not only divorced from political

obligation, it did not even seem to serve the ends of patriotic self-interest. Admittedly it seemed foolhardy to dispense completely with a military establishment, but at least the effort was made to ensure that it did not impinge unduly upon those who had better things to do. Nevertheless, there was some opposition to this situation throughout the years prior to 1848. The legends of the Year II lived on in certain opposition circles and bred a contempt for the armies of passive mercenaries that was being created. Those who wished for a closer affiliation of the Army and the people realised that it could only come as a consequence of a drastic reform of the military organism itself. Such attitudes found their most dramatic expression after February 1848 and the almost bloodless overthrow of Louis-Philippe. On 24 February the Second Republic was proclaimed and the extent and nature of popular dissatisfaction with the Army quickly became apparent.

The demoralised and discredited regiments in Paris were quickly moved away to allay the fears of the people about their possible counterrevolutionary role. And from this time on there was constant popular pressure to ensure that the Army did not reappear in Paris in any shape or form. One of the few consistent and coherent demands of the radical political clubs that had sprung up everywhere was that on no account should the troops be dribbled back into the capital. But this popular mistrust was not directed so much against the Army as such, as against an unreformed army that was held to be the tool of political oppression. Almost everyone conceded that some form of military establishment was necessary, both for national defence and the liberation of the oppressed nationalities. But such an army, it was held, must be rendered compatible with the ideals of a Republic. In February it was still formed around the same reactionary officer-class and the same notions of blind obedience that had prevailed since the Restoration. Until this officer-class was purged and these old notions completely discredited there could never be any hope of a true republicanisation of the Army nor of it transcending its old role of internal social repression. For the radicals the precedents for such a reform were quite clear. Memories of the first Revolution had a great hold on the popular imagination, and surely the armies of the First Republic had shown that purging the officer-corps and throwing all ranks open to those with the necessary talent and *élan* was the way to create an army that genuinely reflected democratic political ideals.

Throughout 1848 and 1849 there were attempts, all over France, to stimulate some sort of reform of the Army. The main form such efforts took was that of electoral propaganda by the various republican-socialist candidates and their supporters. These efforts were not without a certain impact and the radicals gained many supporters within the regiments themselves. But the very nature of the Revolution of 1848, in its political and social dimensions, meant that the attempts at military reform were of a very limited nature. Most of the radical leaders of the period were deprived middle-class elements seeking a place in the sun. They wanted increased opportunities for their own participation in the economic and political life of the nation rather than a total overhaul of the system itself. In the last analysis most of the radicals were a little afraid of the consequences of a total breakdown in military discipline. Just as their main efforts in the political sphere were directed at the reform of society through republican control of the legislature, so also did they seek to reform the Army from within rather than by a direct attack on the hierarchical structure itself. Thus, though they spoke fondly of the armies of the Year II, they in fact had absolutely no intention of imbuing the rank-and-file of 1848-9 with the kind of militant class-consciousness that had animated the middle-class volunteers of 1792. Ultimately the lesser bourgeoisie were attempting to gain a place in the political life of the nation. To obtain it they were willing to enlist the support of the poor peasant and worker, the backbone of the Army, but only if these latter were willing to advance their claims under the former's leadership. They did not want an army that was actively aware of its own interests, but merely one that, through the benevolent influence of a reformed officer-corps, would act in defence of a republican regime it believed to be acting on its behalf.

The limited nature of the radicals' vision was reflected in the kind of men who came forward as republican spokesman within the Army itself. Those demands for reform that did emerge

from the soldiers were of a purely internal character and envisaged no dramatic changes in traditional modes of organisation
and discipline. On the whole the agitation of the so-called demo-
cratic-socialist NCOs and privates was careerist in origin and
concerned solely with their own advancement. Speaking of the
electoral campaign of 1849, one writer has said: '[the candi-
dates] proposed a profound reform; the introduction into the
modes of promotion of that of election alongside seniority and
competitive examination . . . [Some] suggested the creation in
each corps of *conseils d'honneur* which would supervise the good
conduct of the men and bestow honours and rewards.'[2] But
surely one must question the use of the word 'profound' here.
Promotion implies a traditional hierarchical structure, and
good conduct the survival of very traditional military values,
even of passive obedience. An army is only revolutionised in a
meaningful sense if it relates its actions to the wider political
interests of its soldiers. But if a soldier's self-interest is defined
solely in terms of internal norms, functional only to the maintenance of the military system itself, then it matters little who
is given the responsibility of judging men against these norms.
Such a 'democratisation' is quite artificial, having no impact
on the soldier's status within the wider political community.

Thus in the long run the Army remained quite alienated from
the people. The self-absorption of its members, combined with
the basic conservatism of the supposedly radical reformers,
prevented any significant cross-fertilisation with grass-roots
aspirations. From the end of 1849 onwards this alienation
became more and more profound. It was Louis-Napoleon,
elected President of the Republic in December 1848, who
completed it. In a studied campaign of militaristic propaganda,
the promotion of key personnel and particularly good treatment
of the soldiers themselves, he diverted the Army's loyalty not
only from the people at large, but from the very institution of
the Republic itself. In November 1851 a circular was sent to all
generals stressing the importance of passive obedience: 'When
under arms military law is the only law. Responsibility, which is
the lynch-pin of military authority, is indivisible, and is wholly
the concern of the leader from whom an order emanates.'[3]
On 2 December 1851 Napoleon risked all in an attempt to seize

power in a swift and ruthless *coup d'état*. He distributed the last 50,000 francs of his fortune amongst the soldiers, and issued this proclamation:

> Take pride in your mission, you will be the saviours of your country . . . In . . . 1848, you were treated as though you had been conquered. After treating with contempt your heroic impartiality, no-one deigned to find out what were your sympathies and wishes, and that even though you are the elite of the nation.[4]

The Army did not fail him. A new Napoleonic dictatorship began, the Second Empire being initiated a year later.

Thus the Army emerged from the Second Republic with a reputation far better than at any time in the preceding thirty-five years. In the last four years the Army had been seen to act with vigour and determination to protect the propertied classes from the threat of violent social upheaval. Having lost much of its prestige in the ultimate debacle of the Napoleonic Wars, the Army was restored to favour by a second Napoleon riding under the banner of internal defence. Throughout the years of the Second Empire it received an unprecedentedly 'good press', and began once again to attract aspiring officers from the aristocracy and the *haute bourgeoisie*. Military life was once again socially acceptable.

Unfortunately the social cachet accruing to the wearing of gold braid and epaulettes in no way reflected a high level of military competence. After 1851 the Army that had dealt with the ragged insurrections of the previous years with such contemptuous ease felt able to rest on its laurels. Complete faith was placed in an army of long-service regulars whose inability to exist outside the barrack-room was deemed the acme of military proficiency. The decrees on military recruitment of 1855 took over most of the ideas of 1818 and 1832 by which the Army was to remain small and completely isolated from the rest of the community. Replacements were still allowed to spare the middle classes the necessity of having to serve in the rank-and-file. Indeed the laws of 1855 went further than ever before, and the state, for the payment of a flat sum of 2,000 to

2,500 francs, undertook to find replacements itself. A part of this money, generally between 1,500 and 2,000 francs per man, was used to bribe those regulars whose seven-year period with the colours was up, to re-enlist for a further seven years. NCOs' pensions were increased to encourage them to remain in the Army to the bitter end. Clearly the aim was to increase the preponderance of long-term professionals in the line and widen as far as possible the gulf between soldier and citizen. In this Napoleon III succeeded, and by the 1860s the number of men who had served for more than seven years had increased from 45,000, out of 400,000, to 140,000 (from eleven to thirty-five per cent). Clearly such an army had nothing in common with the one discussed in Chapter 4. Far from being a real political obligation, military service had now become a burden to be foisted on those too insecure or too poor to face up to civilian life. As Thiers said, speaking of that class that supplied the vast proportion of the rank-and-file: 'What harm is done to the peasant? Transported into the ranks of the army, he finds there a way of life superior to that which he had at home. But military service is an intolerable tyranny to the man destined for a civil career.' [5]

This military system was not without its opponents. The small but vociferous Republican opposition constantly demanded that military service be made a universal obligation. To some extent this was a mere parroting of the rhetoric of 1792, but it also revealed an awareness of the extent to which the Empire had managed to create a kind of Praetorian Guard for use in case of civil disturbance. An army based upon the population at large, it was held, would be less likely to take up arms against its co-citizens. There was also some opposition from within the Army itself. General Trochu, in *The French Army in 1867*, denounced the apathy and inertia that reliance upon long-term regulars must engender. His ideal was an army of conscripts drawn from all strata of society, who would serve for only two or three years: 'This confirmed soldier, whilst at the same time a young man, is full of energy and honour: he will not give up one day more than the years he owes to the nation, for prior, higher duties call him back to his family. But these years he gives completely, without let or hindrance.' [6]

This book provoked much reaction throughout France and by 1868 even Napoleon himself was a little worried at the almost total lack of a substantial force of adequately trained reservists. In 1861 he had tried to decree that the second portion of the annual contingent of conscripts, whose call-up was largely ritualistic, should undergo at least five months basic training. But the scheme foundered upon a lack of funds and of interest within the army high command. In 1866 he began a series of high-level military conferences in which he again stressed the need for a massive build-up of reservists. He wanted all male citizens to be eligible for service within one of three categories: the line, the reserves, the *Garde Mobile*. But the Assembly, reflecting conventional middle-class opinion, was resolutely opposed to any idea of universal service. It claimed for itself the right to decide the size of the annual contingent, and removed the control of what reserves were to be formed from the Ministry of War. And whilst it agreed to the formation of a third-line *Garde Mobile*, it decreed that its members should not be subject to military discipline, should not receive more than fifteen days training per year, and should never be allowed to go on manoeuvres for longer than sunrise to sunset.

In some respects the Assembly's attitude reflects the kind of concern that has earlier been indicated as being essential to a genuine politicisation of the armed forces. In decreeing these limitations on the *Garde Mobile*'s subjection to regular military life, the Assembly showed itself aware that the genuine soldier-citizen must at all costs remain a full participant in civilian life. Unfortunately they went too far. Anxious as they were to protect the reservists from militarisation and alienation from the civil community, they made their military service of such a ludicrously brief duration that there was absolutely no hope of them acquiring even the most elementary techniques and dis-cipline. By being so opposed to 'militarism' the Assembly ended up by defining satisfactory civil life as the absence of all military preparation, and in effect completely suppressed the idea that political freedom was worth fighting for. During the Second Republic the nation as a whole had been content to allow the Army to become completely divorced from everyday socio-political affairs and so permit it to become the tool of an aspirant autocrat. In the years before the outbreak of the Franco-Prussian War, civilians in turn were made to despise the Army and the very conception of military service at a rank-and-file level. Far from creating a body of soldier-citizens, a people's army, the French simply succeeded in completely divorcing military obligation and political participation. And it should be clear by now that such a state of affairs is completely antithetic to that which will produce an effective democratic fighting force. It led in fact, 'to the moral crisis of the nation which refuses to accept the obligations of universal military service and also to that sort of lassitude . . . and general desire for comfort and security which saps the spirit of sacrifice and discipline'.[7]

Contempt for military life was not the only reason for this neglect of the nation's defensive capacities. It has already been seen how vivid were the memories of the armies of the Year II during the Second Republic, and such memories retained their power even during the years of the Second Empire. But the recollection of bygone French successes now merely persuaded the army commanders and the general public that Frenchmen were natural soldiers, and thus did not need to waste time on manoeuvres or in the barrack-room. In the words of one of the deputies of 1869, the youth of France:

> will always be ready to march on the day of crisis and then its warlike instincts will reveal themselves . . . Let it not be said that their education will be incomplete or that they will not be able to set themselves on march . . . When faced with a serious situation they will studiously take in what they are taught, and will learn more quickly than if they are torn away without immediate reason from the habits of life and work.[8]

The Franco-Prussian War

So the nation slumbered on, with only a tiny minority of its citizens dimly aware that their armed forces were simply not adequate to the demands of modern warfare. It took the outbreak of the war with Prussia, on 19 July 1870, to bring the point home. But by then it was much too late. Within six weeks the French had been completely crushed at the Battles of Wissembourg, Froeschwiller and Forbach, and on 2 September Napoleon capitulated at Sedan. This overwhelming military disgrace completely undermined the Emperor's legitimacy as the head of the state, and on 4 September the Republic was proclaimed and a Government of National Defence established to try and recoup France's military fortunes. By this time the regular army was almost non-existent and so the French fell back on old memories and tried to institute another *levée en masse*, to create a nation in arms and try and drive back the Prussians on a flood of patriotic zeal.

For many of the Republicans newly come to power this was how the war should have been fought from the beginning. As early as 1867 Garnier-Pagès had demanded the complete disarmament of the nation with recourse to a spontaneous *levée en masse* only when France was attacked from outside. As he said: 'When a vigorous *élan* is needed to save the country, in all parts of France they will rise up as a single man, and each citizen will expose his breast to the enemy.'[9] In December of the same year Jules Favre, later Minister of Foreign Affairs in the Government of National Defence, had put forward a *projet de loi* demanding the complete abolition of the standing army and its replacement by a militia. All citizens would be obliged to serve in it, but no one would have to spend more than three years on active service. 'We would have an army, but an army of citizens and of soldiers, invincible at home, incapable of waging war abroad; an army without militaristic spirit.'[10] Léon Gambetta, another Republican steeped in such traditions, took over the Ministry of the Interior in the new government and set about the actual organisation of the national defence.

Certainly, once Bismark's humiliating peace proposals were published by Favre, Gambetta did find much support throughout the country. He replaced all the Imperial prefects, and everywhere local defence committees sprang up eager to arm themselves and take on the invader. 'The population and the local defence committee want arms and I have got to have them,' wrote the prefect at Bordeaux. His colleague at Tarbes wrote: 'My situation is untenable if I cannot distribute at least the 3,000 rifles so long promised.'[11] Many of these defence committees banded themselves together in organisations such as the *Ligue du Midi*, the *Ligue du Sud-Ouest*, the *Ligue de l'Ouest* and the *Ligue du Plateau Central*. In October 1870 the second of these posted a proclamation declaring that its seventy-five delegates 'promise to march as delegates at the head of the armies for the national defence, thus following the glorious example of our fathers in 1792'.[12] The *Ligue du Midi*, in another proclamation of that month, declared that:

> The republican population of the Midi must rise up *en masse* to attempt a supreme effort to prevent the invaders any longer sullying the soil of the fatherland . . . The delegates of the federated departments are nomimated as commissioners-general of the *Ligue du Midi*. They will repair into the departments to preach the holy war, unify the local republican committees and work with them to bring about, by all means possible, a general uprising.[13]

Generally these organisations were led by middle-class Republicans, though they did contain many workers among their membership. Nor were the working-class organisations themselves less susceptible to patriotic appeals. The *Chambre fédérale des Associations ouvrières* and the *Fédération des Sections Parisiennes de l'Internationale*, in September, sent the following message to the Germans:

> Republican France invites you . . . to withdraw your armies; if you do not, we shall have to fight to the last man and spill floods of your blood and ours. We repeat to you what we proclaimed to the European Coalition in 1793: 'The French people will not make peace with an enemy who is occupying her territory.' Go back across the Rhine. On each bank of the disputed river, let Germans and Frenchmen hold out their hands.[14]

Even international proletarian solidarity had its limitations when the prestige of the nation was at stake.

The man chosen, to a large extent by himself, to lead this new national struggle was Gambetta, who took over the Ministry of War as well as that of the Interior. He too was very much aware

of the historical precedents for the fight ahead: 'I have determined to quit the usual paths. I wish to give you young and
active leaders capable by their intelligence and their energy of
renewing the prodigies of 1792.'[15] Again, in a letter to General
Chanzy of 10 January 1871, Gambetta revealed the extent to
which he was influenced by the memory of the ruthless efficiency
of the Committee of Public Safety and its *représentants-en-
mission*: 'You are given full authorisation to remove from his
command any unit commander who does not strictly obey the
orders given or who is unable to run his unit, and by the same
token you have the power to reward on the spot officers and
soldiers who show a spirit of devotion and tenacity.' A second
dispatch assured Chanzy: 'You can make any nominations,
promotions or dismissals that are necessary, in the assurance
that ratification will follow without delay.'[16] By a decree of 13
October all restrictions on promotion were abolished and several
dashing young colonels were made generals. On the 14th all
those units not belonging to the regular army proper were
grouped together in an Auxiliary Army in which anyone could
be appointed to hold any rank.

With regard to the officers, Gambetta, for a short period,
attempted an even bolder tactic, yet again a reflection of the
traditions of the First Republic; in the decrees of 10 August and
12 September, by which the provincial National Guards were
mobilised, these were confirmed in their right of electing their
own officers. Under pressure from Paris this right was extended
to the *Garde Mobile* on 7 September. But such an attack on
traditional modes of military discipline was a little too much
even for Gambetta, and on 18 December the electoral principle
was revoked altogether. Even before this revocation Gambetta
had showed himself far from eager fully to endorse the idea of
elective accountability. On 24 November he described the
relationship between officers and men in these terms: 'You
must have at your head energetic and devoted leaders, as wise
as they are bold. They must be blindly obeyed. They preoccupy
themselves ceaselessly with you. In return they have the right
to demand order, discipline, courage: republican virtues of
which they set you an example every day.'[17] Nor did he apply
the decrees on the election of officers with any firmness. The

local authorities were, in the event, given the right to adjourn
the elections if they deemed that, for military reasons or whatever, 'there would be a danger in holding them'. 'From this it
resulted that the local authorities had the most absolute control
over whether to hold elections or not, and in practice the number of those who found that there was some "danger" was such
that battalions that had elected their officers were the exception.'[18]

Nevertheless, in terms of sheer numbers, the French mobilisation of 1870–71 represented a fair imitation of the massive
efforts of 1793. On 2 November the Government of National
Defence issued a decree mobilising the entire male population
between the ages of twenty-one and forty, exception only being
made for those who were ill or disabled. By the end of the war
only the unmarried men had actually been called to the colours,
but these alone amounted to a little under 600,000. Also, by a
decree of 12 October, the *Garde Mobile* in the provinces had been
called up, and here age restrictions were much more flexible.
Every canton was to supply a battalion, every arrondissement a
legion and every department a brigade. To encourage recruitment the *Mobiles* were allowed parity of pay with the regulars
for the duration of the war. Finally, the government had at its
disposal many bands of *franc-tireurs*, guerrillas or partisans,
which had sprung up all over France even before the end of the
Empire. After the declaration of the Republic there were many
who clearly hoped to unite these bands with the National Guard
and to wage a full-scale guerrilla war. On 21 September Admiral
Fourichon, the Minister of the Navy, advised that the role of
the *Mobiles* themselves, 'is less to fight than to harass the
enemy . . . to obstruct him in his requisitions . . . Above all to
carry out *coups de main* . . to capture convoys, cut roads and
railways, destroy bridges . . . These troops must wage real
partisan war.'[19] In a proclamation issued after his arrival at
Tours, Gambetta expressed a similar conception of the national
war:

We must . . . increase partisan warfare and, against an
enemy so skilled in ambush and surprise, ourselves employ
ruses, attack his flanks, surprise his rear—in short

inaugurate a national war . . . Tied down and contained by the capital, the Prussians, far from home, anxious, harassed, hunted down by our re-awakened people, will be gradually decimated by our arms, by hunger, by natural causes.[20]

It has been estimated that at the height of their activities there were some three hundred partisan bands operating throughout France, incorporating over 57,000 men. But the very independence of these units was the cause of much concern to more traditionally minded members of the government. A series of measures was enacted which tried to imbue their organisation with a basic military discipline. On 29 September they were placed on the same disciplinary footing as the *Mobiles*, whilst on 4 November they were put under the regular military commander within whose area they were operating. Under the terms of this latter arrangement partisan commanders were to submit a regular report on the strength and achievements of their unit. Any unit whose behaviour was unsatisfactory was liable to dissolution.

Such then was the scope of the French attempt to mobilise the whole nation against the Prussians. But in the end the Government of National Defence failed in its task. To a large extent the reasons for this were military. The bulk of the trained, regular army had been put out of the war before even the call for a national uprising was issued; 200,000 men under Macmahon had surrendered at Sedan, and thousands more fell into Prussian hands after the capitulation of Metz and Strasbourg. From the declaration of the Republic to the end of the war the French were consequently forced to rely on units of completely untrained men, be they regulars, *Mobiles* or ordinary National Guardsmen. On many fronts the *Mobiles* fared better than the new line troops, grouped as they were in units based upon the same locality and fighting side by side with their friends and neighbours. But even so they were bound to feel the lack of prior training due to the parsimony and neglect of the Imperial regime. Despite individual acts of great courage they were on the whole no match for either the Prussian line or the *Landwehr* units.

However, the reasons for the French lack of success went deeper than the merely military. In essence what was missing was the political component of a national struggle, in other words a genuine popular commitment to the war. By declaring the Third Republic, the Government of National Defence hoped to arouse those popular enthusiasms that had marked the First and the opening months of the Second Republic. But the mere ritualistic abolition of the Empire, the mere changing of the name of the regime, was not in itself enough to persuade people that they were now members of a state worth fighting for. Even the changes of personnel and the chasing out of office of many Imperial bureaucrats could only have a very limited short-term effect unless those that took their place at least showed themselves willing to inaugurate some measure of genuine socio-political reform. But such was not the case. From the very beginning the Republic placed its faith in the very crudest type of chauvinism, expecting Frenchmen to fight to rid their nation of foreigners simply because they were foreigners, rather than because they would also be fighting for the introduction of a new and advantageous mode of government. It is this that explains the sheer number and stridency of the appeals to past memories. For the Republic leaders had nothing but memories. They lacked any coherent socio-political programme of their own, and thus never saw the *levée en masse* as anything more than a technical problem. They completely ignored the necessity for a dynamic political basis to such a *levée*, and the fact that during the first Revolution there had been such a basis. In the First Republic the peasantry had been fighting for the retention of their freedom from feudal dues; the middle classes had been fighting for their new place in the legislative process; the urban poor, for a time at least, were fighting for the new liberties and relative security promised to them by the Jacobin opportunists. All groups of society had made real economic and political gains, or at least felt that they had a real hope of doing so.

But the Third Republic promised little and gave nothing. The French state was to remain as it was, with or without the Prussians. Consequently the national *soulèvement*, although impressive in terms of sheer numbers, remained a basically amorphous affair, devoid of any firm central leadership or of grass-roots loyalty to such a central *apparat*. Whatever enthusiasm was shown was more for the defence of home and hearth than for the realisation of any social vision. Certainly such a defence can be bitter and dogged, but it is nevertheless almost impossible to combine such parochial fragments into a cohesive force with a centrally directed strategy. Because there is no transcendent political rationale each group puts its trust in local leaders, and limits its military objectives to the protection of the immediate locality. This was particularly the case in the *Mobiles* and the *franc-tireurs*. In the rural departments in particular the *Mobiles* were very loath to be sent on operations outside their own neighbourhood. Even within that neighbourhood their attachment to their plots of land was a grave liability: 'One tried in vain to convoke or reconvoke them, they always found an excuse to return home for some task that they had forgotten, to say goodbye to their families, etc., and finding it hard to leave again, they lingered on.'[21] It would be hardly likely that the guerrilla detachments would be found operating far from their homes, as such warfare depends upon knowledge of the terrain, support of the population and the ability to disperse home again when necessary. But it is still possible, as will be demonstrated in Chapter 8, to give such units a central political direction based around a common set of aspirations. In France there was no attempt to harness such aspirations, and consequently no possibility of centralised political or military control.

> The French companies reflected every hue of the complex political spectrum, from the violently radical *franc-tireurs* of the Seine to Colonel de Cathelineau's legitimists from Vendée, from the wealthy *tirailleurs volontiers* from the Gironde to the companies of Papal Zouaves which Colonel de Charette had brought back to France . . . Even the grooms of the Imperial Household, to the embarrassment of the local authorities, raised a regiment of cavalry.[22]

Such disparate units might win local successes, but there was no hope that they could have been the components of a successful protracted struggle. And in the political vacuum of 1870–71 there was equally no hope of any organisation growing up which could unite, even temporarily, such diverse elements.

The Paris Commune

It is this almost total lack of real political policies from the top, and thus commitment from below, that also helps to explain the disastrous military record of the Paris Commune. Throughout the Second Empire, and particularly in the latter years of the last decade, there had been a growing sense of discontent, and a growing organised militancy, amongst the artisans and workers of the large French towns. There is no space to examine the reasons for this discontent here. Suffice it to say that the shock of military disaster and the nominal fall of the *ancien régime* occasioned a new burst of unrest. Increasingly dissatisfied with the political and military inertia of the Government of National Defence, these workers staged popular insurrections throughout France in March and April of 1871. The most famous of these was at Paris, but the insurrectionaries were also masters of the situation for a time in Lyon (22–25 March), Marseille (23 March–4 April), Toulouse (23–27 March), Narbonne (24–31 March), Saint-Etienne (24–28 March), Le Creusot (26–27 March) and Limoges (4 April).

In Paris, however, the Commune lasted from 18 March to 28 May, and thus gave the insurrectionaries some time in which to try and create a military machine. Once again the Communards were primarily inspired in their efforts by the example of their forefathers during the First Republic. Their central concept was that of the *levée en masse*, the nation in arms as opposed to a reliance on a professional military clique. Even before the final proclamation of the Commune, the Parisians had throughout the siege indicated that for them traditional modes of military organisation had been tried and found greatly wanting. For the Parisians the early weeks of the Franco-Prussian War had revealed the inadequacy of the old notions of strict discipline, passive obedience and rigid hierarchy. The time had now come to rely upon spontaneity and the natural *élan* of the people at large. Time and time again this theme was stressed in speeches and proclamations. On 7 December, at one of the many Parisian clubs, an orator declared: 'They accuse us of lack of discipline; but of what use is discipline? How has it served us up to the present time? It has resulted in our being beaten by the Prussians.'[23]

The organisation chosen to demonstrate the efficacy of this new concept of military cohesion was the National Guard. It had already been called into existence again by the Empress after the early defeats in the field. On 12 August it was reconstituted according to the regulations of 1851. It was to consist of 12,000 men and a headquarters responsible to the Minister of the Interior. Officers were to be chosen from amongst retired regular soldiers, and an account of fifty million francs was to be opened to furnish arms, equipment and pay. On 6 September the Government of National Defence, as part of the general appeal for a national uprising against the Prussians, ordered the formation of sixty new battalions of National Guard. The decree of 12 August had theoretically thrown the Guard open to all citizens capable of bearing arms, but in fact arms had only been distributed to the more prosperous of the volunteers. But the siege, and the logic of republican rhetoric, made an overt class bias unfeasible, and so the call was made for the new battalions. In fact it was answered by some 300,000 Parisians and in the end 194 battalions of National Guard were organised. It is customary to point out that service with the Guard was of great importance to the Parisian workers and artisans because it guaranteed a daily pay of thirty sous, a vital factor in the light of the chronic unemployment, already greatly aggravated by the siege. Be this as it may, it is still worth noting, with Jellinek, that this pay was not in fact decreed until 12 September, after the initial massive response to the appeal for volunteers.[24]

But from the point of view of the Government of National Defence, whose political fervour never went beyond sterile rhetoric, this large-scale arming of the Parisian populace had the most disastrous consequences. As the siege progressed the situation of the bulk of the citizenry worsened, and the extent of the government's unwillingness to attempt any alleviation of this situation became increasingly apparent. But, by creating a new, mass-based National Guard, the Government had laid down the organisational base for the coherent expression of dissatisfaction with this state of affairs. They had in fact set up an alternative grass-roots political structure and, what is worse, a structure whose very existence was predicated upon some form of offensive activity against the Prussians. The social and economic conservatism of the new government swiftly became apparent. After their signature of the armistice at the end of January their patriotism too began to ring a little hollow.

Discontent grew within the ranks of the National Guard. Each battalion had already, in September, elected a Vigilance Committee of four members, who met and discussed military and political questions in an organisation known as the Central Republican Committee of the Twenty Arrondissements. On 4 September this organisation put forward a proposed programme which included the suppression of the police, their replacement by elected municipal authorities, the expropriation of necessary foodstuffs, the supervision of this measure by local committees elected at the street and *quartier* level, the assurance of lodgings to all and a general *levée en masse*. On 7 January 1871, fearing the imminence of a French capitulation to Prussian terms, the Committee posted a proclamation warning that: 'The population of Paris will never want to accept these miseries and this shame. It knows that there is still time, that decisive measures will allow the workers to live, and all to fight. General requisitioning, free rations, attack *en masse*!'[25]

Soon after this the National Guard created another organisation to protect its interests, and the Central Republican Committee relinquished its role as a political and military vanguard. The new organisation was the Federation of the National Guard whose creation was a direct response to the armistice of 28 January. It held its first meeting on 6 February. The preamble to its statutes said:

The duty of a citizen is the defence of his country and the maintenance of internal order, not of a monarchical order, but of an order resting upon frankly republican principles. His rights are those of being an elector and of bearing arms necessary to the accomplishment of his duty; the National Guard must henceforth replace permanent armies which have never been anything other than the instruments of despotism . . . The standing army takes men and turns them into slaves.[26]

In a series of statutes adopted on 24 February the Federation also set up a Central Committee (of the National Guard) made up of one delegate from each battalion. This Committee was also to have a Grand Council of three members, nominated by the Committee, from each of the districts of Paris. This Council was to be responsible for convening the Central Committee itself and for executing its decisions. Within the battalions themselves each company was to have its own group of representatives who would meet once a fortnight for discussion. Such delegates were to be elected by the company. 'In so organising, the National Guard adopted the same form of federation as that of the other popular organisations in Paris, for the effect of the war had been to substitute the National Guard companies for the workshops as the natural group basis.'[27]

Here then is a seemingly perfect integration of the political and military functions. The Federation not only represented the bulk of the now 270 battalions of National Guard, which in turn included a vast proportion of the male population of Paris, but it also made broad political demands a substantial part of its platform, equating the right to bear arms with that of being an elector. Furthermore, as in any genuinely politicised armed force, it tried to organise according to those principles, elective representation at all levels which were to govern everyday political practice. Finally, the identification between civil and military was made even clearer by virtue of the fact that the various legions, battalions and companies were recruited within certain localities, such that each Guardsman fought alongside his neighbours and workmates. In the National Guard of this period one can see at least the embryo of the classic people's army, combining military goals and political aspirations within one organisation.

Yet within three months the whole political and military apparatus of the Commune had been shattered. The reasons for this are many. Some are purely technical. For one thing the Communards never had sufficient arms of any quality, whilst even those they did possess were so lamentably organised that the fire-power of the Commune was always well short of its potential. With respect to the artillery, for example, the Parisians only ever had 320 cannon in service, though there were some 1,740 within the city. They were also badly handicapped by the way the National Guard units were based around particular geographical areas. Whilst this did give each unit a certain additional *esprit de corps*, it undoubtedly also made it more difficult to move the individual battalions and companies away from their particular recruiting area. Naturally enough the Guardsmen were most concerned with protecting their own homes, and thus denied themselves the advantages of any kind of tactical mobility. Apart from one or two isolated forays, the Communards remained within their own localities, gave the Versaillais time to regroup and, when the final assault came, died heroically yet somewhat passively behind their barricades. Having renounced the military habits of the Empire they were eventually reduced to the tragic strategic nihilism revealed in this final proclamation of Delescluze, the third and last of the Commune's military organisers:

> Enough of militarism, no more bespangled and gilded staff-officers . . . Make way for the people, for those who fight with their bare hands. The hour of revolutionary warfare has struck! The people know nothing of scientific manoeuvring; but when they have a rifle in their hand, paving-stones beneath their feet, they fear not all the strategists of the monarchical school.[28]

For the purposes of this book, however, what is of interest in the military activities of the Commune and the National Guard is their basic confusion with regard to the division of the military and the political. Up until the insurrection of 18 March and the flight of Thiers, the Central Committee of the National Guard represented both a political and a military opposition. But as soon as the way was open for the creation of a new municipal government, the Central Committee tried to renounce its own role in such a central authority. For the first few days, until the elections could be held, it was forced to act as a temporary executive, and between 20 and 23 March it enacted several short-term socio-economic measures. But its heart was not in it and it clearly wished to hand over such functions to the Commune as swiftly as possible. A proclamation of 27 March read: 'The Commune represents political and civil power in Paris. It is the emanation of the power of the people. The Central Committee represents the military forces. It puts into effect the orders given by the Commune.'²⁹ On 5 April they were even more specific: 'We did not wish and do not wish for any political power, because the idea of sharing [power] would be the germ of civil war within our walls.'³⁰

But the behaviour of the Central Committee rather belied this impression of political abnegation. In the face of the military failures of the Commune itself, and its rather feeble record of actual socio-economic reform, the Central Committee increasingly asserted itself as a political force in its own right. As early as 1 April several of its members appeared before the Commune demanding recognition of their rights with respect to the administration of the National Guard, including the right to nominate the *Chef de l'État-Major*. The minutes of the meeting of the Committee on the 10th reveal that several present thought that: 'The Central Committee is always a part of the struggle, despite its having said that it had given way to the Commune . . . The Central Committee is always a revolutionary power, it is not at the mercy of the voting, like the Commune.'³¹ In many parts of Paris the sub-committees of the Central Committee were more influential than the municipal authorities of the arrondissement, and these latter rarely attempted to assert themselves. The Committee waged a particularly vigorous battle against Rossel, the Commune's second Delegate for War, and on 5 May succeeded in persuading him formally to leave all matters pertaining to the adminstration of the National Guard in their hands. At their meeting of the 2nd of that month they even went so far as to demand that the Commune abolish the Ministry of War, leaving the Central Committee in charge. As they said:

We have finally resolved that, if the Commune does not go along with us . . . we will take things into our own hands, reminding it that the National Guard, represented in us, was the sole lawful source of resistance in Paris. In a word the men of 18 March are taking in hand again the revolution that they made, and are going to act in a revolutionary fashion.[32]

The Commune itself was quite in accord with this reluctance to share political power. Indeed its members became most jealous of those few administrative military functions that the Central Committee insisted on still performing. Thus from 4 April the Executive Council of the Commune itself included as one of its members a so-called Delegate for War. Between this date and 25 May there were three different incumbents in this office, Gustave Cluseret, Louis Rossel and Charles Delescluze. All three were more or less hostile to the Central Committee and to the somewhat anarchic organisation of the National Guard. Even before the nomination of a Delegate for War the Commune's Military Commission, set up on 29 March, had put to the whole assembly, 'a proposition tending to distinguish the powers of the Commune and the Central Committee, and totally to deprive the Central Committee of political powers, only leaving its administrative control over the National Guard'.[33] On 5 April Cluseret insisted upon conscription into the Guard for unmarried men between seventeen and thirty-five years of age. On the 6th he abolished the rank of general in the Guard, and also dissolved the arrondissement sub-committees: 'Considering that in the present crisis, public security demands the unity of military command, and that this unity is everyday compromised by the orders issuing from the arrondissement sub-committees.'[34] On the 7th the Commune decided to place civil delegates with all military commanders, though this in fact remained a dead letter. On the 9th Cluseret struck a blow at the power of the Central Committee delegates within the Guard by giving the individual unit commanders absolute responsibility for the signing of orders. Whilst on the 11th the Commune itself put a check on the influence of these commanders by making them ineligible for a seat within the assembly. On 16 April Cluseret set up a court martial to enforce strict military discipline and actually went so far as to arrest one of the members of the Central Committee.

Cluseret's successor, Rossel, was equally antipathetic to the autonomous nature of the Guard and its own political spokesmen. On 29 April, he claims in his memoirs, he wrote to the Executive Commission foretelling that: 'There was no more hope of success except in an absolute reform of the system of pay . . . the re-establishment of discipline by harsh examples, directed chiefly against senior officers, and the immediate organisation of a small military body capable of holding its ground and taking the offensive.'[35] He wanted a small army of 20,000 men, formed into eight regiments, and supported by some forty cannon. He wanted a force to live in military barracks, and proposed the thorough examination of all elected officers whose commissions had not been confirmed by the Ministry of War. In mid-May one of the Commune's best field commanders, Dombrowski, tightened up the military organisation by forbidding all local councils of war, and by insisting that: 'Orders emanating from above will be carried out without discussion.'[36] Finally, on 17 May the Commune insisted that: 'To safeguard the interests of the revolution, it is essential to associate the civil element to the military . . . Our fathers understood perfectly that this measure alone could preserve the country from military dictatorship.'[37]

Clearly the whole military leadership of the revolutionary forces within Paris was seriously flawed by this squabble over the exact powers of each organisation. Whatever the reasons for the disagreements it seems obvious that such an arrangement rendered impossible any full integration of political aspirations and military tasks. As long as the units which formed the backbone of the Commune's military strength disputed the very extent of the Commune's authority over them, there was little chance of the Commune delegates being able to formulate a set of political demands and principles that could rouse the National Guardsmen from their stubborn parochialism. Until the Commune could formulate such a set of demands they would never be able to unite the Guard behind them and cut the ground from under the feet of the Central Committee. As it was both Commune and Central Committee remained impotent and confused. Each seems to have been intuitively striving towards an amalgamation and centralisation of the political and military apparatus, yet each seemed convinced that when the other attempted it, it was a bid for either political or military dictatorship. In the end both components of the military struggle were fatally weakened. The Commune (political) never achieved sufficient grass-roots support to formulate and impose a radical and coherent programme of reforms which would unite the armed forces behind it. It degenerated into a mere talking-shop. The Central Committee (military) spent so much time guarding against the encroachments of the Commune's Military Commission that it never had the time to attempt its own politicisation of the National Guard.

But whilst the struggle of the Communards was fatally undermined by this division of responsibility within revolutionary Paris, and the even more enervating jealousies it engendered, the root problem was a factor that runs throughout the history of nineteenth-century France. The First Republic had left its memories but the lessons drawn from these memories were not the right ones. People recalled the successes of the massive *levée en masse* rather than the smaller but much more important example of the National Guard as a class militia. The French radicals lost sight, through ignorance and fear, of the essential dynamics of a truly revolutionary situation. They began to equate revolutionary upheaval with merely a large-scale patriotic mobilisation, rather than with conflict within the society itself. In both the Second and the Third Republics no group emerged that was prepared to speak out decisively for the interests of one particular class or to formulate a socio-political programme that would assert the absolute necessity of fighting, if needs be, on behalf of those interests. Real political demands were lost in a mish-mash of patriotism and sentimental appeals to national unity. No one ever offered the workers, artisans or even poor peasants anything worth fighting for, and so there was no chance of an effective revolutionary army being created. In the Second Republic the radicals' interest in the Army degenerated into a purely internalised careerism, within an essentially unchanged structure. In the Franco-Prussian War the appeal to national solidarity soon wore thin as the rank-and-file quickly appreciated that this new Republic on behalf of which they were called to fight had absolutely no concrete reforms to offer them. In the Commune the lack of a clear socio-economic perspective even prevented the revolutionaries from solving the basic problems of revolutionary leadership. When Delescluze calmly stepped over his barricade and walked towards the Versaillais troops and his certain death, he gave the Commune its most appropriate symbol. Paris had become a glorious tomb for martyrs, but could never have been the womb of a revolutionary republic.

Chapter 7   The Russian Civil War
1917—20

CHRONOLOGY

1917

9–13 Feb   General strike in Petrograd. Mutiny of two regiments of the garrison. Formation of the Executive Committee of the Provisional Government.

29 Oct   Creation of the Revolutionary Military Commission of the Petrograd Soviet.

7 Nov   Flight of Kerensky's troops from Petrograd. Arrest of the Provisional Government. Opening of the Second Pan-Russian Congress of Soviets.

8 Nov   Formation of the Council of Peoples Commissars (Sovnarkom). A decree is passed placing all land at the disposal of the local Land Committees.

9–13 Nov   Defeat of the counterattack by the Cossack Division of the First Army Corps.

15 Nov   Victory of the Red Guard in Moscow.

27 Nov   Initiation of peace talks with the German High Command.

5 Dec   Truce with the Germans signed at Brest-Litovsk.

20 Dec   Establishment of the Cheka.

23 Dec   The French and British sign a secret agreement giving each other zones of influence within Russia.

1918

9 Jan   Peace talks recommence at Brest-Litovsk.

19 Jan   Dissolution by the Bolsheviks of the Constituent Assembly.

10 Feb   The Russian delegation refuses to sign the proposed treaty at Brest-Litovsk.

19 Feb   A further decree on land policy.

2 March   Beginning of a new German offensive.

4–7 March   Both sides agree to renew peace talks.

16 March   Signature of the Treaty of Brest-Litovsk.

20 March   The Soviet Government moves to Moscow.

19 April   The Japanese occupy Vladivostock.

13 May   A decree is enacted ordering the peasants to hand over to the state all grain and seed surplus to their individual requirements.

29 May   Introduction of universal compulsory military service.

7 June   The mutiny of the Czech Legion.

28 June   Over 2,000 large-scale industrial enterprises are nationalised.

14 July   French and British troops land at Murmansk.

11 Aug   The Fatherland is declared in danger.

19 Aug   Red forces retreat from Kazan before the combined advance of the Czechs and the forces of Admiral Kolchak.

20 Aug   Trotsky's armoured train is assembled.

1919

15 March   The Inaugural Conference of the Third International begins in Moscow.

26 March   Kolchak begins a new offensive in the East.

16 May   Finnish troops enter Russia.

18 May   Denikin begins a general offensive across the River Manytch.

27 May   Rodzianko's troops threaten Petrograd.

17 June   Mahkno's revolt begins.

21 Aug   Minsk is occupied by the Poles.

26 Sept   The defeat of Kolchak's Southern Army.

14 Oct   Denikin almost reaches Tula, after capturing Kiev, Kursk and Orel.

24 Oct   Yudenich begins his second offensive against Petrograd.

9 Nov   A Soviet counteroffensive around Petrograd begins, whilst Budenny's cavalry drives Denikin back to the Don.

1920

January   The Allies lift the economic blockade on Russia.

9 Jan   Kolchak is arrested.

16 April   Pilsudski's Polish Army marches into the Ukraine and captures Kiev.

14 Aug   After driving Pilsudski back across the Polish

frontier the Russians reach the outskirts of Warsaw. But they are defeated in the three-day Battle of the Vistula.

Aug–Nov The Red Army repulses Wrangel's attempted offensive in the Crimea and the Caucasus. The Civil War is effectively over.

In the previous chapter the discussion of the military effectiveness of the Commune was limited to the purely internal features, of the Parisian forces themselves. The contradictions and shortcomings that were delineated were in themselves a quite sufficient explanation of the eventual total defeat of the Communards. But had the Parisians actually been able to remain masters within their own walls, they would, sooner or later, have had to face the problem of carrying the revolution beyond Paris into the rest of the country. To do this effectively they would have had to sally forth into the countryside and grapple with the peculiar conservatism of the French peasantry, who at that time still constituted the vast percentage of the population. As it was, the problem was never faced. The Parisians were forced, both by the Prussian and later the Versaillais siege, to conduct their revolution purely within their own walls. Their demands and the few measures they took in pursuance of them were limited to purely parochial concerns. At no stage were the grievances of the peasantry of any importance in the debates of the revolutionaries. Partly through force of circumstance, and partly through a limited geographical and social perspective, the Communards were condemned to wage their revolution in the name of Parisian autonomy rather than of national regeneration. Strategically, this gave them the advantage of interior lines of communication and a strong sense of civic solidarity. Politically, however, it isolated them from the other classes and social groups within the country as a whole on whom they might have counted for support. Neither the proletariat and petit-bourgeoisie of other urban centres nor the peasantry throughout France could be expected to rally with any fervour to a revolution conducted in the name of Parisian autonomy. As Trotsky himself pointed out in a pamphlet written at the height of the Russian Civil War: 'The Commune . . . was the expression of the dictatorship of the revolutionary city over the country.'[1] But, as such, it doomed itself to political isolation from the very beginning.

The Russian Revolution and the Peasantry

Russia too was primarily a peasant country, but here the Bolsheviks, and Lenin in particular, realised that there was no point in seizing power at all if the party programme did not go as far as possible towards guaranteeing the support of the rural masses in the event of counter-revolutionary resistance. Lenin clearly saw that if the Bolsheviks did not fully endorse the aspirations of the broad mass of the Russian peasantry, any *coup d'état* within Saint Petersburg itself would be doomed to eventual failure. Only the most comprehensive espousal of rural demands could guarantee the necessary cannon-fodder in the event of armed reaction. But in April 1917, when Lenin began to realise the full importance of this point, the Bolsheviks did not have any particularly strong support amongst the peasantry. Their chief political spokesmen were the Social Revolutionaries, a party formed at the turn of the century and made up of a broad assortment of radicals, populists and anarchists. But since the February Revolution and the overthrow of the Tsar, it had become plain that rural unrest was probably the most critical feature of the situation in Russia. Throughout the country, fired by the creation of a new, supposedly radical government—in April the Social Revolutionary, Chernov, had been appointed as Minister of Agriculture—the peasants were vociferously putting forward their demands, and insisting upon a far-reaching redistribution of the land. It thus became of prime importance for the Bolsheviks to harness this chronic discontent and replace the SRs as the spokesmen for the peasantry.

Their campaign began in April. At their party conference of that month they passed a resolution inviting the peasants actually to take over the landlords' estates, albeit in an organised and peaceful way. In so doing, 'the Bolsheviks were . . . the only party which gave its blessing to the forcible expropriation of the landlords by a peasant revolution'.[2] In August Lenin's attack on the SRs' base within the peasantry was intensified. He adopted *in toto* their own agrarian programme which advocated the expropriation of all landowners' estates, their nationalisation and the redistribution of land to all the people on a basis of equality. In so doing Lenin was simply following the dictates of tactical expediency. In theory the Bolsheviks were the vanguard of the socialist, proletarian revolution, a vital feature of which was the full socialisation of the land and the abolition of private property. But for the moment, with agrarian unrest mounting from month to month, and all of it directed at the acquisition of a private plot of land for each peasant family, it was clearly in the Bolsheviks' interest to play down this feature of their programme.[3] For the time being it was expedient to echo the demands of the SRs, whilst avoiding their fatal hesitancy over the legality of direct peasant initiative. The latter point was of particular importance after July. For the nature of the rural unrest began to change. Instead of struggling for changes in rent conditions, this movement became merely another way of driving out the landlord:

The veto on buying and selling land and forest gives way to direct seizure. The mass wood-cuttings and mass grazings acquire the character of a deliberate destruction of the landlord's goods . . . Over forty-two per cent of the cases of destruction recorded by the militia between the February and October Revolution occurred in the month of October.[4]

This development was of crucial importance to any party concerned with the tactice of a possible seizure of power. At first:

The tenant was struggling for an alleviation of the conditions of rent . . . [He] started out by recognising the landlord as property-holder and boss. But as soon as the possibility opened of carrying the thing through to the end—that is of taking the land and occupying it themselves—the poor peasants ceased to be interested in questions of rent . . . It was these rural workers and poor tenants who by joining the general movement gave its ultimate determination to the peasant war and made it irrevocable.[5]

It was part of Lenin's tactical genius to recognise the importance of this, and make rural demands a central feature of the Bolshevik programme. As Nevsky said in September, demanding that the Petrograd party committee begin the publication of a newspaper aimed specifically at the peasantry: 'We must fix things so that we shall not have the experience of the French Commune, where the peasantry did not understand Paris and Paris did not understand the peasantry.'[6]

This land policy was finalised on 8 November, in a decree submitted to the Second All-Russian Congress of Soviets. All landlords', state, church and allotment land was placed at the disposal of the Land Committees and Soviets for redistribution to the peasantry. Existing peasant smallholdings were exempt from confiscation. In theory the Bolsheviks were still for the full collectivisation of the land, for both doctrinaire and economic reasons. But for the time being peasant opinion was the key consideration. As Lenin said: 'We, as a democratic government, cannot evade the decision of the rank-and-file of the people, even if we do not agree with it.'[7] On 19 February 1918 a further decree was promulgated which once again, whilst it clearly defined the long-term aim of the agricultural policy to be the full socialisation of the land, for the time being left all the problems of the actual redistribution in the hands of village, district or county soviets.

On the basis of such an approach to agrarian discontent the Bolsheviks were able to take, and cling on to, power. Because of their straightforward advocation of peasant seizures of land they were able to rest their authority upon a vast network of sympathetic local organisations at the most basic level of Russian society—the village. Because of this vital bedrock of support it was almost impossible for anti-Bolshevik elements to mobilise swiftly a force capable of overthrowing the still very flimsy Soviet regime. Whilst many of the peasants could hardly be characterised as being pro-Bolshevik, they could see still less advantage in turning against a regime that had sanctioned their long-sought solution to the land problem. Too many of them would possibly have something to lose if the Bolsheviks were overthrown. It has been estimated that some three million landless peasants received land after the Revolution. Furthermore, whilst the amount added, *per capita*, to the peasant holdings was rather low, there was such an addition and, moreover, a general levelling down of the size of peasant holdings.[8]

In essence then the Russian Revolution was a peasant revolution, and the peasantry formed the rank-and-file of the armies that the Bolsheviks had to create to defend their seizure of power. Without their initial concessions to traditional peasant demands the Bolsheviks would have had no hope at all of enlisting them, whether voluntarily or by compulsion, for the short or the long term, in defence of the Revolution. Even so, as will be seen, their success with the peasantry was at best qualified, but without the original concessions rural apathy would have forced them from power within a matter of weeks. But, even given this basic reliance upon the rural masses, the armed defence of the Russian Revolution was in fact quite different from the other peasant revolution dealt with in this book—the Chinese Civil War. The Chinese Communists moulded their strategy to fit peasant habits and attitudes throughout the years of civil war. They fought a peasant war to make a peasant revolution. The Russians, on the other hand, having ridden to power on the crest of a peasant revolution, found themselves having to resort to a mode of warfare specifically designed to overcome the basic characteristics of the peasantry and undermine their traditional values and preconceptions. This state of affairs had three basic causes.

The first of these was related to the basic contradiction in the Bolshevik policy towards the peasantry, that has already been noted. Whilst they could temporarily, in the interests of first gaining power, avoid the issue of the total abolition of private property and the full transition from private agriculture, the Bolsheviks realised that the longer they kept it in the background the more difficult would it become to effect the transition at all. They simply could not allow the peasants to become too familiar with tending their own plots. For if Russia was to progress economically such a mode of agriculture was simply not adequate. As Lenin pointed out in May 1917:

Dire necessity is knocking at the door of the entire Russian people. This dire necessity consists in the fact that it is impossible to continue farming in the old way. If we continue as of old on our small farms, even as free citizens on free land, we shall still be faced with inevitable ruin . . . Individual husbandry, on individual plots, even though it be 'free labour on free land', offers no way out of the terrible crisis . . . It is essential to go over to joint cultivation on large model farms.[9]

Trotsky too was continually aware that the revolutionary forces that the Bolsheviks had utilised so ably could in the end stand solidly in the way of a full transition to socialism:

Only yesterday the ordinary man was nothing, he was the slave of the Tsar, of the nobility, of the bureaucracy, part of the manufacturer's machine. In the life of the country he was the person who payed the tithe and the taxes. Today, free, he for the first time feels himself to be someone, and he starts to think that he is at the centre of the universe. He tries to get for himself all that he can, he only thinks for himself and would be inclined to forget that he is part of the popular classes.[10]

This was part of a speech made in March 1918. In his *History of the Russian Revolution* he made a strikingly similar point with regard to the army of the *ancien régime* between the two revolutions of 1917:

For millions of soldiers the revolution meant the right to a personal life, and first of all the right to life in general . . . In this sense . . . the fundamental psychological process taking place in the army was the awakening of personality . . . this volcanic eruption of individualism, which often took anarchic forms . . . this flood of mass individualism.[11]

Clearly such attitudes would have to be rigorously contested by any party that saw future development in terms of the sublimation of individuality to the common good. And in so far as those attitudes presented themselves in clearest relief amongst the peasantry, it was against them that the Bolsheviks would have to conduct their campaign of propaganda and coercion.

The second reason for the Bolsheviks' rather ambivalent relationship with the peasants was of a much more mundane nature. As the Civil War progressed, the Bolsheviks and the urban populations as a whole found themselves faced with an acute shortage of grain. After October, the Ukraine, the centre of Russian grain production, had passed out of Soviet control, and it proved increasingly difficult to extract whatever surplus remained from the peasantry. In mid-1918 the People's Commissar for Supply described the situation quite bluntly:

> We encountered the fiercest resistance of the population which was unwilling in any event to give up the grain . . . We came to the conclusion that the measure on which we had staked so many hopes, namely, exchange of goods, was not likely to prove particularly useful. Many cases occurred . . . where the peasants, seeing that we had no goods, declared: 'We will not give grain without goods.' But when we brought the goods, we did not get the grain, and they distributed the goods amongst themselves.[12]

After the failure of the effort to obtain grain through barter, the Bolsheviks adopted two other methods. Between May and December 1918 they attempted to turn the peasantry against itself by making the rural poor, organised into Committees of Poor Peasants, responsible for ensuring that the wealthier tillers within their own areas were not holding back any grain or other surplus produce. The former were to be rewarded for their services by being given allocations of grain from that which had been seized. At first this was to be free and later at a discount on the price fixed by the state. In August 1918 the struggle against hoarding was intensified and began increasingly to take on the character of a war against the peasantry as a whole. Trade unions, factory committees and town soviets were instructed to form their own detachments of workers who were to visit the grain-producing areas and obtain it at fixed prices or requisition it from the *kulaks*. Always the *kulaks*, or rich peasantry, were named as the targets of the requisitioning squads, and the whole operation was described as an essential component of the struggle between the poor and the rich in the countryside, the transition from the rural bourgeois revolution to the rural socialist one. But in essence it was a struggle between town and countryside. In January 1919 the Petrograd and Moscow soviets had some 350 detachments of about 15,000 men touring the villages in their areas. In the last analysis these detachments had neither the time nor the experience to be too selective about what type of peasant they accosted. As Lenin candidly put it: 'We really took from the peasants all their surpluses, and sometimes even what was not surplus, but part of what was necessary to feed the peasant, took it to cover the costs of the army and to maintain the workers.'[13]

A clear indication of the fairly clean division between town and country in this respect has been provided by Tibor Shanin. Speaking of the peasant resistance to the requisitioning squads, and of Bolshevik rhetoric on this subject, he points out that:

> The so-called *kulak* rebellions seem nearly always to have been general peasant uprisings, in which no class-distinctions can be traced . . . In the major peasant rebellions of 1919–21 . . . which were against both the Whites and the Reds, all strata of the peasantry seem to have risen by localities with remarkable unity and with no trace of internal class divisions.[14]

Certainly, from the scanty evidence available, peasant resistance does seem to have been widespread in the years of War Communism. In 1922 Lenin himself, speaking at the Fourth Congress of Comintern, spoke of: 'The peasant uprisings which earlier, before 1921, were, so to speak, a general phenomenon in Russia.'[15] In a table appended to his chapter Meijer has listed just some of the peasant uprisings in the Civil War. They spread over the period June 1918 to March 1921, and occurred in places as far apart as Minsk and Siberia. In the five areas for which numbers of participants are given, something between 115,000 and 150,000 peasants took part.[16] Shanin points out in

a footnote to his chapter on the revolutionary period that
between July and November 1918 alone at least 108 peasant
uprisings were reported.[17] Finally, Meijer again, in his annota-
tions to the Trotsky Papers, mentions ninety-three anti-Soviet
uprisings in the countryside in the single month of April 1919,
thirty-eight of these in the Kiev region.[18]

Scattered references to such uprisings seem squarely to place
the responsibility for them upon those in charge of the actual
administration of War Communism. In December 1918
Lozovskii pointed out:

> If we take what is in the counter-revolutionary risings in the
> villages . . . looking at them as Marxists should, then we
> see that in the village there are only two per cent *kulaks*,
> and that these are risings of toiling peasants, who could
> not but rise out of self-preservation . . . The risings
> occurred because of the absurd idiotic measures of the local
> powers.[19]

Trotsky himself was made fully aware of the excesses of the
requisitioning squads. In a telegram to Lenin of December 1918
he remarked: 'All news from on the spot testifies that the
extraordinary levy [on grain] has extremely upset the local
population . . . This is what the majority of the *gubernijas*
say. In view of the bad position with regard to food it would
appear essential to call a halt to enforcing the extraordinary
levy.'[20] In March of the following year he telegraphed to Stalin:
'I again repeat that an inspection team of the highest authority for work in the rear of the Eastern Front is essential for
calming the peasant elements . . . The movement has acquired
a broad character. The medium peasants are exasperated by the
manifest malpractices of the official institutions.'[21] But if the
leading Bolsheviks understood, and to some extent sympathised
with the reasons for peasant resistance, this in no way implied
that they could afford to take a lenient approach to it. All anti-
Soviet activity was a threat to national unity and the war
effort. It was thus absolutely essential that the rural masses
be kept firmly in check. Soviet power at this time was too brittle
to allow any compromise with peasant parochialism.

This brings us to the third reason for the Bolsheviks' basic hostility towards the peasantry. Whether Imperial or Revolutionary, any Russian army was in the end forced to rely upon the peasantry for the recruitment of its rank-and-file. Certainly the vast percentage of the Imperial Armies of the First World War had been made up of peasants, and as the Civil War progressed this was no less true of the Red Army. In 1920 Trotsky spoke of 'our army, four-fifths of whom are peasants'.[22] In 1921 Tukhachevsky pointed out that: 'Our peasant masses, the majority of them illiterate, are the principle source of recruitment for the Red Army.'[23] The same was true in China during the Civil War, but in this instance Mao Tse-tung and Chu Teh were able slowly and painstakingly to create a peasant army over the course of thirteen years. They were able to train their men as they went along, first giving them experience of small-scale combat, weeding out undesirables, creating veteran, dedicated, elite units, sacrificing quantity to quality and retreating to inaccessible base areas in moments of great peril. The Russians could afford none of these luxuries. In preparing the ground for the October putsch the Russians had assiduously encouraged the disintegration of the old army, coupling their demand for land to the tillers with that for immediate peace. When Civil War broke upon them in 1918 only four regiments remained in battleworthy condition. And because the Bolsheviks had already seized state power and taken over many of the administrative functions of the government, they were unable to retreat to the hinterland before the White offensives without completely destroying their credibility. Having seized power they were forced to try and maintain it. To do this they had to create large armies, in the shortest space of time. Such large armies were of necessity to be composed of peasants. Unfortunately these same peasants were at best war-weary, at worst defeatist, their morale completely undermined by four years of war and by the Bolsheviks' own propaganda and subversion. But the latter had no time for a sustained campaign of revolutionary propaganda, for the long-term creation of a genuine politically motivated armed force. The peasantry simply had to be made to fight, and so for yet one more reason they found themselves the object of the most intensive state pressure to forgo their natural inclinations.

Such was the basic situation in Russia throughout the Civil War. With all this in mind it is possible now to go on to see exactly how the Bolsheviks coped with the military problems inherent in such a state of affairs.

The Idea of a Proletarian Army

As has been seen, many of the Bolsheviks, particularly Trotsky, were aware of the shortcomings of the peasantry in so far as they could be deemed a progressive class within the framework of a socialist revolution. Some outside observers were even more outspoken. In her pamphlet *The Russian Revolution*, written just after the October Revolution, Rosa Luxembourg said: 'The Leninist agrarian reform has created a new and powerful layer of popular enemies of socialism in the countryside, enemies whose resistance will be much more dangerous and stubborn than that of the noble large landowners.' [24] To certain elements within the Bolshevik party the unreliability of the peasantry necessitated that it be vigorously excluded from any participation in the armed defence of the revolution. Even Trotsky, though conscious of the inevitability of having to employ the peasant masses in such a role, was fully aware of its practical dangers.

In the early days of the Revolution, in particular, many hoped to be able to pin their hopes exclusively upon an army made up of authentic proletarians. Indeed, the first genuine revolutionary armed units were the so-called Red Guard detachments of Moscow and Saint Petersburg, formed in the unstable days of February 1917. Each city was able to muster some 10,000 Red Guards. And in the early days of the Revolution, as the Bolsheviks hotly debated what kind of armed forces were suitable for a socialist regime, great stress and reliance was placed upon those Red Guards. In mid-December the General Staff of the Petrograd Red Guard even proposed that their detachments should form the nucleus of a new army, and be expanded to a strength of two corps. At about the same time Kedrov, the Deputy People's Commissar for Military Affairs, put forward a plan for the raising of a Socialist Guard from whose ranks peasants would be rigorously excluded.

It is difficult to ascertain how seriously these plans were taken by the Bolshevik leadership. Certainly Lenin does not seem to have come to power with any clear conception of the components of a revolutionary army. In his *Letters from Afar* he left the problem on a very vague level, stating merely that: 'When the workers and all the people as a real mass, take up this task in a practical way they will work it out and secure it a hundred times better than any theoretician can propose.'[25] Whatever the theory behind the new army, the Bolsheviks in fact found themselves forced to rely, in the early stages upon the urban masses. On 4 January the Military Affairs Commissariat, faced with the imminence of fresh German and Austrian attacks, formulated a defensive plan built exclusively around the population of Moscow and Petrograd. The Red Guard units were to be rushed to the front along with an extra 300,000 men to be raised within the next ten days in these two cities. On 11 January Krylenko issued a manifesto calling for the formation of a Revolutionary National-Socialist Army. He envisioned 'a new army—the people in arms, the rudiments of which are to be found in the Red Guards'.[26] As late as 4 March 1918 Trifonov, a leading member of the Red Guard, was demanding that the Red Army should be raised 'through our proletarian centres of organisation and through the ideological direction for the foundation of the Red Army'.[27]

At this stage the Bolsheviks were still relying on volunteers for the rank-and-file of their army. Naturally enough they expected the bulk of these volunteers to come from among the organised, more class-conscious urban population. But such men simply did not come forward in sufficient numbers. In Petrograd the response had been quite encouraging: 5,500 volunteers by February, and three times that number by early March. But in Moscow no more than 3,000 volunteers came forward. This, and the poor performance at the front of these rather anarchically constituted detachments, led the Central Executive Committee of the Soviets (VTsIK), on 29 May 1918, to introduce compulsory military service. But even so the Bolsheviks were still doubtful as to the efficacy of such a compulsory mobilisation outside of the main urban areas. Thus Trotsky cautiously decided to try an experimental mobilisation in Moscow itself, the seat of the Soviet Government since 7 March, before extending it to the provinces and the unpredictable peasantry. He and his extraordinary Commission decided upon a target figure of 10,000 to 12,000 men from the eighteen to forty age-group. Everything was carefully prepared and the test mobilisation was a thorough success. Some 10,000 recruits were raised without any undue objections.

But when the mobilisation orders were extended to fifty-one districts of the Volga, Urals and West Siberian Military Districts, and made incumbent upon worker and peasant alike, the results were far less gratifying. The final total of recruits fell far short of the fairly modest 275,000 that had been looked for. The Bolsheviks found themselves compelled to look once more to the cities for their troops. A new mobilisation plan was drawn up by the Supreme Military Soviet, under the leadership of Trotsky, and adopted on 23 July. First of all 25,000 workers, aged between twenty-five and thirty-five, were to be raised in Moscow and Petrograd. Once this figure had been reached mobilisation in these cities would cease, and would be transferred to the urban centres of the Moscow, Petrograd, Vladimir and Nizhni Novgorod provinces. Thus, of the fifteen mobilisations carried out between 12 June and 29 August 1918, no less than eleven of them were confined solely to the workers. On 2 August there was also a special mobilisation of workers who had been non-commissioned officers in the Imperial Army. All in all the Red Army acquired a little over 540,000 men and 17,000 NCOs. A report from the Urals Military District Commissariat of June 1918 emphasises the effect of this reliance upon urban recruits: 'Of the more or less regular Red Army units at the front there were the 2nd . . . and the 7th Ural Regiment . . . The remainder of the troops consisted of separate . . . detachments containing from twenty to a hundred men, for the major part workers from this or that individual factory or plant.'[28]

For the first months after the Revolution, then, the Bolsheviks relied upon the urban working-class for their revolutionary recruits. But notwithstanding purists such as Kedrov and Trifonov, or Smilga who even in 1920 was opposed to the creation of a militia army based upon local recruitment because the urban workers would be submerged in a sea of peasants, this class character of the early Red Army should not be seen as a

doctrinal or theoretical decision. From at least mid-1918 onwards the Bolshevik leaders and their military advisers were
committed to mobilising all strata of Russian society, simply
because only in this way could they mobilise sufficient forces to
repulse the counter-revolutionary offensives. In June 1918 the
Fifth All-Russian Congress of Soviets even abolished the previous distinction between workers and peasants and the bourgeoisie, by which the latter, although liable to call-up, were to
be made to serve in labour battalions. The compulsory principle
was now to apply equally to 'every honest and healthy citizen'.
But for the first year or so of the Revolution Bolshevik power
was relatively weak, particularly outside the key urban areas.
They simply did not have the personnel or the authority to
compel the peasantry to come forward. These latter were too
much involved in the redistribution of the land and the protection of their gains to look outside the confines of their own
villages. Moreover, in so far as they had ever been attuned to
Bolshevik propaganda, one of the slogans they remembered with
the most affection was that calling for an end to the war and
the demobilisation of the Imperial Armies. Thus the Bolsheviks
were forced to fall back on the urban working class simply
because the peasantry was unwilling to fight and the government was unable to force them. In the great military crisis of
1917 the peasant soldiers had voted with their feet. Throughout
much of 1918, having regained their villages, they simply
abstained.

There was, however, one aspect of the Bolshevik mobilisation that did retain a deliberate class character. This was the
formation of armed detachments of workers, acting under the
authority of the People's Commissariat of Supply, who were
to go into the countryside to collect, by force if necessary, the
grain surplus. Their class character was heavily underscored
by Lenin: 'The outstanding worker, as the mentor of the poor
peasant . . . should go to the "people" . . . We need a mass
"crusade" of outstanding workers to every corner of this vast
country. We need ten times more iron detachments of the conscious proletariat unreservedly devoted to communism.'[29] In
July 1918 Tsyurupa, the People's Commissar for Agriculture,
described them in this way: 'We do not regard these detach-

ments merely as a military force; we see in these detachments people who go into the country armed, it is true, but at the same time as agitators who will conduct propaganda in the country, who will bring our ideas into the country.'[30]

Nevertheless, the significance of this class basis should not be taken at too theoretical a level. Whilst it suited a revolutionary Marxist party to stress the vanguard nature of these proletarian formations, one should never forget that their prime purpose was to collect food. In the last analysis the significance of their social composition was not that they were from the working class *qua* class, but that they were from the towns. And the towns depended upon the countryside for their food. Thus, whilst the Bolsheviks could regale these detachments with the most high-sounding rhetoric about their missionary role, at the end of the day it was simply a question of pure survival. In its most basic form it was a confrontation between town and countryside in which questions of progaganda and proselytisation were subordinated to the problem of moving, by whatever means necessary, the bulk of the peasants' crop to the urban centres.

The Role of Partisan Warfare

The peasantry are central in any assessment of the nature of the Russian Revolution, and it has been shown how, from almost the very beginning, the Bolsheviks wished to incorporate the peasants into the armed forces of the Soviet state. But it has also been seen to what extent the central authorities were at odds with the rural population, and how they felt threatened by their individualism, possessiveness and war-weariness. Thus, whilst the Bolsheviks were eager to mobilise the peasantry in defence of the Revolution, they were extremely anxious that this mobilisation should proceed according to suitable organisational precepts.

When the Civil War began to be fought in earnest and the White counter-revolutionary forces began to press in upon the peasantry and threaten their revolutionary gains, the masses in the countryside showed a spontaneous willingness to defend themselves. But their mode of resistance matched their conception of social reality. To the peasant the world outside his own village and plot of land meant little. So, though he was willing to defend tenaciously that plot of land, he saw little point in remaining under arms once the immediate danger had passed. He thus inclined to a mode of warfare that did not demand that he serve except for very short periods of time and which did not take him far from his home. Even when his horizons were not limited by an intense parochialism, he had too many seasonal tasks to perform to wish to be kept away from his village for long. Thus, when left to his own devices the peasant always opted for some mode of partisan or guerrilla warfare, by which he only mobilised when immediate danger threatened, never went far beyond his own small area and could demobilise almost at will.

But for the Bolsheviks such a mode of warfare, precisely because it so suited the peasant temperament, was inimical to their own conception of the revolutionary process. Guerrilla warfare was based around small bands of peasants who were loyal to their own leaders and only interested in the preservation of their own plots of land. They operated according to their own tactical judgements and paid little attention to the strategic directives of the central authorities. But such an attitude was quite unacceptable. Because the Bolsheviks had come to power through a *coup d'état*, their hold on the country as a whole was at best rather tenuous. They could have no hope at all of consolidating that hold if they allowed the peasantry to indulge in totally decentralised guerrilla operations. The problem was stated graphically by Trotsky in a report to the Central Committee of the Bolshevik Party in March 1919, when he defined the revolution as: 'The fearful difficulties of the dictatorship of a hungry, internally-rent working class alongside an ill-informed, discontented and mutinous peasantry. We see these difficulties on all sides. In the military sphere they assume their most concentrated form.'[31] He summed the problem up, years later, in his autobiography:

We had continuously to fight the methods of the irregulars—a fight that demanded the utmost persistence and unwillingness to compromise, sometimes even the sternest measures. The chaos of irregular warfare expressed the peasant element that lay beneath the revolution, whereas the struggle against it was also a struggle in favour of the proletarian state organisation as opposed to the elemental petty-bourgeois anarchy that was undermining it.[32]

In a speech to the All-Russian Congress of Military Commissars in June 1918, he emphasised the link between the unleashing of peasant individualism and the erosion of central authority:

> The question of the organisation [of the army] is hampered by a purely psychological question: all the previous period of the war has considerably unsettled the discipline of work; in the lower strata of the people there has been formed an undesirable element of *déclassé* peasants and workers . . . We must not conceal the fact that in many cases the revolutionary movement has weakened temporarily the capacity for systematic and methodical labour. Elemental anarchism, idleness, depravity, these are the features which must be fought with all our strength.[33]

Trotsky also vehemently attacked all those who advocated guerrilla warfare as a genuinely revolutionary method of fighting. In his thesis presented to the Eighth Congress of the Communist Party in March 1919 one finds once again Trotsky's single-minded concern with the problem of maintaining a strong central authority:

> The ideological opposition of partisan detachments to a methodically organised, centralised army (preached by the Left SRs and their ilk) represents a caricature of the political thought or lack of reflection of the petty-bourgeois intelligentsia . . . The conquest of political power has given the proletariat the chance to use the state apparatus to build methodically a centralised army whose unity of organisation and command can alone guarantee that we obtain the best results . . . To put forward the guerrilla spirit as a military programme is to recommend a return from heavy industry to the artisan's workshop.[34]

His whole introduction to his collected military writings, published in Russia in 1922, can be seen as a retrospective attack on the so-called Left Opposition within the party, who stressed the importance of a decentralised army based on volunteers and elective principles. For Trotsky: 'The tendencies of the Left Opposition [were] in fact those of the peasant intelligentsia.'[35]

The very vehemence and consistency of Trotsky's attack on the guerrilla mode gives a clear idea of the extent to which it formed a part of the military reality of the revolution. This was particularly true at the beginning of the war when partisan-type detachments, of workers as much as of peasants, were the only type of unit the Soviets were able to muster. The small number of recruits, the lack of trained officer-cadres and the weakness of the central organisation all militated against the possibility of being able to put any organised, large-scale units into the field. For the first few months the Red Army was necessarily based around the *otriad*, or small detachment. As a report from the Urals Commissariat pointed out: 'The first period of the struggle with the Czeckoslovaks might be called the *otriad* period, then we conducted the war in primitive style, without any kind of previously worked-out plan, with detachments of twenty to a hundred men.'[36] But such units were not only politically dangerous; against the disciplined and well-trained Czech troops they also proved to be militarily incompetent. A report from Vatsesis in this sector pointed out that: 'The fighting in Kazan demonstrated the complete incapacity of the workers' detachments . . . The soldiers proved utterly lacking in discipline . . . They proved incapable of fighting in a mass because of lack of preparation and discipline.'[37] In June the two regular regiments on the Eastern Front met and adopted five unanimous resolutions demanding that rank-and-file committees be abolished, field courts be set up to punish deserters severely and commanders down to platoon level be men of previous military experience. On 2 June the Revolutionary Military Soviet of the Eastern Front was set up, and all available forces were organised into four armies. All volunteer and partisan units were ordered to amalgamate into regular formations, and to take their proper place in an orthodox chain of command rather than try and deal directly with Moscow as had hitherto been the case.

The early history of the fighting in the Ukraine against Krasnov, Denikin and Alekseev showed a similar reliance upon the guerrilla mode. Bolshevik reports are full of complaints about it. In April 1919, in a report to Lenin, Vatsesis described the overall situation on this front: 'The Ukrainian Front is made up of units from the numerous Ukrainian formations. Many of these units are headed by *atamans* [Cossack chiefs] and reactionary peasant leaders, both overt and covert. On paper the Ukrainian army is a fairly large one, but it is without any organisation and formed on irregular lines.'[38] In his pamphlet *All Out for the Fight against Denikin*, written in 1919, Lenin remarked that: 'Partisanism, its vestiges, remnants and survivals, have been the cause of immeasurably greater misfortune, disintegration, defeats, disasters, and losses in men and military equipment in our army and the Ukraine army than all the betrayals of the military experts.'[39] Once again Trotsky was quite adamant about the implications of such a mode of warfare in the Ukraine. In a report to the Central Committee of May 1919 he wrote:

> The moment has now arrived where it is necessary to state, firmly and clearly, that the Revolution has derived all that can be derived from the improvised insurgent detachments, and that henceforth these detachments become not only dangerous but positively disastrous to the cause of the Revolution . . . There must be no stopping short at the most savage measures—shooting, drafting to the units of rear levies, imprisonment in concentration camps.[40]

On the 17th of the same month he demanded that the partisans 'be liquidated and their theorists got out of the way by conducting a thorough campaign of agitation in favour of discipline and order'.[41] In September he gave a broad clue as to his reasons for his intense distrust of the bands of peasant guerrillas not tied to any central command and gave a rather uncharitable interpretation of their ability to form and disperse at will:

> It must be said that everyone in the Ukraine except the soldiers possesses rifles and ammunition. The state of the

soldier is the state in which the Ukrainian peasant finds himself until such time as he receives a rifle with which to return back to his own village, where the rifles find their way into the hands of the *kulaks* and the so-called middle peasants, i.e. potential *kulaks*.[42]

These were the main areas of partisan activity, but it did also occur in other parts of Russia. Writing of the Caucasus, Trotsky said, after the Civil War: 'Never perhaps has *partisan-schchina* cost the workers and peasants so dearly as in the North Caucasus. Thus the main cause of our failures in the South was not so much the organisational defects of the Army of the Southern Front as the treacherous—in every sense of the word—role of *partisanschchina*.'[43] Writing to Lashevich and Jurenev on the Eastern Front in July 1919, Lenin said: 'Special measures should be taken: firstly, to ensure against pilfering of arms by the Urals workers so as to prevent the growth among them of a disastrous partisan mentality; secondly, to see that the Siberian partisan movement does not demoralise our troops.'[44] To this end, on 19 July, the Central Committee issued a decree putting all the Siberian irregular and partisan detachments under centralised command.

Much stress is placed in the various remarks cited above on the military ineffectiveness of the partisan forces. Certainly there was some truth in this. But it is more profitable to look for an explanation of the Bolshevik attitude in the other feature of these bands that is so often remarked upon—that is their essentially peasant composition. It was this, coupled with the naturally anarchic organisation of the bands, that worried the Bolsheviks. This point is perhaps best evidenced by the history of Makhno's guerrilla bands in the Ukraine from 1918 to 1921.

Makhno's guerrillas represented the very worst features of peasant anarchism and anti-centralisation (in Bolshevik eyes), but they were in fact militarily effective. In 1917 Makhno founded the Gulyai-Polye Association of Peasants and established a militia to aid the Bolshevik forces fighting the Germans. When the Germans actually invaded the Ukraine Makhno and his friends held a conference at Tagenrog at which they resolved

to initiate a guerrilla campaign against the invaders. Aided by
the fact that the Ukrainian landlords were returning in the
wake of the advancing Germans, Makhno soon had some 1,500
peasants behind him, organised in village fighting squads. But
the political tenor of these bands became increasingly anti-
Bolshevik. At their Congress in January 1919 the following
resolution was passed:

> With deep regret the Congress must . . . declare that
> apart from external enemies a perhaps even greater danger
> threatens the revolution of the Ukrainan peasants and
> workers. The Soviet Governments of Russia and of the
> Ukraine, by their orders and decrees, are making efforts
> to deprive local soviets of peasants' and workers' deputies
> of their freedom and autonomy . . . The Bolshevik Party
> . . . [is] demanding a monopoly of the revolution.[45]

Despite the frequent mention of 'workers' in this and other
resolutions, the bulk of Makhno's support came from the peasantry. Almost all the delegates at this Congress and the four
others in February, April, May and October were peasants.
At the peak of his military success in winter 1919-20, fourteen
of Makhno's twenty principle subordinate commanders were
themselves peasants. The main demands of the guerrillas were
concerned with exclusively peasant questions. They approved
the re-establishment of the former agricultural communes,
were opposed to the Bolshevik nationalisation of the vineyards,
sugar-beet plantations and livestock and were particularly
hostile to the enforced requisitioning of grain. In Order Number
One of August 1919, not only did their enemies include the rich
bourgeoisie but also all those who were thought to uphold an
unjust social order, such as Bolshevik commissars, members
of the Cheka or the punitive detachments.

But they were militarily successful. They had support from
the local peasantry and utilised this support. The same Order
Number One stipulated that no insurgent must act for personal
profit, there must be no arbitrary or independent requisitioning
and behaviour at all times must be orderly and disciplined. In
late September and early October Makhno was able to effect

a massive drive through the opposing White forces, and for the next four months his bands reached a peak of effectiveness. His strength varied between 20,000 and 50,000 men, formed into triangular brigades of three three-battalion regiments. His tactics were of the classic guerrilla type, and are well described by Footman:

> Infantry were carried in carts and both infantry and cavalry could travel at twice the speed of regular army troops ... If attacked ... [they] would retreat, leave a small unit in front of the enemy to act as a decoy, pass the main body round the flanks, and counterattack from the rear ... If surrounded with no chance of a breakout a unit would bury its arms and stores and disappear, as peasants, into the surrounding villages, waiting to reform as soon as the enemy had passed on. At the peak of Makhno's hold on peasant loyalties it was almost impossible for the enemy to locate insurgent formations: the peasants would not talk.[46]

But all this time the Red Army was slowly consolidating its control over the rest of the country, and the peasants were becoming increasingly weary of the incessant fighting, be it against Germans, Whites or Bolsheviks. In March and April 1919 the Red Army began to blockade the partisans, and in September they attempted to disembarrass themselves by ordering Makhno's army to join the offensive on Poland. Makhno refused and in mid-January 1920 was outlawed by the Central Committee of the Ukrainian Communist Party. But it was not until the Bolsheviks began to distribute more land to the poor peasants, cutting the state-farms by half in number and two-thirds in acreage, that Makhno's support began to fall away decisively. The Bolsheviks slowly increased their stranglehold, and in August 1921 Makhno passed over into Romania.

In the end Makhno was defeated by the regular army. But one must be wary of being persuaded to take Bolshevik strictures about partisan ineptitude at their face value. He had managed to keep his forces intact for some three years, and in the process had afforded invaluable assistance to the Red

Army. What terrified the Bolsheviks was the spontaneous anti-*étatisme* that Makhno's guerrillas represented, and the inherent threat to their own frantic efforts to consolidate their newly won power, feed the cities and begin the long march towards a truly socialist economy.

The Drive for a Regular Army

Bolshevik concern over decentralising tendencies did not limit them to combating the worst excesses of peasant individualism and fighting against uncontrolled guerrilla warfare. It also prompted them to make a positive effort to regularise the Red Army formations as much as possible. As the Civil War progressed all the supposedly socialist innovations in the organisation of the Army were rejected by the Central Committee and the Supreme Military Soviet. Successively, on the question of volunteers, the election of officers and the employment of the officers of the *ancien régime*, the Bolshevik leadership opted for the solution most commensurate with the creation of an orthodox, disciplined regular army, with an emphasis upon military expertise rather than socialist principles.

There were those who tried to put the Civil War forward as a unique military experience that taught its own lessons about the nature of revolutionary war. But both Lenin and Trotsky were adamant that war was war no matter what its socio-political milieu, and that certain principles held good for all types of military confrontation. Chief among these was the notion that the *sine qua non* of military effectiveness was the ability to pass orders down a fixed chain of command and expect that these orders would be instantly obeyed at all levels.

The question of volunteers has already been touched upon in the previous section, where attention was drawn to the effect of a total reliance on voluntary enlistment upon the organisation of the various units. Referring to troops of this kind in the Kazan sector, in early 1918, Vatsesis noticed:

The complete incapacity of the workers' detachments. Local party comrades in high posts displayed the greatest energy, but their efforts were wasted in the chaos of unpreparedness. The soldiers proved utterly lacking in discipline

... The whole burden of defence fell upon the [regular] Latvian Rifles ... As regards Russian units they proved utterly incapable of fighting in mass because of lack of preparation and discipline.[47]

The history of the First Corps in Petrograd during the same period gives a further idea of the chaos that stemmed from the use of volunteers, and a reliance upon the primacy of local initiative. As Erickson says: 'Partisan units, special guard units, Red Army units and militias were all in the market for men and poached ceaselessly from each other. Government and party agencies, wholly unclear about organisational procedures and objectives, meddled and overlapped with each other.'[48] On 29 May VTsIK introduced a decree declaring universal military conscription, and in the next weeks almost all important organisations and Bolshevik leaders came out vehemently against the idea of a volunteer army.[49]

The second target of the Bolshevik drive for a regularised military structure was the principle of the election of officers. In the early stages of the Revolution the election of superior military personnel had generally been considered as an indispensable concomitant of a democratic revolution. In early May 1918 the First Red Army, for example, was made up of detachments of between 700 and 1,000 men, each with a commander and two assistants nearly all of whom had been elected by their men. In the previous December the Military Affairs Commissariat had issued a draft decree in which they envisioned the creation of 'a free army of armed citizens, an army of workers and peasants with broad self-government and elected soldiers' organisations'.[50] Their concept of a full democratisation of the Army included the abolition of formal officer-ranks, the annulment of decorations, the transfer of power to soldiers' committees and the election of all 'officers'. On 4 January 1918 the Petrograd Soviet came down in favour of a new socialist army which would be built on 'elective principles, on the principles of mutual comradely respect'.

But in the stormy days of open civil war the Bolsheviks were not confident that either the workers or, in particular, the peasants could be relied upon to choose officers who were either militarily capable or politically reliable. As Trotsky pointed out: 'The election of leaders by units with little political education and made up of young peasants that had just been called up, would inevitably have become a chancy affair and would certainly have created a situation favourable to the intrigues of isolated adventurers.'[51] In the *ABC of Communism*, written in 1920, Bukharin and Preobrazhensky made a very similar point. After having agreed that: 'In the struggle against militarism, in the campaign against the privileges of the officers' caste, our demand for the election of officers proved of enormous importance . . . [and] contributed to the general disintegration of the Imperialist armies', they went on to point out that:

> The matter of real importance is that we should know what will make the army, in its present condition, the most efficient fighting force. From this point of view, will it be best to elect the officers, or to appoint them from above? When we take into consideration that our Red Army is mainly recruited from amongst the peasantry . . . and the low level of class consciousness among the peasants who have joined the army—it will become obvious to us that the practice of electing officers cannot fail to exercise a disintegrating influence on our forces.[52]

As early as December 1917 the Bolsheviks were making some preliminary efforts to erode the absolute right of the soldiers to elect their own officers. Two decrees were issued on the general problems of 'elective command' and the 'equalisation of rights'. It was laid down that henceforth regimental, battalion and squadron commanders were to be elected by the existing unit committees, thus placing the actual election at one remove from the rank-and-file. Commanders of units larger than a regiment were only to be elected by the members of the nearest higher committee. Even more significantly, it was decreed that non-specialist personnel should have nothing to do with the nomination or election of specialist staff or of chiefs of staff. On 29 April 1918 the Bolsheviks took the final step and completely abolished the elective principle.

Yet another way in which the Army was moulded into something remarkably similar to the Imperial Army that it had replaced was the tendency of the Bolsheviks to have recourse, to a greater and greater extent, to the officer personnel of the Imperial forces. Once again they had found themselves caught out by the very precipitateness of their coming to power. Almost up to the coup itself they had thought exclusively in terms of terrorism and urban insurrection, and had not seen the point of devoting any attention to military affairs. To the Bolsheviks, between February and October, the only significance of the army was as a bastion of the old regime. As such the essence of their task was to destroy the army rather than ponder on the problems of revolutionary warfare. They were only concerned with the problems of the creation of the political apparatus that could take over in the event of the complete collapse of Tsarism or bourgeois constitutionalism. The army was only of importance in so far as its collapse would contribute towards the creation of a power vacuum. Of course all revolutions contain their purely destructive element. But there is a basic distinction between those revolutions that aim at the destruction of the incumbent government's will to resist through the creation, over a period of time, of their own military forces and those that simply hope to profit from the chaos caused by the spontaneous disintegration of the existing repressive *apparat*. The Russian Revolution was clearly of this second type.

Because of this the Bolsheviks had to plunge into their civil war, in defence of the Revolution, without being able to produce sufficient officer-cadres of their own, men who had been hardened and tested in the actual experience of a slowly expanding civil war. They had to wage war on many fronts from the very beginning, and never had the opportunity to retire completely to lick their wounds. Having taken power in the first place, such a retirement would have been an admission of complete defeat. Thus capable officers had to come from somewhere. The only source was the old army.

From the very beginning, from purely patriotic motives, many Imperial officers sided with the Bolsheviks in the struggle against the Germans. Quite a few stayed on even after the sig-

nature of the Treaty of Brest-Litovsk, partly because of the
Allied intervention and partly because many felt that their
loyalty was to the government in power, no matter what its
political complexion. Some Bolsheviks were opposed to this
utilisation of 'counter-revolutionaries' in the army of a socialist
state. As late as 1919, when it had become an established fact,
Tukhachevsky reported to the Revolutionary Military Council
that:

> Such an expedient might have been useful if the old officer
> corps had really been up to the task and had really known
> its job. But in fact it possessed none of the requisite qualities.
> It was composed, in the majority, of elements with the most
> limited military education; moreover they were un-
> imaginative and without initiative. [53]

Throughout the Civil War the Military Opposition, primarily
Stalin and Voroshilov, violently lashed out against the preponderance of ex-Imperial officers, the so-called 'military
specialists', within the Red Army.

But Lenin and Trotsky were adamant. The Revolution could
not survive without the co-operation, albeit somewhat un-
committed, of such men. On 29 July 1918 an order was issued
by Trotsky setting on foot the general mobilisation of all ex-
officers, and shortly afterwards all Imperial NCOs were also
called up. By the end of November 22,315 officers and 128,168
NCOs were serving with the Red Army. Between June 1918
and August 1920, 48,809 ex-officers were taken into service
along with 214,717 ex-NCOs.[54] Both Lenin and Trotsky stuck
by this policy to the end. The former declared himself completely opposed to the 'ignorant . . . belief that the working
people are capable of overcoming . . . the bourgeois order . . .
without learning from bourgeois experts . . . without going
through a long schooling side by side with them'.[55] Trotsky
too emphasised the purely technical aspects of the problem,
underplaying ideological implications as much as possible. In
March 1918 he said: 'As industry needs engineers, as farming
needs qualified agronomists, so military specialists are indispensable to defence.'[56] In a telegram to Lenin, of August of
that year, he was even more blunt:

Many of them commit acts of treachery. But on the railways, too, instances of sabotage are in evidence in the routing of troop trains. Yet nobody suggests replacing railway engineers by Communists . . . It is essential to make the entire military hierarchy more compact and get rid of the ballast by extracting those general staff officers that are efficient and loyal to us and not on any account by replacing them by Party ignoramuses.[57]

Basically he was for keeping ideological problems out of the councils of the military as completely as was possible. On the question of the complaints of the Military Opposition he wrote to the Central Committee in December 1918: 'The issue has to be settled either on an individual basis or by Party action and not by means of wholesale accusations which poison the atmosphere in the military establishments concerned and have the most harmful effect on the conduct of the work.'[58]

Gradually the employment of the military specialists and the whole regularisation of the military structure, came to be accepted at almost all levels. Gradually more and more Imperial officers made their way up in the Soviet command structure and began to reinforce Trotsky's doctrine by their own emphasis upon the command techniques and traditions learnt under the *ancien régime*.[59] One of the most forthright statements of such attitudes came from Bonch-Bruevich, himself a former Imperial officer, in June 1919:

The army cannot by virtue of its structure be 'socialist', even were it to consist of the foremost socialists; the structure (organisation) of each combat-fit army must satisfy solely the requirements of present-day warfare and active combat, which are factors which have nothing in common with socialism—and, indeed, whether the army does or does not consist of socialists is of no consequence as regards classifying its combat-fitness. The name must classify the nature of the object to which it relates—in the given instance, that of the army.[60]

Discipline and the Role of the Party

There was, then, a constant tendency within the Soviet High Command to play down the connection between political and military affairs. At bottom, military affairs were regarded as a matter best left to the experts, and to a large extent governed by their own specific laws. On the question of 'military doctrine' Trotsky constantly emphasised the importance of the mundane realities of supply and logistics. At the height of the Civil War he wrote:

> We must now devote our whole attention to improving our material and to making it more efficient rather than to fantastic schemes of reorganisation. Every army must receive its rations regularly . . . We must teach our soldiers personal cleanliness . . . They must learn their drill properly . . . They must be taught to make their political speeches short and sensible, to clean their rifles and to grease their boots . . . They must learn to wind their puttees properly . . . and once again they must learn to grease their boots . . . If anyone wishes to . . . describe this practical programme as 'military doctrine' he is welcome to do so.[61]

In a telegram to Lenin, Ptjaev, a member of the Military Revolutionary Council of the Western Front, suggested that: 'In the interests of increasing the might and combat-fitness of the Red Army it is a thousand times more expedient to have no more than one million Red Army men in all, but well-fed, clothed and shod ones.'[62]

But no matter how much Trotsky might have dreamt of an apolitical army, concerned only with the problems of purely military efficiency, he was actually very aware of the extent to which politics must in fact inevitably intrude into military life. For no army can effectively exist in a total political vacuum, but must have some sort of external authority to which to give its allegiance; if not, its rationale will become totally introverted and the Army will assume a Praetorian role, making and unmaking rulers according to the sole criterion of the troops' personal well-being. Clearly such a development was anathema to the Bolsheviks. Authority had to reside in the civil organs of Soviet power, the political expression of the dictatorship of the proletariat. What was more, because the Bolsheviks had come so recently to power, because they lacked a deep-rooted legitimacy and the authoritativeness that goes with it, it was necessary for them to make very sure that the Bolshevik Party and the Soviet regime in general was seen to act decisively and to wield effective power. For, in the last analysis, deference to power had to precede respect for authority, fear had to precede legitimacy. The record of the military specialists during the Civil War was a proud one, but it was not inevitable that this would be so. It was really only made possible by the most rigid surveillance and political control. The Bolsheviks also managed, by and large, to keep peasant discontent at a relatively low level, but once again only by the most repressive terror against them. They managed to create effective fighting armies made up almost entirely of peasants, but only by enforcing the strictest discipline in the ranks.

To accomplish all these tasks the leadership had recourse to three principle organisations—the Cheka, the Commissars and the Bolshevik Party itself. The Cheka, or All-Russian Extraordinary Commission, was established on 20 December 1917 by a decree of the Soviet of People's Commissars for the purpose of combating counterrevolution and sabotage. Under the leadership of Dzerzhinsky this organisation waged an unceasing war against all anti-Bolshevik elements, most of their efforts being devoted to the sending of punitive detachments into the villages to ensure the prompt delivery of grain. Dzerzhinsky himself admirably summed up the role of the Cheka in the Civil War:

The Cheka is not a court. The Cheka is the defence of the Revolution as the Red Army is; as in the Civil War the Red Army cannot stop to ask whether it may harm particular individuals, but must take into account only one thing, the victory of the Revolution over the bourgeoisie, so the Cheka must defend the Revolution and conquer the enemy even if its sword falls occasionally on the heads of the innocent.[63]

Whilst the Cheka dealt with the peasantry outside the Army, that section of it actually at the front was kept up to the mark by a combination of strict disciplinarianism and the personal example of dedicated Party zealots. Trotsky himself was a sincere advocate of both methods. With regard to discipline, his whole philosophy of life seems to have been predicated upon the necessity for an unceasing control over the bulk of the population. In *Terrorism and Communism* he wrote:

> As a general rule man strives to avoid labour . . . One may even say that man is a fairly lazy animal . . . Antonio Labriola, the Italian Marxist, used to picture the man of the future as a 'happy and lazy genius'. We must not, however, draw the conclusion from this that the Party . . . must propagate this quality in their agitation as a moral duty. No! no! We have sufficient of it as it is. The problem before the social organisation is just to bring 'laziness' within a definite framework, to discipline it.[64]

Certainly this notion of human capabilities extended to the Army. In his autobiography he wrote: 'An army cannot be built without reprisals. Masses of men cannot be led to death unless the army command has the death penalty in its arsenal . . . The command will always be obliged to place the soldiers between the possible death in the front and the inevitable one in the rear.'[65] In a telegram from the front in August 1918 he wrote: 'The lack of revolvers creates an impossible state of affairs at the front. There is no hope of maintaining discipline without having revolvers.'[66] He was equally emphatic about the undesirability of any debate or dissent amongst the rank-and-file. Orders had to be obeyed instantly and unquestioningly. In a message to one front in 1919 he noted: 'According to reports, the Army newspaper was an organ of discussion and criticism. I recommend that the critics be immediately removed from the newspaper and it be transformed into a militant organ for the inculcation of firm discipline.'[67] In a speech to the Fifth Congress of Soviets in July 1918 he gave a clear definition of the selflessness and obedience he expected from the troops. Refuting leftist assertions about the healthy nature of guerrilla tendencies he said: 'What does true healthiness consist of? In the fact that the revolutionary can say: "I am dissatisfied and indignant, but I will submit today to the general situation and to the orders of the power that I created. And I will so submit as a disciplined soldier." ' [68]

But nevertheless Trotsky realised that naked force was not enough, and there were efforts to persuade the rank-and-file that the Party was right. The main method of doing this was to send Party members up to the actual front and place a few of them with each unit, there to inspire the troops with their personal example. Trotsky was a fervent proponent of the salutary effect of personal example:

> Just as it was not in our power, especially in the first period, to supply this army with all its needs from a single centre . . . just so were we unable to inspire this army, got together under fire, with revolutionary enthusiasm. It was necessary to win authority in the eyes of the soldiers . . . Where tradition is lacking, a striking example is essential. [69]

In the very early days Party men were comparatively rare at the front and Trotsky had to rely upon small groups brought from the capital, and thrown into the battle at the most critical points, where, 'they simply outdid themselves, stepping into the breach and fairly melting away before my eyes through the recklessness of their heroism'. [70] But gradually small groups, known as 'red cells', were formed in many of the regiments and moved around to others where necessary. Their task was simply to inspire their comrades by personal example, and to stress the ultimate social and political aims of the Revolution continually. As an order of December 1918 put it: 'A soldier who is a Party member has just the same rights as any other soldier—but not a hairsbreadth more. He has only incomparably more duties.' [71] In the winter of 1918–19 the Bolsheviks intensified their efforts to send Party men to the fronts. In three months Petrograd alone sent some 3,000 men. In June 1917 there had been about 26,000 Party members in the Army, whilst at the end of the following year there were at least 50,000, organised into about 1,500 'red cells'. By the end of the Civil War this latter figure had reached 7,000.

To some extent their efforts were counterproductive, particularly as the Soviet conduct of military operations became more regularised and self-confident. For many of the cell members felt that their privileged political position entitled them to interfere in purely military operational questions. The problem grew serious enough to compel the political leadership, in January 1919, to issue a decree explicitly ordering cell members not to interfere in questions of organisation and tactics. They were to restrict their activities to raising the political consciousness of their units. There seems little doubt that they did make a substantial contribution to Bolshevik military successes, though one must none the less be cautious about accepting at face value the preponderant place given to the role of ideological enthusiasm in many Soviet accounts.

The role of the Party in the Army was not limited to the formation of the 'red cells'. It also provided the vast percentage of the famous political commissars. Between the time of the Eighth Congress and July 1919, for example, about 1,800 Party members were sent to the front as commissars. Of 500 commissars sent out between 1 July and 10 October 1918, 300 were Bolsheviks, ninety-three sympathisers, thirty-five Left SRs, five various and sixty-eight belonged to no formal political organisation at all.[72] On 8 April 1918 the All-Russian Bureau of Military Commissars was set up, and in mid-January 1919 Political Sections were established within each division, although it was several months before they became effective.

To some extent the commissars performed the same role as the cadres of the 'red cells'. Trotsky reported enthusiastically in September 1918:

Wherever there is a good or tolerably good commander and good commissars, the soldiers fight. The presence of workers who are Communists is most beneficial. There are many supremely devoted and courageous men among them. When a commander wants to say that such and such a post is occupied by a reliable person, he says: 'I have got a Communist there.'[73]

But their prime purpose was to exercise Party authority over the specialists, and to ensure that none of them attempted to betray the Revolution. For, in the last resort, only sheer terror could be absolutely relied upon to impress the ex-officers. Trotsky made it a point to remind them that any disloyalty would invoke reprisals against their families, whilst Lenin asked, in a telegram to Trotsky: 'Should you not announce to them that from now on we shall adopt the example of the French Revolution and commit for trial and even sentence to be shot . . . the Army Command at Kazan and the senior commanders in the event of the operations meeting with delay or failure?'[74] On the establishment of the All-Russian Bureau, the functions of the commissar were quite clearly laid down:

> The military commissar is the direct political organ of the Soviet authorities attached to the army . . . The military commissar sees that the army does not isolate itself from the entire Soviet system and that individual military establishments do not become conspiratorial centres . . . The commissar takes part in all the activities of the military directors.[75]

If the Civil War is examined in the light of the most basic theme of this book—the relationship between war and politics in a time of revolutionary unrest—one crucial fact emerges. Though the Bolsheviks were fighting in the name of a revolutionary transformation of society, it was not this fact that determined their military policies. For, having seized power so precipitately, they found themselves engaged, almost despite themselves, in a life and death struggle for sheer political survival. It was the need to survive that underpinned all their military policies rather than any broad considerations about what constituted a truly democratised army, or how genuinely to engage the socio-economic aspirations of the rank-and-file. Having retrospectively sanctioned the spontaneous rural revolution, they were given a short breathing-space in which the peasants chose to tolerate a government that was not actively against them and did not interfere too much in their massive expropriations and redistributions.

But sooner or later the Bolsheviks had to face up to the logic of the military situation and bear down upon that same peasantry whose parochialism and contempt for all forms of central authority conspired to undermine all Bolshevik efforts to assert their own authority. When this was combined with the absolute necessity of alleviating the terrible food shortage in the cities and at the fronts, and with the short-lived Soviet belief in the possibility of a swift transition to collective agriculture, the government found itself in opposition to very broad sections of the rural population. Yet only this population could supply the necessary troops for the defence of Bolshevik power. Therefore the peasantry had to be forced to co-operate, and the whole of the political effort was directed to this end. The Russian Civil War, therefore, is not to be seen as a genuine people's war in which military and political institutions are a reflection of grass-roots aspirations. In the Soviet armies these institutions were an instrument of authority, and the whole of the military organisation was specifically designed to mini- mise discussion and dissent. The Bolsheviks could only tailor their organisational structures to the demands of survival (i.e. rigid, authoritarian centralisation) rather than to popular attitudes and aspirations.

Trotsky, as ever, was completely aware of the implications of all this:

> The army is, to the highest degree, an artificial organism which always develops vast centrifrugal tendencies . . . Under the conditions of an intense and implacable civil war . . . permissible differences of opinion are within the army of the revolutionary class, reduced to the absolute minimum. The army is an artificial organism, and the unity of thought and planning which sustains this artificial organism must be maintained with a firmness all the more relentless, the more savage, against the objective condi- tions that tend to undermine the army.[76]

Chapter 8 The Chinese Civil War
1926–49

CHRONOLOGY

1921

1–5 July   First Congress of the Chinese Communist Party (CCP).

1923

June   The Third Congress of the CCP ratifies a proposal to amalgamate, though as a distinct organisation, with the Kuomintang (KMT).

July   The peasants of the Haifeng–Lufeng region attempt to reduce rent and abolish the *corvée* system. They are organised by Peng Pai.

1924

May   Creation of the Whampoa Military Academy.

1925

11–12 Jan   The Fourth Congress of the CCP makes their Party's first pronouncements on the importance of the peasant question.

12 March   The death of Sun Yat-sen and a split within the KMT.

20 March   Chiang Kai-shek arrests important CCP cadres within Canton.

3 May   Several demonstrators in Shanghai are killed by the British. There follow widespread nationalist protests and strikes.

1926

15 May   The KMT Central Executive Committee limits the extent of CCP participation in the government and the Party.

1 July   Chiang begins the Northern Expedition against the warlord cliques in North-east China.

1927

18 March   The Northern Expedition forces are in control of ten provinces in South and Central China.

21–22 March   The Nationalists, with help from the workers, seize Shanghai.

March   Mao Tse-tung writes the *Report on the Peasant Movement in Hunan.*

12 April   Chiang conducts a savage purge of Communists in Shanghai. There are also purges and executions in Kanchow, Hangchow, Canton and Peking.

30 June   The CCP, following the Moscow line, issues a conciliatory statement about the role of the KMT.

15 July   The KMT left-wing establishes itself at Wuhan. The Nanking rightists group under Chiang decides to expel the Communists.

1–5 Aug   The Communists attempt a putsch at Nanchang using dissident troops in the area. This is a failure.

Sept   The KMT hold a Conference for National Unity after which the Wuhan group gradually disintegrates.

8 Sept   The CCP begins the Autumn Harvest Uprising. A failure.

Nov   Mao and the remnants of his forces reach the Ching Kang Shan area.

11–13 Dec   The Canton Commune. The CCP stages a workers' insurrection in Canton where they briefly seize power.

1928

April   Chu Teh, who had attempted to set up Soviet base areas like the Ichang–Leiyang–Pinghsien–Yunghsing area in the aftermath of the Autumn Harvest Uprising, joins Mao in the Ching Kang Shan. The Fourth Red Army is set up.

Sept   A purge by Mao of dissidents in the Party in the Ching Kang Shan base.

Dec   Mao evacuates the Ching Kang Shan and moves to the Kiangsi–Fukien border area.

1929

9 July   A CCP resolution, under the influence of Li Li-san, demanding bolder action in the towns and the military organisation of the workers.

1930

7 Feb   The first provincial soviet set up in the Kiangsi–Fukien base.

11 June   Another CCP resolution stressing the Li Li-san line.

July   A series of communist attacks on the towns of Changsha, Wuhan and Nanchang. By September the offensive has ground to a halt.

1 Oct   The beginning of the first KMT Encirclement campaign against the Kiangsi base.

Dec   A purge of opponents of Mao in the Kiangsi base, following the Fukien Incident.

1931

Jan   The CCP, following Moscow's instructions, denounces the Li Li-san line.

May   The Second Encirclement Campaign.

July   The Third Encirclement Campaign.

Sept   Another purge of dissident elements within the First Army.

18 Sept   The Japanese in Manchuria expel the Chinese forces there.

7 Nov   The first meeting of the All-China Soviet Congress at Juichin.

1932

28 Jan   The Japanese attack Shanghai.

15 April   The Chinese Soviet Republic declares war on Japan.

1 May   Agreement between the Nationalists and the Japanese.

June   Beginning of the Fourth Encirclement Campaign.

1933

Jan   The CCP Central Committee takes refuge in the Kiangsi base.

27 Feb   The Japanese invade and annex Jehol.

March   End of the Fourth Encirclement Campaign.

1 Oct   Beginning of the Fifth Encirclement Campaign.

Nov   Mao demands that the Communists support a group of dissident Nationalist generals who are urging war against Japan. He is overruled by the Central Committee.

1934

14 Oct   The CCP begins to evacuate the Kiangsi base.

19 Oct   Vanguard elements break through the Nationalist lines. Beginning of the Long March.

1935

Jan   Mao is made Temporary Chairman of the Central Committee.

Oct   Mao reaches North Shensi with the First Front Army.

13 Nov   An anti-Japanese declaration by the CCP and an alliance with the KMT is proposed.

9 Dec   Students in Peking demonstrate against the Japanese.

1936

25 Jan   A circular letter from the CCP to Chinese armies in Manchuria suggesting joint anti-Japanese action.

5 May   A further proposal to the KMT of combined anti-Japanese action.

3 Oct   The Second and Fourth Front Armies reach North Shensi.

1937

10–21 Feb   Exchange of proposals for joint action by the CCP and the KMT. Hostilities between them come to an end.

28 July   The war with the Japanese begins in earnest.

21 Aug   Signature of Sino-Russian non-agression pact.

22 Sept   The KMT endorses the CCP manifesto of 15 July. The Red Army becomes the Eighth Route Army.

1938

21 Oct   The Japanese take Canton.

25 Oct   The Japanese take Hankow.

1939

Jan   First meeting of the Border Region (National) Assembly after general elections.

1941

Jan   Nationalist troops disarm Communist soldiers of the New Fourth Army in South Anwhei.

May   The beginnings of a Party reform movement that was to last three years. Upwards of 80,000 members purged.

Nov   First meeting of the Second Border Region Assembly.

1942

28 Jan   The Central Committee formalises its policy of limiting land-reform to reductions in rent.

1944

March   Mountbatten begins the reconquest of North Burma.

27 Nov   Chiang rejects Communist terms for a new national government.

Dec   The CCP is now in control of twelve regional administrative structures.

1945

1 March   Chiang insists there can be no legal recognition for the CCP until it integrates its administrative structures into those of the government.

July   The Japanese begin to retreat from China.

13 Aug   Japan capitulates.

28 Aug   Mao visits Chungking for negotiations with the Nationalists.

31 Oct   Large-scale fighting between Communists and Nationalists in Honan.

20 Nov   The CCP refuses to attend a joint Political Consultative Conference.

25 Dec   General Marshall arrives in China to try and bring the Communists and the Nationalists together.

1946

10 Jan   Ceasefire.

July   Total breakdown of ceasefire.

28 Aug   Nationalists occupy Jehol province.

1947

6 Jan   Marshall withdraws.

5 March   CCP delegation leaves Nanking.

19 March   The Nationalists seize Yenan.

July–Aug   Communist troops return into Central China.

1948

24 April   The Nationalists are forced to evacuate Yenan.

24 Sept   The capital of Shantung falls to the Communists.

2 Nov   The Communists complete the defeat of the Nationalist forces in Manchuria.

1949

10 Jan   Surrender of 200,000 Nationalist troops in Honan.

15 Jan   Surrender of Tientsin.

23 Jan   Surrender of Peking.

24 April The Communists occupy Nanking.

3 May   The Communists occupy Hangchow.

27 May   The Communists occupy Shanghai.

30 May   The Communists occupy Sian.

1 Oct   Mao reads the declaration of the People's Republic of China.

In the Russian Civil War the Bolsheviks were forced to recruit their armies predominantly from among the peasantry, simply because Russia was still basically a rural country. By their timely concessions to peasant demands the Bolsheviks were at least able to obtain their tacit support. More importantly, because the *ancien régime* had collapsed so totally the Bolsheviks were more easily able to impose their own regime and force the peasants to provide food and manpower within a centralised, and to a certain extent repressive, political structure.

Bolshevik successes, like those of the Jacobins of the Year II, owed more to prodigies of *ad hoc* administrative coercion than to any consistent reliance upon a thoroughgoing integration of military service and the aspirations of the ordinary rank-and-file.

China too was almost entirely a rural society, and any thorough revolution would have to initiate measures to satisfy the chronic discontent of an increasingly impoverished peasantry. But in China, the incumbent regime, though corrupt and incompetent, was far from disintegrating. The revolutionaries could not hope to seize power in a swift *coup d'état*, as in Russia, and then tighten their administrative grip on the peasantry. Power could only be seized when the revolutionaries had a large military and political *apparat* of their own, equal to the task of meeting the incumbent forces in open conflict. It would take many years to build up such an *apparat*, and to give themselves the necessary time and room for manoeuvre the revolutionaries had to carve out for themselves impenetrable base areas where they could slowly and surely build up the requisite military forces and political structures. Such forces needed food and recruits and so the base areas had to be created amongst the peasantry. But the revolutionaries had no effective coercive machinery and so they slowly had to win the support of the peasants. They had, in other words, to identify their struggle with that of the peasantry for greater economic security. If the rural population was to fight in the revolutionary army it had to be able to see that such military service contributed to the satisfaction of the peasants' most basic social and economic grievances.

Only by satisfying these conditions could the Chinese Communists hope to overthrow the Kuomintang state. A few Communist leaders, notably Mao Tse-tung, realised this at an early stage, but it was many years before they were in a position to put such theories into practice. Until 1934 and the beginning of the Long March the revolutionary and military history of China was bedevilled by many misconceptions and opportunistic theories that precluded the possibility of bringing about an effective social revolution. To understand the significance of the Maoist line it is necessary to discover why other military-revolutionary policies were inadequate in the light of the actual conditions of twentieth-century China.

Putschism and Opportunism

Chinese Communist policy before 1934 and the triumph of Maoism was based upon two successive doctrinaire assumptions. In both cases the Communists tried to fit the Chinese situation into orthodox Marxist categories and to ignore the fact that any successful Chinese revolution would have to be based upon the peasantry. In each case they acted upon the assumption that the revolutionary dynamic was inherent in social classes other than the peasantry, and made their alliances accordingly. Throughout the whole period the Communists assumed that the true socialist revolution in China would be almost exclusively based around the proletariat. So from the beginning great efforts were made to recruit Party members from among this class. But it was fairly clear, even to the Chinese Communists and their Russian advisers, that the Chinese working class at this time was hardly large enough to justify hopes for an imminent proletarian revolution. Thus it was assumed that China must first go through a nationalist revolution that would clear the way for the emergence of an indigenous bourgeoisie. This class would then be free to set about the creation of a national industrial base and this in turn would guarantee the growth of a large working class. Then the eventual triumph of the socialist revolution would be inevitable. Acting in the name of this long-term strategy the Communists decided to ally themselves with the Kuomintang (KMT), the foremost nationalist party within China. At its Third Congress, in June 1923, the Party formally announced that it was prepared to collaborate with the KMT and accord the latter the leading role. In the following autumn Chiang Kai-shek, then the Chief-of-Staff of the KMT, went on an official visit to Moscow. At the First Congress of the KMT in January of the following year the delegates agreed to allow members of the Chinese Communist Party (CCP) to join their Party, and in the months that followed they were given many key posts in the governmental and Party structures.

But CCP policy was based upon a rather unrealistic assessment of the historical process. Whilst there was some validity in adhering to the Marxist dictum that the bourgeois revolution must precede the proletarian, it was utopian to expect the KMT to look with favour upon an ally whose ultimate aim was the destruction of the very society for which the Nationalists were fighting. From the very beginning many within the KMT were intensely suspicious of their new allies. In November 1925 two groups, the Western Hills Group and the Society for the Study of Sun Yat-senism, emerged within the KMT both of which demanded the expulsion of the Communists. On 29 March of the following year Chiang Kai-shek staged a coup in Canton where he arrested many Communist cadres and their Soviet advisers, and had strike pickets in the city disarmed. On 15 May the KMT Central Committee decided to limit the extent of CCP participation in the Party and its institutions. On 29 July martial law was declared in Canton and the workers were refused the right to assemble. The anti-Communist drive was renewed in 1927. On 12 April Chiang had all the pro-Communist trade-unionists in Shanghai disarmed, and some three hundred people were killed in the sporadic fighting that ensued. There followed purges of Communists in Shanghai, Canton, Kanchow, Kukiang and Hangchow, and these soon spread to other cities. On 28 April thirty-six Communists caught sheltering in the Soviet embassy in Peking were strangled after a summary trial.

Obviously these and similar incidents marked the end of full collaboration between the KMT and the CCP, and the beginnings of Communist disillusionment with the potential of bourgeois revolution in China. Even so the leadership strove to retain some links with the 'progressive' Chinese bourgeoisie. For a brief period in 1927 they attempted to ally with the so-called 'left' KMT elements who had insisted on maintaining their own government in Wuhan in opposition to the Chiang apparatus in Nanking. As late as June 1927 the Central Committee issued a declaration vowing that:

> The KMT, being an alliance of workers, peasants and small capitalists against imperialism, ought naturally to assume the leadership of the national revolution. The Communists belonging to the KMT hold governmental posts . . . only as members of the KMT . . . Mass organisations . . . must

submit to the leadership of the KMT authorities . . . The trade-unions or pickets cannot apply legal or adminis- trative sanctions, make arrests, pass judgements, or patrol the streets without the permission of the Party or the government.[1]

But in July the Wuhan government also tired of their Com- munist allies and they were expelled from its Party. By the end of the year the KMT was united once more, and the Communists were vigorously excluded.

The first revolutionary initiatives of the CCP had met with total failure. Though they were undoubtedly correct in stressing the potential of the indigenous middle classes, they were a little short-sighted in assuming that such a moderate, though anti- imperialist, coalition as the KMT would look with any favour upon the Communists' socialist millennium or their seeming subservience to a foreign government. But the CCP could still not bring itself to break its links with Marxist or Soviet ortho- doxy. If there was no hope of a progressive bourgeois revolution then clearly the Communists would have to count upon the proletariat alone. They had in fact stressed the importance of the working class even in the period of alliance with the KMT. The trend of events was at first very much in their favour. Between 1916 and 1922, for example, the number of workers in the big cities had doubled from one to two million. At the same time there was a dramatic increase in the number and extent of strikes. The records for 1918, albeit incomplete, speak of twenty-five strikes, involving 10,000 workers. Whereas the so-called 30 May Movement of 1925 in response to foreign atrocities sparked off some 135 strikes from Hong Kong to Peking, involving at least 40,000 workers. Thus membership of the CCP, whilst a mere fifty-seven in 1921 and 342 in 1923, had reached 19,000 by 1925 and 93,000 eighteen months later. After their disillusionment with the KMT the Communists began to put the alliance with the Chinese working class at the very centre of their programme. In August 1927, at the Emergency Conference of the CCP, it was 'decided that the leadership of the Chinese Revolution had passed to the proletariat'.[2]

But even though it was growing very fast, the working class

in China was still very small in relation to the population as a whole. Moreover, whatever organisational bases the Communists had been able to establish amongst the workers had been severely disrupted by the anti-Communist offensives of the KMT. Key cadres were dead, imprisoned or had gone underground, whilst many of the workers themselves were very reluctant to expose themselves to police and army repression. So the Communists found themselves compelled to seek other allies to supplement their dwindling forces in the cities. The only possible choice was the peasantry. In forming such an alliance the Party was taking the first steps along the road to the Maoist conception of the Chinese Revolution. But it is most important to bear in mind that at this time the peasantry was only regarded as the cannon-fodder of the revolution. Revolutionary power was still envisaged in terms of the dictatorship of the proletariat, and the key revolutionary acts were still to take place in the cities. Peasant unrest was merely to create a climate of uncertainty and chronic instability in which the cities could find the inspiration and the freedom of manoeuvre to act. A Comintern directive of 1929 summed up this basic theme of early Communist policies *vis-à-vis* the peasantry: 'The struggle of the peasant masses must be closely linked to the revolutionary struggle of the urban proletariat. Moreover, our tactics in the countryside should correspond to the work of the Party in winning over the urban proletariat in the process of its day-to-day economic struggles.'[3] As Schram says: 'Although it was realised that for the moment the peasantry in the countryside was more active than the working class in the cities, this was regarded as an unnatural state of affairs ... to be remedied as soon as possible. "Proletarian hegemony" remained an unquestioned dogma.'[4]

This dogma pushed the Party inevitably in one strategic direction. Whilst the rural unrest was not a self-sufficient phenomenon, it could be utilised to aid the urban masses. And this aid must come swiftly if the Communist bases within the cities were not to be entirely lost. Thus there followed, over the next eight or nine years, a consistent policy of trying to use the peasantry to storm the cities. Sometimes not even the peasantry as such was used. On 1 August 1927 a Front Committee formed the previous month in Nanchang attempted to take over that city with certain military units commanded by Communist sympathisers. On the 5th the approach of loyal Nationalist troops forced them to abandon the city completely. A little over a month later the CCP once again tried to ensure themselves a permanent urban base in a series of attacks known as the Autumn Harvest Uprising. The prime targets were a series of cities in Hupei province. Once again the attempt proved abortive. Mao Tse-tung, who had been ordered to form a military force for the purpose, pulled his men out of the campaign, in defiance of Party orders, before they were all uselessly squandered. He took them into the mountainous Ching Kang Shan region where he set up the first Communist rural base in Central China.

The Communists also decided to take action in Canton to coincide with the hoped for Autumn Harvest successes. Despite the miserable failure they did not go back on this decision. Even though they could only muster 2,000 poorly-armed militia against a possible opposition of 50,000 Nationalist troops, the local Provincial Committee approved a plan for an insurrection on 7 December. It began on the 11th in the early morning. The rebels set up a local Soviet government and 'announced the most revolutionary measures concerning confiscations, nationalisation, redistribution of wealth and cancelling of debts'.[5] By the 13th, however, government forces had recaptured the city, and between 5,000 and 8,000 rebels are said to have perished in the brutal repression that followed.

Clearly the whole 1927 campaign had been the most disastrous failure. In February 1928 the Comintern Executive Committee stated the obvious:

The greatest danger of the present situation lies in the fact that the vanguard of the labour and peasant movement as a result of a wrong appraisal of the present situation . . . may be torn away from the masses, run too far ahead, split up its forces and allow itself to be smashed into separate detachments . . . It is necessary to fight energetically against putschism among some sections of the working class . . . against playing with insurrections.[6]

The Sixth Congress of the CCP agreed and the Secretary-General held responsible for this wrong appraisal, Chu Chiu-pai, was replaced. His successor was a mere figurehead, and effective responsibility fell to Li Li-san.

At about this time Mao Tse-tung moved his forces from the Ching Kang Shan to a new base around Juichin and Tingchow in the Kiangsi–Fukien border region. There Communist influence expanded amongst the peasantry and the Red Army grew accordingly. Despite the mistakes of his predecessor, Li Li-san was incapable of regarding this as anything but proof of the imminence of large-scale Communist victories and the vulnerability of the towns and cities. The so-called Li Li-san line was formulated, complete with the old urban fixation and stress upon insurrectionary activity. In March 1930 he wrote: 'The villages are the limbs of the ruling class. The cities are their brains and hearts. If we cut out their brains and hearts they cannot escape death; but if we simply cut off their appendages, it will not necessarily kill them.'[7] In June he was even more specific: 'The great struggle of the proletariat is the decisive force in the winning of preliminary successes in one or more provinces. Without an upsurge of strikes of the working class, without armed insurrections in key cities, there can be no successes in one or more provinces.'[8] So the Central Committee in Shanghai decided that once again the time was ripe for armed assaults on the cities. The targets chosen this time were Changsha, Wuhan and Nanchang. At the same time, strikes, later to develop into insurrections, were planned for Shanghai, Nanking, Canton, Tientsin and Tsingtao. The offensive began in late July. The only success was in Changsha which the rebels managed to hold for ten days, mainly because its garrison was ludicrously small. Elsewhere failure was total, and once again Mao took it upon himself to disobey Party orders and avoid what he knew would be a futile attack on Nanchang. Once again also the Party reacted strongly to this fiasco. Li Li-san was bitterly attacked at the Fourth Plenum of the CCP Sixth Central Committee, the attack being led by a group of young Chinese 'Bolsheviks' recently returned from Moscow. He fell into relative obscurity and power devolved upon a new group of men led by Mif, the Comintern delegate, Wang Ming and Po Ku.

But even at this stage the CCP retained some kind of urban orientation, and the Central Committee remained in Shanghai. But arrests were becoming more and more frequent, whilst membership of the left trade-unions, once at least two million strong, had fallen away to a mere 50,000. In early 1933 the Central Committee gave up the uneven struggle and moved to Juichin, the capital of the Kiangsi–Fukien base, or Chinese Soviet Republic as it was now called. But it took massive defeat in the Nationalist Fifth Encirclement Campaign to finally bury this obsession with urban centres. From the time of the Second Encirclement Campaign in May 1931, and the attendant Communist successes, the Wang Ming group was constantly urging that the time for cautious guerrilla warfare was past and that the Red Army must adopt a forward offensive strategy based upon seizing the towns. Indeed this policy had some initial successes. The Red Army was able to capture the cities of Changchow, Lo An, Li Chuan, Chien Ning and Tan Ning in early 1932. But such gains proved ephemeral in the absence of a sympathetic and organised base in the surrounding countryside. By 1934 the Kiangsi Soviet Republic had been reduced from ninety to six counties and the Nationalist grip was tightening with every day. In terms of real political power urban bases were mere mirages in a desert of apathy and oppression. The irrelevance of the Central Committee's line had by now become all too apparent and Mao Tse-tung was at last given the chance for an unhindered application of his own strategies and tactics to the revolutionary struggle.

Dealing at such length with the early failures of the CCP emphasises the point that the Chinese Civil War does not begin with Mao Tse-tung and the Maoist guerrilla line. In the first place it is important to remember that this line was not simply conjured up out of thin air but was a response to the first disastrous failures of an urban-orientated policy. Secondly, even these failures are instructive in terms of the general concerns of this book, and help to highlight the reasons for the success of the Maoist line. In adopting an insurrectionary policy aimed at the swift seizure of the main urban centres the Central Committee was flying in the face of the real balance of forces within China. For one thing the cities were simply not important enough in terms of the whole Chinese economy such that occupation of them implied real political control of the country at large. But there was in actual fact never any danger of the Communists ever occupying more than a handful of cities at a time. For whilst they realised that they needed rural manpower to supply the assault troops, the successive members of the Central Committee never appreciated that such troops would never fight with any enthusiasm or come forth in significant numbers unless Communist policy was directed to the satisfaction of their own most basic demands. Certainly the Communist leaders did at least realise that the Communist armies would have to draw their recruits from amongst the peasantry. But they never appreciated the vital corollary that such recruits needed something concrete to fight for. As was emphasised in the previous chapter, peasants are parochial, traditionalist and fatalistic. They were not prepared to fight for a revolution that concentrated on distant urban centres or that defined its ideal society in terms of the liberation of the proletariat. They would only fight in a revolutionary army that stressed the importance of their own preoccupations about rural reform. Certainly the towns had to be taken eventually. But such seizures meant something only in the context of a militant, radicalised countryside, and thus the whole of the initial Communist effort had to be directed to the task of arousing the rural masses. When Mao said that the countryside had to surround the towns he gave a clear indication of the siege-like nature of the operation. And sieges are not based upon swift assaults but a slow and painstaking process of erosion.

But before going on to discuss Maoist policy itself there is yet another aspect of the history of the Chinese Civil War that is of interest in relation to the general theme of this book. For, somewhat ironically, in the early years of the Revolution the Nationalists had been more aware than the CCP leadership of the necessity of attempting to create a viable revolutionary armed force through an integration of political aspiration and military service. In 1924 the First National Congress of the KMT accepted the idea of raising a modern army organised along Russian lines. During this period of Russian tutelage the problem of politicising the armed forces was a primary military issue for the Nationalist leadership. In May 1924, in an attempt to create politically conscious cadres for the army, the Whampoa Military Academy was set up, with an initial enrolment of 499 student-officers selected from amongst 3,000 applicants. These officers were used to supply the command-structure for a new Russian-armed force of regulars. Beginning as a brigade this force was enlarged into a full army corps after the establishment of the Nationalist government. As a part of the command structure the Nationalists set about the creation of a system of political commissars. Each commissar with an army corps had a hundred assistants who were responsible for spreading National-ist propaganda within the ranks. Their powers were great and they were entitled to countersign, and if necessary even countermand, the orders of the military commanders them-selves.

To this extent at least the Nationalist Army forms a part of the tradition of politicised military structures that has been traced in the previous chapters. Nevertheless, the KMT forces could not really be called a people's army in the true sense of the term. The attempt to integrate political participation and military service was extremely crude. Thus, whilst the com-missars stressed that the KMT was fighting for some vaguely defined better society, no attempt was made to implement any real reforms. KMT social programmes remained at the level of grandiose rhetoric, and the network of commissars never became more than an artificial appendage to a traditional mercenary body. This became more and more manifest after the Northern Expedition against the dissident Chinese warlords. In the hallowed tradition of Chinese politics most of the soldiers in the defeated warlord armies were absorbed wholesale in to the KMT units where they were bombarded with vacuous National-ist propaganda. Liu says:

All factions [in the KMT] accepted with confidence . . . the institution of the political commissar system . . . They adopted a plan of gathering armed forces by every con-ceivable means and then inserting commissars at the various levels of the newly absorbed groups . . . Thus the KMT could afford to swell its ranks with heterogeneous groups of men, in full confidence that they would be won over to the party.[9]

But this is a very over-optimistic assessment of their success. For one thing the sheer number of bandit and mercenary elements absorbed into the army stretched the commissar system to its limits. Too many men were absorbed too swiftly for the commissars to be able to give them anything but the most trivial education in Nationalist principles. As Gittings points out: 'Unlike the [later] Communist army, the KMT's national-revolutionary army never went through the slow process of organic growth which alone could preserve qualitative homogeneity during quantitive expansion.'[10]

Even more importantly, it soon became fairly apparent that KMT principles meant little in practice. They could have done, for in the early days of the Northern Expedition Nationalist progress was more like a triumphal march as peasant associations came out in full support of the army, and the warlord forces simply melted away. But if Chiang had wished to keep this support he would have had to effect some concrete reforms to impress his sincerity on the peasantry. This he failed to do. Indeed he was incapable of doing any such thing. During the Northern Expedition he had not only absorbed the rank-and-file of the warlord armies, but he had also made alliances with their leadership. They were for the most part arch-conservative landowners, totally opposed to any concessions to the debt-ridden, land-hungry peasantry. Thus while there were some reforms of a sort—the government built nearly 6,000 miles of new railway, over 30,000 miles of road and rebuilt the telegraph system—these were purely on a technical level. They were designed for the express purpose of facilitating the movement of troops. KMT policy soon came to represent a mere militarisation of the Chinese system without any of the reforms that would encourage a mass-based participation in, and support for, that system. Although Chiang had at one stage recognised the necessity for encouraging the growth of a politically motivated army, at a crucial stage he turned away from the masses and their aspirations and embraced a policy of repressive and predatory militarism.

Early Ideas on Peasant Revolution

The agricultural crisis in China in the 1920s and 1930s and the gradual pauperisation of the rural masses is fundamental to an understanding of the Chinese Revolution. The population was expanding so that land *per capita* was steadily declining. There was also a steady decline in the total area under cultivation. Because land was in such short supply rents rose rapidly. Worse, many peasants could not afford to keep themselves in the period between sowing and harvesting and had to borrow money, at staggeringly high rates of interest, to tide them over. But this was not the end of the story. The Chinese peasant was suffering the effects of the gradual commercialisation of agriculture, as middle-class elements in the cities invested in land itself and in the raising of commercial crops.

> The introduction of commercial crops and the commercialisation of land affected land prices, tenure conditions and rent charges. Prices for land doubled and tripled in some areas, and secure tenure was replaced by short-term contracts. At the same time rents increased outright or rose through the use of such mechanisms as advance collections or the payment of rent deposits to ensure rights of permanent tenure.[11]

All this meant that the peasant had a continuous need for money to ensure that he was able to hang on to his patch of land. The middle classes were unable to make much investment in indigenous industrial development because of the low tariffs created by the 'unequal treaties', and because of the extent of Japanese investment at all levels in the economy. Therefore, in the majority of cases, 'it stayed in the village and became the usurious class, lending money to the peasantry. In that field it could get immediate profits, at so high a rate of interest as to make the whole system iniquitous. As a result its members often became landlords, in addition to lending money'.[12] On top of all this the China of the 1920s and 1930s was largely controlled by the warlords in particular areas. Each one issued his own paper money, always without any adequate metallic reserve, and so inflation was rampant. Further, the warlords depended totally on their armed forces for both internal repression and inter-provincial prestige and security. To pay for the upkeep of these soldiers it was necessary to extract revenue from the peasants in the shape of taxes. The taxes were heavy enough, but in many cases the demands of the military budget forced the warlords to collect them two, five, seven or in the case of Szechwan thirty-one years in advance.

Under these circumstances it is hardly surprising that rural China was in an almost continual state of ferment. It had be-come evident even during the Northern Expedition for which, as it passed through the countryside, the peasantry came forward in droves to act as guides, informers or actual soldiers. The Expedition precipitated a mushrooming of the organised peasant movement. In Hunan in November 1926 the peasant associations had just over one million members, whilst in 1927 some two million were involved in outright seizures of land.

At about this time Mao Tse-tung himself was in the province of Hunan, and in March 1927 he presented a study of the peasant movement there. In it he stressed the importance of peasant militancy for the prospects of revolution in China. He criticised those within the CCP who still maintained a somewhat vacil-lating attitude towards the peasantry: 'All talk directed against the peasant movement must be speedily set right. All the wrong measures taken by the revolutionary authorities concerning the peasant movement must be speedily changed. Only thus can the future of the revolution be benefited.' But in one very important respect this excursion into an analysis of the revolutionary potential of the Chinese peasantry differs from the later line. He goes on to say: 'In a very short time . . . several hundred million peasants will rise like a mighty storm, like a hurricane, a force so swift and violent that no power, however great, will be able to hold it back. They will smash all the trammels that bind them and rush forward along the road to liberation.'[13] The crucial words here are 'in a very short time'. Mao had still not developed the concept of protracted warfare that underpins his mature conception of the road to revolutionary power. Indeed, throughout the report, he speaks of rural militancy as con-tributing to the overthrow of 'rural feudalism' and the development of the 'national revolution'. In other words, whilst avoiding the hesitancy of many of the CCP leaders with regard to the peasant movement, he was in no way asserting that this movement could lead directly to the communist seizure of power.

In fact the leadership soon caught up with Mao as he expressed himself in this report. After a reorganisation of the Central Committee in August 1927 it issued the following pronouncement: 'At the following time . . . the preparation by the Party of systematic, planned peasant insurrections, organised on as wide a scale as possible, is one of the main tasks of the Party.'[14] These insurrections, as has been seen above, were only regarded as a background for the important task of seizing the cities. Nevertheless, in two important respects, they had much in common with Mao's concept at this time. Both he and the leadership agreed that rural unrest was only a prelude to the organisation of the socialist revolution, and both agreed that this prelude could be expected in the immediate future.

Soon after this the Autumn Harvest campaign was set in motion, and it was the abject failure of this insurrectionary movement that forced Mao to think again about the imminence of the rural cataclysm. Indeed, he made a crucial choice during the uprising itself. He was in command of a force of some 2,000 men, organised into four regiments. He had been ordered to take the city of Changsha, but in the face of a determined counterattack, heavy losses and the desertion of one entire regiment, he abandoned this venture and in the last few weeks of 1927 retreated with the remnants of his force into the Ching Kang Shan, a mountainous semi-desert region. Having taken this step Mao explicitly embraced a double conception of future revolutionary activity in China. Firstly, it was to be intimately concerned with the peasantry and secondly, it was to take the form of prolonged military activity.

The Role of Guerrilla Warfare

Mao's original conversion to the guerrilla mode was due to practical considerations. Having gathered together a tiny military force for the Autumn Harvest Uprising he was unwilling to squander that force in a futile frontal assault. But in disobeying Central Committee orders he had already committed himself to a policy of keeping some kind of armed force in permanent existence, rather than raising one piecemeal according to the tactical requirements of a particular time and place. He had in short eschewed the insurrectionary mode.

The theoretical justifications for this decision were not long in coming. The military-political concept at the heart of these justifications was that of the base area. According to Mao the political situation in China was unique in that power was not in the hands of a single central authority but of a diverse selection of warlords, each very jealous of his own prerogative within a limited area. These warlords were in a constant state of rivalry and sometimes of open war, such that they, let alone the central government, were never able to concentrate more than a fraction of their forces against any revolutionary group. Thus the Communists could create for themselves the room for manoeuvre to set up some kind of permanent revolutionary base. As Mao said in October 1928:

> The prolonged splits and wars within the White regime provide a condition for the emergence and persistence of one or more small Red areas under the leadership of the Communist Party amidst the encirclement of the White regime . . . Some comrades often have doubts about the survival of Red political power and become pessimistic . . . If we only realise that splits and wars will never cease within the White regime in China, we shall have no doubts about the emergence, survival and daily growth of Red political power.[15]

He stated the point again in an article of the following month:

> China is the only country in the world today where one or more small areas under Red political control have emerged in the midst of a White regime which encircles them. We find on analysis that one reason for this phenomenon lies in the incessant splits and wars within China's comprador and landlord classes. So long as these splits and wars continue, it is possible for an armed independent regime of workers and peasants to survive and grow.[16]

But because this was a strategy dictated by what Mao referred to as the 'objective conditions' within China, he was very aware that one must adopt tactics that meshed with these conditions. Thus:

An independent regime must vary its strategy against the encircling ruling classes, adopting one strategy when the . . . regime is temporarily stable, and another when it is split up. In a period when the ruling classes are split up . . . our strategy can be comparatively adventurous and the area carved out by military operations can be comparatively large . . . In a period when the regime . . . is comparatively stable . . . our strategy must be one of gradual advance.[17]

This is what one might call Mao's political analysis of Chinese society, and out of it arose his fundamental concept of the possibility of maintaining, for a varying period of time, an independent, self-sufficient Red area within which to conduct political propaganda and initiate a series of socio-economic reforms. Further:

Since the struggle [in such areas] . . . is exclusively military, both the Party and the masses have to be placed on a war-footing. How to deal with the enemy, how to fight, has become the central problem of our daily life. An independent regime must be an armed one. Wherever such an area is located, it will be immediately occupied by the enemy if armed forces are lacking or inadequate, or if wrong tactics are used in dealing with the enemy.[18]

The question of right and wrong tactics introduces Mao's sociological analysis of China's revolutionary potential. The tactics he chose were those of guerrilla warfare, designed to make the most of an army of badly trained, badly equipped and parochially minded peasants. Just like the overall strategy, the tactics themselves were chosen to fit in with the objective conditions. And just as the independent regimes as a whole had to advance boldly or consolidate according to the strength of the opposing White regime, so did the individual guerrilla units have to mould their tactics according to the strength and purpose of the opposing units. In the base in the Ching Kang Shan guerrilla tactics were reduced to four simple slogans: 'When the enemy advances, we retreat. When the enemy halts and encamps, we trouble them. When the enemy seeks to avoid battle, we attack. When the enemy retreats, we pursue.'[19] This unity of the strategical and the tactical, the political and the sociological, was admirably summed up in an interview between Edgar Snow and Peng Teh-huai in 1937. Speaking of the reasons for the development of guerrilla warfare, Peng said: 'Although the strategic areas of China are all more or less dominated by the imperialists, this control is uneven and not unified. Between the imperialist spheres of influence there are wide gaps, and in these partisan warfare can quickly develop.' Speaking of the actual tactics of guerrilla warfare he noted: 'Many a Red "short attack" has been carried out with only a few hundred men against an enemy of thousands. Surprise, speed . . . and the selection of the most vital and vulnerable spot in the enemy's "anatomy" are absolutely essential to the complete victory of this kind of attack.'[20] By organising in the 'wide gaps' between the White spheres of influence, the Communists were capitalising upon the weaknesses of their enemy. By attacking the 'vulnerable spots' in the enemy's formations, they were making the most of their own troops, deficient in both training and equipment.

But guerrilla warfare was not just a response to the material weaknesses of the Communist peasant armies. It also took account of the nature of peasant society as a whole and the extent of its potential for organised, armed resistance. And it is in this selection of a mode of warfare absolutely in harmony with the basic characteristics of peasant society that Mao's genius is revealed.

Firstly, guerrilla warfare is suited to a peasant society for purely technical reasons. Almost by definition such a society will be very dispersed, terrain will be very difficult in large sections of the country and communications will be very primitive or non-existent. In such circumstances it will be exceptionally easy for the revolutionaries to appear as from nowhere and then to effect swift retreat. By the same token the incumbent forces will find it difficult to concentrate their forces or to pursue the enemy. As Peng Teh-huai said: 'Partisan warfare has developed because of the backwardness of the hinterland. Lack of communications, roads, railways and bridges makes it possible for the people to arm and organise.'[21]

The second basic reason for the affinity between a peasant society and the guerrilla mode was anthropological. Mao recognised that the peasant was only interested in the cultivation of his own plot of land, within his own village. In a document written in January 1934 he said: 'Only since we have distributed the land to the peasants . . . has their labour enthusiasm blossomed forth and great successes in production been achieved . . . [We work] within the framework of a small peasant economy . . . Of course we cannot yet bring up the question of state or collective farming.'[22] But as the peasant's horizons hardly stretched beyond his own village, he was little interested in fighting for anything outside of it. Mao increasingly fought against this 'localism' and attempted to develop mobile, regular forces prepared to undertake long-range operations. In this he eventually succeeded. Nevertheless, from the very beginning he was forced to concede that a vast percentage of his forces would be of the local guerrilla type, unwilling to operate far from their own villages. In the Ching Kang Shan period the troops were divided into guerrillas, mobile within a *hsien* (district), and 'rebel detachments' attached to each village and mainly concerned with police work and local defence. In the Kiangsi period the armed forces consisted of fairly mobile guerrillas and of the so-called Red Guards. All citizens aged between eighteen and forty were required to serve in the latter, but in practice only certain model units of young, able-bodied men ever undertook actual military operations. Roughly the same system applied in the Yenan period, although by this time the mobile troops had reached a higher level of regularisation. The local troops, 2,222,000 in 1945 as opposed to 910,000 regulars, were again divided into model units and others. Only the model units actually fought, whilst the remainder were responsible for transport, supplies, evacuation, security, etc.

Certainly the creation of the regular detachments might have been necessary for the actual seizure of power. But because

Mao was engaged in the slow erosion of Nationalist power he was able to build up such forces slowly and accommodate his principles to the realities of a peasant society. Indeed he had to accommodate them in this way. In the Russian Civil War, because the Bolsheviks had already seized state power before they grappled with rural attitudes, they were able to impose some kind of repressive regime upon the peasantry and force them into line. But in China the Communists had no power base at all apart from the support of the peasantry. Therefore they were in no position to force the peasants to indulge in a mode of warfare at odds with their natural inclinations. Guerrilla warfare was the only possible way of mobilising the Chinese peasantry. As Mao said in December 1936:

> In defining our policy . . . we should not repudiate guerrilla-ism in general terms but should honestly admit the guerrilla character of the Red Army. It is no use being ashamed of this. On the contrary this guerrilla character is precisely our distinguishing feature, our strong point, and our means of defeating the enemy. We should be prepared to discard it, but we cannot do so today.[23]

At all stages Mao was prepared to evaluate the nature of the objective conditions at the expense of any conception of doctrinal orthodoxy.

The Development of Attitudes towards the Peasantry

We have so far discussed Mao's analysis of Chinese society in terms of the political and sociological considerations. But the problem also had an economic dimension. When examined in these terms the peasantry was far from being a unified whole. There were wide gulfs in peasant society, dividing the rich, middle and poor peasant, the landed and the landless. But as the guerrilla war widened in extent and intensity Mao came to realise that the only way effectively to utilise the full potential of the peasant movement was to ensure that all sections of the rural population participated in it. In other words, though it might make some sense in terms of the vision of the future society to turn peasant against landlord, poor peasant against rich peasant and to insist upon equal land distribution to all, in political and military terms such internal dissension merely sapped the strength of the revolutionary base. Mao swiftly came to the conclusion that the immediate task was of a military nature and everything else would temporarily have to be subordinated to that policy which came nearest to guaranteeing military success.

Thus there is discernible over the period of protracted military struggle a gradual softening of Mao's line on the peasantry, and a steady attempt to include as broad a spectrum of rural society as possible into the revolutionary movement. His attitude to the rich peasants is a case in point. In 1926 he was fairly dogmatic about the counter-revolutionary role of the rich peasants who, 'usually combine . . . [their] interest with that of the small landlords'.[24] Consequently the rich peasantry had to be destroyed as a class by confiscation of their land and redistribution to the other peasant classes. During the Ching Kang Shan period: 'At the level of the villages . . . [agrarian] reform was carried out to the letter. Confiscated lands were divided into three categories— good, middling and poor—and shared out as equally as possible . . . The landlords who escaped physical liquidation were excluded from the sharing out of the land, and rents were abolished.'[25] The rich peasants suffered heavily under such measures. Mao's link between them and the landlords became a self-fulfilling prophecy as they, and even broad sections of the middle-peasantry, became totally alienated from the Communist movement and looked to the warlords to re-establish their property rights. But the Central Committee of the CCP was more aware than Mao of the dangers of such a policy. In May 1929 they ordered him to stop confiscation of rich peasants' land, and the Land Law of Hsingkuo county of April 1929 did in fact contain such a stipulation.

The fall of Li Li-san caused a dramatic change in Central Committee policy. It now demanded an all-out attack on the rich peasants and a constant effort to maintain the fervour of the masses against them. The old attitude was dubbed the 'rich peasant line' and Land Investigation movements were set in motion to seek out rich peasants and the proponents of leniency towards them. But Mao had by now begun to appreciate the benefits of a more tolerant attitude and he was opposed to this new onslaught. From 1932 or so he was in constant disagreement with the Central Committee on this point. Thus, although the government of the Soviet Districts of north-east Kiangsi agreed, in 1932, to confiscate the land of the rich peasants it refused to concede to an absolutely equal redistribution of that land. Because the rich peasants had the capital and the equipment to exploit whatever land they might receive, the government 'made a distinction which it was impossible to check: rich peasants would get land of the worst quality'.[26]

If the Central Committee was still to the left of Mao with regard to the rich peasants, there does seem to have been a consensus on the question of the middle peasants. The Land Law passed by the First Soviet Congress in November 1931 was remarkably moderate in this respect:

> The First Congress considers that equal distribution of all the land is the most radical way of destroying all feudal relations of slavery connected with the land . . . ; even so, local soviets . . . must explain all the aspects involved to the peasants. Not until the peasants at the base and above all the mass of middle peasants desire it and give it their direct support, can this land reform be applied.[27]

Mao himself was fully in agreement with this flexible attitude. His policies towards the middle peasants became even more moderate after the opening of hostilities with Japan and the formation of the KMT–CCP United Front between 1935 and 1937. From this time on the task of the CCP was of an increasingly overt military nature, and all social and economic policies had to be assessed in terms of the basic priority of mobilising a genuinely national resistance to the Japanese.

> During the war the Communists did not contemplate the redistribution of land or any other class-orientated measures that would have radically altered the pattern of land ownership. Instead, the economic policies implemented by the Communist Party during the Sino-Japanese War were designed to create maximum unity . . . As Mao put it, 'The

agrarian policy is a dual policy of demanding that the
landlords reduce rent and interest, stipulating that the
peasants pay this reduced amount of rent and interest.[28]

From 1937 onwards this was for a long time the sole concern of
the Communist agrarian policy. At about this time Mao bluntly
stated: 'It must be explained to Party members and to the
peasants that this is not the time for a thorough agrarian
revolution . . . The landlords shall reduce rent and interest, for
this serves to arouse the enthusiasm of the basic peasant masses
for resistance to Japan, but the reductions should not be too
great.'[29]

Right through until 1946 this remained the policy of the CCP.
The Central Committee resolution of 28 January 1942 summed
it up admirably, describing the principles that underpinned it in
these terms:

The Party recognises that the peasants constitute the basic
strength of the anti-Japanese war . . . They must be helped
and their living conditions improved. Most landlords are
anti-Japanese and some are even in favour of democratic
reform. They must be allowed to keep their political rights
and their interests must be protected. The capitalistic
mode of production is a relatively progressive mode of
production in present-day China. The rich peasants are the
capitalists of the rural areas and are an indispensable force;
their work must be encouraged. Legislation must provide
for the reduction of land-rent and stipulate that rent be
paid. The landlord must keep his right to dispose of his
land in accordance with existing legal provisions.[30]

But it is important to see this liberal attitude towards the
rich peasants and the landlords in its proper context. The key
sentence of the 1942 pronouncement is that which relates to the
progressive economic role of the rich peasantry. One of the most
important considerations for the survival of the base areas was
the question of the economic viability. They had to be made
self-sufficient, and this demanded that those with any capital or
equipment extra to their personal needs be given the opportun-

ity to make use of that surplus for the good of the community. But they would only do that if they also saw some possibility of personal profit. Thus the richer elements within the soviets had to be given some considerable measure of economic freedom. From 1930 or so, as has been seen, Mao consistently advocated such a policy.

But he did not at any stage lose sight of his long-term political goals. If the landlord, the rich peasant, the petty capitalist was to be given a considerable measure of economic liberty, the strictest of checks were to be kept on his political role. During the Kiangsi period Mao's political line was quite clear: '[He] never conceived of a policy of alliance with the rich peasants; he believed in restricting them. He would be willing to give them as good treatment as possible to enable them to become loyal citizens of the Soviet regime, but he was opposed to expanding their political power.'[31] Lo Fu, Mao's chief ally in this matter, adopted a similar dual policy to the hired labourers, the nominal proletariat of rural China. Despite the land redistributions there always continued to be a group of landless labourers in the soviet areas, a group whose economic demands set them at odds with the middle and even poor peasants. But the support of these latter groups was fundamental to Communist success. If such antagonisms were allowed to come to the surface all hopes of unity within the base areas would vanish. So Lo Fu conceived a policy of once again trying to minimise the economic contradictions, in the interests of productivity and temporary class harmony, whilst stressing the political supremacy of the poorest groups. He coined the slogan that the Party, 'represents the farm labourer, depends upon the poor peasant, allies with the middle peasant'.[32] Thus whilst the poor peasants should be allowed full enjoyment of their economic gains, including the use of hired labour, at the same time this hired labour should be one of the most important groups within the political organisations of the soviet areas. Moreover Lo Fu maintained that this dual policy of economic appeasement and political exclusion was relevant to Communist policy in its broadest outlines. On the whole question of poor peasant versus landlord and capitalist he insisted that, in the soviet areas, 'capitalism not only exists but has inherent in it [the possibility] of further expansion. Should the proletariat often carry on a struggle against the capitalist for the improvement of its livelihood, then not only can it not destroy the capitalist but it will soon restrict its own development'.[33] At the same time he maintained that capitalism should only be given a free rein as long as political power remained firmly in the hands of the Party, the living expression of the ultimate demands of the poorest sections of the population.

This important qualification about the political role of the rich peasant, landlord and capitalist was also basic to the economic liberalism of Mao that was discussed above. As Wolf points out, regarding the policy in the Yenan period, although the Communists 'became even more liberal in their handling of land reform than they had been earlier . . . the reform also introduced new forms of organisation—village councils, work teams, peasant unions—which gave the peasants and the landless political leverage in influencing the course of village decisions'.[34]

Like everything else this policy was dictated by developments in the military sphere. Thus, once the Japanese had been beaten, and as the internal balance of forces swung more and more in the Communists' favour, Mao became less and less concerned with the maintenance of class harmony within the soviet areas. As the threat from without became decreasingly serious, the Communists had more room for manoeuvre to use their grassroots political support to translate their economic visions into reality. In November 1945 Mao was still advocating a limited policy of rent reduction. The first signs of change came in May 1946 when a distinction was drawn between 'formerly' and 'recently' liberated areas. It was decreed that in the first category there would once again be a policy of confiscation of excess land. In December 1946 the Draft Land Law of the Shensi–Kansu–Ninghsia Border Region empowered the government to purchase landlords' excess land compulsorily. In some respects this Draft Law can be seen as a slight softening of that of May in that compulsory purchase replaced confiscation. For even in February of the following year Mao still maintained that 'during and after the land reform, appropriate consideration . . . should be given to ordinary rich peasants and middle and small landlords.'[35] But prospects for Communist success became brighter with every month, and in the Land Law of October 1947 their policy veered sharply to the left. The Law terminated the ownership of all landlords' land, abolished loans contracted before 10 October, authorised the seizure of the surplus land of rich peasants and stated that all lands in the liberated areas were to be distributed on an equal basis. Jen Pi-shih, a leading member of the Central Committee, wrote: 'The Communists must not forbid or prevent the masses from getting even with those who have oppressed them and whom they hate. Instead, they should sympathise with them or they will be cut off from them.'[36] Clearly the days of liberalism of the Lo Fu brand were ended once and for all. The prospect of total military victory brought the possibility of a land reform more far-reaching than anything that Mao had considered since the days of the Ching Kang Shan.

The Role of the Party

The political, sociological and economic considerations that have been discussed so far demonstrate the indissoluble links between military and socio-political factors in the Chinese Revolution. The existence of the massive KMT and warlord armies demanded that any revolution in China would have to be of a military nature. The essentially rural composition of Chinese society dictated the resort to a guerrilla mode of warfare. At the same time the military demands for a unified fighting front and a large reserve of manpower forced the Communists temporarily to adopt certain conciliatory economic measures. Yet even here political considerations also intervened, and economic conciliation went hand-in-hand with a certain political isolation. This latter point is crucially important. Although the very nature of the Chinese Revolution forced the Communists to accord a high priority to military matters, it should in no way be thought that this implied that the Maoist line was, in any conventional sense of the term, militaristic. Militarism implies that all social, political and economic questions are subordinate to the demands of the military structure and its continued existence. Under a militaristic regime the elite groups predicate their existence upon maintaining the society on a permanent war-footing where various characteristics such as obedience, hierarchical organisation, xenophobia, are seen to be self-evidently functional to the survival of that society. Such characteristics were of importance in the soviet areas in the Civil War, but what is important is that they were never put forward as self-evident or permanent truths. For the Communists the struggle had a political and economic goal which, once it was reached, would render obsolete the necessity for a large-scale military organisation. In a militaristic regime the sense of struggle is perpetuated, usually artificially, to justify the existence of the incumbent elite groups. In China the struggle was on an economic level and as such was relevant to broad sections of the population. Certainly to win this struggle it was necessary to indulge in organised military activity, and such activity had to be an important consideration in the shaping of day-to-day policy. But this only implies a partial, temporary militarisation of the society, during which the basic aims of the struggle always transcended the demands of the military organism as such.

One of Mao's clearest expressions of the political role of the Red Army came in December 1929, in the article *On Correcting Mistaken Political Ideas in the Party*. In the first section he denounced what he defined as 'the purely military viewpoint'. These remarks are basic to his policy throughout the Civil War and are worth quoting at some length:

The purely military viewpoint manifests itself as follows: these comrades regard military affairs and politics as opposed to each other and refuse to recognise that military affairs are only means of accomplishing political tasks . . . They think that the task of the Red Army . . . is merely to fight. They do not understand that the Chinese Red Army is an armed body for carrying out the political task of the revolution . . . The Red Army should certainly not confine itself to fighting; besides fighting to destroy the enemy's military strength, it should shoulder such important tasks as doing propaganda work among the masses, arming them, helping them to establish revolutionary political power . . . The Red Army fights not merely for the sake of fighting, but in order to conduct propaganda work among the masses, organise them, arm them.[37]

In other words, for Mao, the existence of the Red Army had always to be seen, from within and without, as a logical extension of the most basic social and economic aspirations of the mass of the people. It was to be a true people's army in that its existence was only functional to the pursuance of popular political objectives. This subordination to grass-roots political opinion expressed itself at the most basic levels. In 1928 the following eight rules were drawn up to govern the army's relations with the civilian population:

(1) Replace all doors when you leave a house. (2) Return and roll up the straw matting on which you sleep. (3) Be courteous and polite to the people and help them when you can. (4) Return all borrowed articles. (5) Replace all damaged articles. (6) Be honest in all transactions with the peasants. (7) Pay for all articles purchased. (8) Be sanitary.[38]

Again and again this question of identifying the Red Army with the popular struggle was underlined by the Party leadership. In January 1934 Mao wrote:

Our comrades should in no way neglect or underestimate the question of the immediate interests, the well-being, of the broad masses. For the revolutionary war is a war of the masses; it can be waged only by mobilising the masses and relying on them . . . We must lead the peasants' struggle for land and distribute the land to them . . . safeguard the interests of the workers . . . develop trade with outside areas, and solve the problems facing the masses—food, shelter and clothing, fuel, rice, cooking-oil and salt, sickness and hygiene, and marriage.[39]

In 1937 he wrote: 'Without a political goal, guerrilla warfare must fail, as it must if its political objectives do not coincide with the aspirations of the people and their sympathy, co-operation, and assistance cannot be gained.'[40] In May 1938 he wrote:

> Political mobilisation for the War of Resistance must be continuous. Our job is not to recite our political programme to the people, for nobody will listen to such recitations; we must link the political mobilisation for the war with . . . the life of the soldiers and the people, and make it a continuous movement . . . [Of the] conditions indispensable to victory . . . political mobilisation is the most fundamental. The Anti-Japanese National United Front is a united front of the whole army and the whole people, it is certainly not a united front merely of the headquarters and members of a few political parties; our basic objective . . . is to mobilise the whole army and the whole people to participate in it.[41]

There is absolutely no doubt that these policies were carried out and were extraordinarily successful. A Japanese Army report of 1941 said:

> The main anti-Communist forces today are the Japanese Army and the Nanking Government, and they certainly do not possess the confidence of the broad masses . . . Today [the Red Army] . . . champions army–civilian integration everywhere, and is continuously organising local armies. As a consequence it is extraordinarily difficult to separate bandit from citizen in Communist destruction work.[42]

In 1944 an official American observer noted: 'The communist governments and armies are the first governments and armies in modern history to have positive and widespread popular support. They have this support because the governments and armies are genuinely of the people.'[43]

But there were no romantic notions of the spontaneity of the masses or undue concessions to the anarchic instincts of the peasantry. The above remarks of Mao of May 1938 give a broad hint in this respect. Whilst much stress is placed upon the necessity of attuning to popular attitudes, the whole passage is predicated upon the root notion of 'mobilisation'. This pre-

supposes two things. Firstly that there is a group of revolutionaries to do the mobilising, and secondly that their role is much
more than one of merely passively responding to inputs from
outside. This group is of course the Party. Thus, for Mao,
although the Party had to be at all times responsive to peasant
demands, if it was to survive, that survival was also of crucial
importance to the peasantry. Without the leadership of the
Party the revolutionary struggle might merely dissolve into a
fruitless series of anarchic, unconnected peasant insurrections.

In some respects this is very reminiscent of the problems that
faced the Bolsheviks during the Russian Civil War. But where
they were compelled to stamp out guerrilla warfare at the
earliest possible stage, the Chinese Communists were forced to
rely in large part upon this mode of warfare because of their
need to build their revolution from the bottom upwards. But
even for them guerrilla warfare had its limits. Though it is by
definition a fragmented, decentralised mode of warfare, Mao
tried at all times to ensure the maximum subordination to
Party control and discipline. Thus one of the 'mistaken ideas'
that the Party warned against in 1929 was the 'ideology of
roving rebel bands'. 'This ideology manifests itself as follows:
some people want to increase our political influence only by
means of roving guerrilla actions, but are unwilling to increase
it by undertaking the arduous task of building up base areas
and establishing the people's political power.'[44] If Mao was
unable to go as far as Lenin and Trotsky in their implacable
opposition to all manifestations of guerrilla warfare, he was
certainly in agreement upon the undesirability of any armed
forces divorced from central control. In December 1936 he had
the following to say about the harmful effects of guerrilla
warfare:

> One [of its aspects] is irregularity, that is, decentralisation,
> lack of uniformity, absence of strict discipline . . . As the
> Red Army reaches a higher stage we must gradually and
> consciously eliminate them so as to make the Red Army . . .
> more regular in character . . . Refusal to make progress in
> this respect and obstinate adherence to the old stage are
> impermissible and harmful.[45]

As the Army became more regularised Mao became increasingly emphatic about the necessity for strict Party control. In 1937 he spoke of the struggle against 'the tendency towards new warlordism in the Eighth Route Army. This tendency is manifest in certain individuals who . . . have become unwilling to submit strictly to Communist Party leadership, have developed individualistic heroism.'[46] In November 1938 he made his famous remark to the effect that 'political power grows out of the barrel of a gun'. But the corollary to this is of much greater significance: 'Our principle is that the Party commands the gun; the gun shall never be allowed to command the Party.'[47] To ensure that the Party did exercise control, political officers were attached to all units, who were responsible for the education of the troops and were also the Party's direct representatives within the Army. They were mainly concerned with the formulation of local policy and the transmission of Party directives to lower levels. Beneath them were political departments at the divisional and regimental level, and political instructors at the battalion and company level. These were the men responsible for the actual implementation of policy and propaganda work among the rank-and-file.

This system had been abandoned after the alliance with the KMT against the Japanese, but it was very soon reintroduced in response to the emergence of 'warlordism'. Party control over the Army was intensified between 1942 and 1944 during the so-called Cheng Feng Reform Movement. The movement was basically aimed at heightening discipline within the Party. It tried to stress the importance of democratic centralism and vigorously denounced 'extreme democratisation [stemming from] . . . the erratic nature of the petty bourgeoisie (agricultural production and urban petty capital)'.[48] But the movement also concerned itself with Army–Party relations, and a Politbureau resolution of 1942 demanded the full integration of the political staffs within and without the Army.

In the future, the Main Armed Forces must carry out the decisions and resolutions of Party committees at all levels of government. The Main Armed Forces must also carry out the resolutions of the lower-level Party committees and

lower-level governmental units . . . of the area where they
are stationed . . . In the guerrilla areas . . . there must
be a unification of Party, governmental, military, and mass
structures . . . When there are hostilities [those cadres]
. . . are to participate in the work of the army and the
guerrilla units; when there is a lull, they are to carry out
their former tasks in Party, government, or mass organisations . . . Within the army it should be thoroughly understood that without the integration of the Party, government, and mass organisations, the army by itself would
not be able to fight for a single day.[49]

The Chinese Civil War represents the most perfect integration
of civil and military concerns that has been discussed in these
pages. It was a genuinely military revolution. Military activity,
after the debacles that arose from the doctrinaire lines that
prevailed before the Long March, was dictated by the considerations of socio-economic revolution. The armies had almost to be
created from scratch, and it was clear that the rank-and-file
would have to come from among the rural masses. The only way
to tempt these men to come forward was to accommodate their
economic aspirations. Moreover, these aspirations had to be
accommodated immediately. So base areas had to be established
wherever feasible so that the Red Army soldiers could be given
something concrete for which to fight. It is interesting to note
that in this respect the Land Law of the Ching Kang Shan
period explicitly stated, in Article Two, that every Red Army
soldier should be allocated a plot of land. Further, in the hope
of attracting men with some military experience, it was also
decreed that the land of soldiers in the counterrevolutionary
armies should not be confiscated as these men 'had been drawn
into . . . the struggle against the soviets because of their ignorance'.[50]

But beyond a certain point civil policy had in its turn to bow
to the demands of military conflict. Thus once a base area had
been established by dint of economic reforms it became an
increasingly high priority for the incumbent government or
clique to eliminate it. But the more pressure that was put on it
the more it became necessary for the Communists to engage all

classes in it in the struggle for its survival. This necessitated conciliatory policies towards the more prosperous elements, and attempts to persuade the poorer groups to sublimate their more radical economic demands beneath a full participation in various mass organisations. Similar considerations held true in the war against Japanese aggression. If the Communists wished to appear patriotic they had to be prepared to work with the KMT. But if such an alliance was to have any operational meaning the Communists could not afford to alienate the Nationalist ruling elite by pursuing too radical social and economic policies. But as the balance of military power swung in their favour, during and after the war with Japan, the Communists could afford to disregard this elite and prepare themselves for the final push by once again insisting on the implementation of a drastic agrarian reform programme. Radicalism had been necessary to create the first revolutionary bases, and radicalism was necessary to seize revolutionary power. The potential of genuine people's war, the full appreciation of the integral links between social, political and military organisation and between popular aspirations and military effectiveness, had been made manifest, and the established world order had received a blow from which it can never fully recover.

Chapter 9   Conclusion

Throughout all the previous chapters the pre-eminent importance for military affairs of various social and political factors
inherent in the very revolutionary situation has been stressed.
The forms of military organisation and modes of combat were
not discrete phenomena explicable in terms of abstract, time-
less 'rules of war'. They were rather reflections of social reality
at a particular time and in a particular country. With this in
mind it is possible to organise the factors that have been
isolated in the various chapters under two broad sub-headings.
The first of these relates to general ideological considerations.
Revolution must represent the possible fulfilment of grass-roots
aspirations. Revolutionary power can only be effective if it is
based upon a manifest willingness to satisfy such aspirations.
If the exercise of revolutionary power demands that some sort
of armed force be created then that army will only fight with
any enthusiasm if military service is generally seen to be an
indispensable method of satisfying rank-and-file grievances.
The people at large will only fight in the revolutionary army if
the act of being a soldier is made inseparable from the desire to
be a more fulfilled citizen. But it is utopian to suppose that
effective political power rests only upon a benevolent identification with popular desires. This is a necessary condition but not
a sufficient one. The exercise of power also demands effective
administrative structures and strong central leadership, particularly in a time of bitter social upheaval. Thus the second
sub-heading relates to organisational factors and the mechanics
of revolutionary power. If the engine of revolutionary war
cannot run without the fuel of popular support, nor can it last
very long if the machinery itself is not well maintained.

Ideological Factors

The very first case-study presented an example of the crucial
importance of the ideological question. Much more important
than the relative ease with which the Parliamentarians were

able to equip themselves for open warfare against the King was the whole set of fears and aspirations that gave them the original impetus to challenge the legitimacy of royal authority. And once the challenge was thrown down these same ideas brought forth a corporate spirit and willing submission to discipline, as well as a sublime chiliastic fervour that made the crack regiments of the New Model Army almost invincible on the field of battle. The very resort to war itself and the ease with which the Puritan stalwarts transformed their churches into fighting regiments can only be understood in the light of their conception of the forthcoming millennium. For one thing these millenarian notions implied a division of society into the forces of good and evil, a division that could be seen to be increasingly manifest as the Puritans fought with their own sense of sin, and the imminence of possible chaos if the forces of the Lord were not ever vigilant and prepared. In a time of political crisis it was easy to identify one's secular enemy with Antichrist and the Beast. Once this identification was made it was even easier to justify a resort to open rebellion in the name of the final struggle of good and evil. Once this struggle was begun all the Puritans' past training on the spiritual beachhead of his organised church afforded a perfect basis for implacable military efficiency.

On this very general cultural level the English Civil War offers possibly the most perfect integration of the civilian and the military. The Puritans were able to develop a military organism more attuned to the most basic preoccupations of their revolutionary culture than has appeared in any western society since. Only the Chinese Revolution has achieved a comparable affinity between basic modes of thought and the mode of military organisation. In that case, after the early disasters of urban-orientated putschism the Communist Party developed a type of warfare that was specifically adapted to take account of peasant capabilities and limitations. Peasants' horizons rarely extend beyond their own village or group of villages and thus they are most unwilling to travel any distance away from home. Similarly they are constantly preoccupied with the annual tasks of sowing and harvesting and thus are loath to be away from home for any length of time. Guerrilla warfare takes account of all this and is based around swift, local mobilisations that are thrown against a particular target, after which the peasant soldier is allowed to melt back into his own village and take up the routine tasks of everyday life.

Thus the book begins and ends with military revolutions that most reflected this indisposable fusion of general cultural pre-occupations and military obligation. But to define ideology in such broad terms does not tell the whole story. Millenarianism and peasant parochialism between them do not exhaust the possibilities for a genuine ideological mobilisation. Even in the two cases at issue so far, such general considerations do not explain everything. In each case one has also to account for the existence of concrete social and political aspirations. And in the other chapters it is such aspirations alone that are often found to be the root cause of revolutionary success, or that at least go a long way towards explaining the policies of the leadership.

In the English Civil War the emergence of such concrete issues in fact marked the end of the period of authentic military revolution. In the beginning millenarianism had remained a vague faith in the inevitability of the emergence of a good society. The very existence of an open armed struggle could be clearly interpreted as the final battle with Antichrist, for this was the only kind of just war countenanced by Puritan thought. It was clearly written in the Bible that this struggle would presage the re-establishment of God's Kingdom on earth. But as the war went on, even though the New Model Army went from victory to victory, even though the Beast was physically liquidated, no new society appeared of its own accord. The revolutionaries were forced to examine within their own minds, and in terms of their own human capabilities, exactly what they expected such a new society to be like. Questions of social, economic and political reconstruction and reorganisation became their main preoccupation, questions moreover that would have to be solved by the revolutionaries themselves. In short the struggle was secularised. But this secularisation had one very important result. It revealed that those who had been able to band happily together under the banner of an amorphous, religious chiliasm were not in fact comrades-in-arms when it came to more concrete social and political issues. In these terms their interests were in fact very diverse. There were those who had fought to obtain for themselves some material stake in the nation and there were others who realised that the satisfaction of all such demands, even were it possible, would be a threat to their own economic position. Grandees and Levellers met and split irrevocably during the Putney Debates. The cohesive revolutionary army disappeared from English history.

In this particular case the ideological factor was of a very ambiguous significance. At first, on a general cultural level, it welded the Army together. Later, as the actual political issues were defined in specific terms, it divided and destroyed that army. But the basic point remains that this ideological factor is of the utmost importance in any assessment of the history of the Civil War. Any so-called military history of the conflict that limits itself to a discussion of tactics, orders of battle, terrain and battlefield decisions runs the risk of completely missing the point. Indeed such an approach is shot through by a massive irony. War is perhaps the one field of human endeavour which most depends on concerted human action, and in which the basic human problem of life and death is most to the fore. It seems a little ludicrous, therefore, to study war without reference to any other of the most pressing preoccupations of human society. War is not an emotional and intellectual vacuum. Quite the reverse; the imminence of death or conquest forces men to examine closely their most basic assumptions about the nature of human relationships.

In the Chinese Revolution there was no problem of a basic contradiction at the ideological level. The Chinese revolutionary leadership was forced to take account of the concrete aspirations of the rank-and-file but they were able to use these aspirations as another method of increasing the cohesion and morale of their armed forces. For they adapted their programme to embrace peasant demands from the very beginning. The Maoist line took account of both the most basic anthropological features of the society and of the specific reforms that were demanded by its members. On the ideological level Maoist guerrilla warfare was specifically and exclusively designed to answer the grass-roots aspirations of the population. It was people's war in the fullest sense of the term. Military service and the modes of military organisation and combat were, at all times, seen to be functional to the solution of the most basic civil problems of the mass of the soldiery. Military service became a political act. One returns again and again to the complaint of Edward Sexby at Putney: 'If we had not a right to the kingdom, we were mere mercenary soldiers.' The ordinary soldiers of the New Model Army came to realise that they were indeed no more than mercenaries, and in the absence of a durable grass-roots organisation the Army fell apart, what was left of it being sent away to Ireland to remove the risk of mutiny at home. But the soldiers of the Chinese Communist armies were explicitly told that they did have a right to the kingdom; and the armies were held together, through the most terrible privations, for over twenty years. Eventually it became only a matter of time before the Nationalist armies disintegrated in the face of their advance.

In terms of the linking of civil concerns and military service, in terms of the translation of political demands into military obligation, the Chinese Revolution is our paradigm. But this is not to say that questions of ideology are unimportant in a discussion of other military revolutions. The English Civil War has already been dealt with and stress was put upon the affinity between the Puritan *weltanschauung* and the demands of military efficiency. This is the only other case-study in which such broad cultural considerations are of any positive importance. But in all the other periods under discussion it is vital to have a clear understanding of the concrete social and political aims of the revolutionary armies in order to interpret the significance of the particular mode of military organisation.

Thus in the early days of the American War of Independence and the French and Russian Revolutions there was some integration of ideological preoccupations and organisational modes. The first combatants in America grouped themselves in fairly autonomous militia units whose concern with the accountability of their officers and whose right to judge for themselves whether a particular operation or manoeuvre was justifiable were a perfect reflection, particularly in the New England units, of the aggressive egalitarianism of the ordinary colonist. But this egalitarianism was a threat to the economic interests of the colonial elite. So, even though both groups could unite under the nationalist banner and both could see that the expulsion of the British might mean an improvement of their lot, there was a basic disagreement over the concrete implications of such an improvement. Just like the Parliamentarians in the English Civil War, the colonists were able to unite for a while in the name of vaguely formulated slogans. But in both cases the realities of actual political reform eventually caught up with the insurgent group. The elite was forced to clamp down upon grass-roots radicalism to avert the danger of any excessive adjustments to the *status quo*. The Grandees were able to get by with a few exemplary executions. The American leaders had to wage a constant battle against decentralising tendencies within the Army, and enforce a rigid discipline and hierarchical organisation.

The same sort of contradictions were evident during the French Revolution. The vast political changes it occasioned were made possible by the temporary alliance of peasantry, bourgeoisie and urban poor against royal and aristocratic privilege. But once feudalism and absolutism had been swept away the alliance began to fall apart. The peasantry opted out to till their fields in peace, leaving the middle classes and the *sans-culottes* to decide the wider issues of how the French economy as a whole was to be managed. To ensure that their own blueprint was followed the bourgeoisie swiftly set about creating its own armed force, with the dual function of containing aristocratic reaction and excessive lower-class radicalism. There appears once again an excellent example of a genuinely revolutionary army in which military service was functional to the satisfaction of social, economic and political aspirations. The only essential difference from, for example, the Chinese Communist armies was that the French armed force represented the middle strata of society rather than its most oppressed lower elements. Given this distinction the National Guard was just as much a class in arms as the Eighth Route Army. The Chinese Army reflected civil aspirations in its endorsement of eventual far-reaching rural reform and in the prominent place accorded to the poorest peasants in the mass-based political structures. The National Guard mirrored such demands in its anti-aristocratic and anti-plebeian posture and in the democratic structure of the battalions themselves. By serving in the National Guard the bourgeoisie were protecting their wider class interests, whilst at the same time the terms of that service were completely in accordance with their visions of political participation.

Such a tight integration of civil and military life was possible as long as the National Guard was only needed for internal duties and thus required only a relatively small complement. But once it was needed for national defence it became clear that the bourgeoisie alone could not afford to try and keep the monopoly of armed revolutionary force. The extent of the foreign aggression demanded that the lower classes be brought into the fray. But the inherent contradiction between bourgeois and *sans-culotte* visions of what constituted post-revolutionary society militated against any possibility of these new armies of national defence being revolutionary in any real way. Although the leadership had to appeal to lower-class patriotism and stress the dangers of a return to royal absolutism, it could not afford to embrace *sans-culotte* demands for economic redistribution or permanent regulation of the economy. Thus in the mass armies of the Year II civil concerns were played down as much as possible and the revolutionary leadership concentrated on imposing a fairly rigid discipline and orthodox hierarchical structure upon the regiments. Civil representatives were attached to the armies but they were the representatives of centralised bourgeois power and their role *vis-à-vis* the rank-and-file never extended beyond authoritarian paternalism, exclusively concerned with the soldiers' military life. Thus, as in the English Civil War and the American War of Independence, the disparate nature of the socio-political vision of the rank-and-file and the leadership sooner or later forced that leadership to assert its own authority within the military organism. Discipline and the demand for unquestioning obedience reflected the class struggle within the country and the Army.

Discipline had a very similar significance in the Russian Civil War. Once again the cultural configurations of the peasantry, the vast proportion of the population, had been mirrored in the early appearance of guerrilla warfare, as the peasants felt their gains threatened by the White offensives. But the desperate food shortage in the towns and at the fronts forced the Bolsheviks to impose an urban dictatorship upon the countryside. Central power had to be made as effective as possible if the revolution was to survive. The effectiveness of such power rested partly upon the pre-eminence of Bolshevik authority within the armies. This in turn necessitated a ceaseless struggle against any mode of warfare based upon the concept of local autonomy and peasant notions of an atomised society. In such a struggle it was only natural that the leadership's emphasis should be upon the regularisation of the Army and the formation of conventional military units based upon conventional chains of command. In such a regular army it was also only natural that the Bolsheviks should find themselves compelled to employ experts who had served in the pre-revolutionary army. But such experts were potential agents of White counter-revolution. Thus the political leadership was forced to send its own representatives into the Army to operate a strict surveillance over the activities of the ex-Imperial officers. It is in this light that one should assess the role of the commissars. As in the armies of the First Republic their *raison d'être* was not so much to heighten the ideological consciousness of the rank-and-file as to assert the absolute supremacy of the central leadership. The awakened consciousness of the rural masses might have been vital in eroding Tsarist authority in the months just prior to the October putsch, but in the Civil War proper this consciousness was a direct threat to Bolshevik power. Peasant aspirations had to be ruthlessly subordinated to the demands of a regular military apparatus. In other words, in the Russian Civil War, as at various stages of the military period of the English, American and French Revolutions, the ideological factor came to be significant for largely negative reasons. The character of the grass-roots revolutionary consciousness came to be a problem for the leadership rather than a source of inspiration for a truly revolutionary army.

In terms of ideological factors the Prussian reforms have a unique significance. They represent an attempt to create a political ideology around which to build a revivified military structure. By emancipating the serfs, creating elective representative assemblies and throwing the officer-corps open to all classes, the Prussian leaders hoped to create a mass national consciousness that would render all citizens eager to bear arms in defence of the state. But, just because the initiative for these reforms came from the incumbent elite, they had inevitably to fall short of a truly revolutionary reorganisation of society. Ideologies simply cannot be manufactured to order to suit the interests of ruling groups. When this is attempted there will almost inevitably come a stage when popular aspirations will overtake the leadership's conception of what constitutes adequate reform. The very act of granting political concessions will highlight the contradictions inherent in the organisation of the society. In Prussia this fact was nowhere more in evidence than in the reformers' timid attempts to initiate a guerrilla war. It has already been made clear that such a mode of warfare depends on a complete identification with the most basic modes of behaviour and aspirations of the people at large. The reformers realised full well that in Prussia such aspirations took little account of the interests of the landowners. But in the last analysis the reformers were the representatives of the landowning class and so they were forced to hedge about their plans for a guerrilla uprising with such qualifications that it became an operational nonsense.

Organisational Factors

Whilst ideological factors are clearly of immense importance in explaining the exact organisation of a particular revolutionary army, it is also fairly clear that there is no particular correlation between military victory and the extent to which the army resembles an authentic people's army. Certainly it is the contention of this book that the existence of such a military organism is a sufficient condition for victory, as in England and China. But it does not seem to be a necessary condition. In America, France, Prussia and Russia revolutionary armies which were unable to effect a full integration of civil demands and military obligation were nevertheless very successful upon the battlefield. What then are the other considerations, beyond the merely technical which have been dealt with in the introduction, which can explain the military successes of these armies?

The best way to approach this problem is through an examination of the one military failure discussed in these pages, the

Paris Commune. Clearly the insurrection that created the Commune was a reflection of intense grass-roots discontent within Paris, and indeed France as a whole. The spontaneous rebirth of the National Guard was an adequate testimony to the willingness of the Parisians to fight for an improvement of their conditions. In other words, there did exist the ideological preconditions for the creation of a people's army. What there did not exist, however, was an effective, united revolutionary leadership. In terms of effectiveness, what leadership there was never even began to formulate a detailed programme of reform that could answer the demands of the lower classes. The absence of such a programme was all the more glaring because the revolutionaries had actually taken power. The old central government had withdrawn its writ from Paris and its citizens were able freely to set about electing a local body to represent their interests. In these circumstances the maintenance of revolutionary morale depended absolutely upon the passing of tough measures that could be seen to answer to the needs of the people. If the revolutionary assembly failed to enact such measures the people could not be expected to fight on its behalf.

Yet another organisational prerequisite is that the revolutionary leadership be united at the military and political levels. Just as military service should be seen to be functional to social and political emancipation to make service in the revolutionary army possible, so there should be political and military unity at an institutional level to make that service effective. Again such unity was manifestly absent during the Paris Commune. Both the Commune itself and the Central Committee of the National Guard were constantly at odds with one another, each fearful of the possibility of political or military dictatorship by the other. The National Guard was given neither rationale, organisation nor leadership. Perhaps even if all these things had been present the Parisians would still have been unable to carry their revolution beyond the confines of Paris. But it is certain that their absence rendered it completely impossible and made the task of the counterrevolutionaries that much simpler.

With this failure in mind it becomes easier to assess the true significance of the *représentants-en-mission* and the Bolshevik commissars. Whilst they are not particularly analogous to the chaplains of the New Model Army or to the Chinese military commissars, in that their role was not important in ideological terms, they are nevertheless a direct manifestation of the reasons for military success in France and Russia. For they were the vanguard of an effective revolutionary organisation or party. There could be room for some disagreement about whether or not the Jacobins constituted a political party, but it is quite certain that the group was characterised by a remarkable unity of thought and action. This was particularly true of the actual executive, the Committee of Public Safety, and the men that it chose to be its representatives within the military forces. Because of their ruthlessness and dedication they were able to institute and maintain a military mobilisation quite unprecedented in European history up to that date. They straddled both the political and the military spheres and were able to ensure that their policies in the one were tailored to the demands of the other.

The Bolshevik Party was similarly important during the Russian Civil War. Only the existence of a cohesive organisation providing resolute cadres at all military and political levels could have saved the revolution. Once again also the participation of Party men in both the military and civil command structures ensured that the activities of each could be most effectively co-ordinated. Certainly the officers of the Red Army were made autonomous with regard to purely operational decisions, but the commissars and Party men in local and central government made sure both that these decisions were taken in a correct political context and that civil affairs were regulated in a manner most likely to aid the military effort. Without such a dedicated and disciplined Party apparatus, and without a leadership capable of assessing together the military and civil priorities, it is unlikely that the revolutionaries would have been able so completely to annihilate the White forces. What Bolshevik discipline took away from grass-roots commitment it put back in the form of institutional stability and efficiency.

The organisational factor is also of some relevance to the other revolutions under discussion. It has been already dealt with as far as the English Civil War is concerned. The Puritans lacked any formal political organisation through which to govern the Army but this was hardly necessary during the war years. The very nature of the Puritan view of the world had inherent organisational implications. The very fact that they laid such a great stress upon the creation of a disciplined compact group of believers provided them with the perfect institutional base for the development of an aggressive military machine.

In the American War of Independence, however, the insurgency seems to have survived despite its organisational structures. For the Continental Army the benefits of firm central political control were conspicuous only by their absence. Inter-state rivalries and jealousies constantly undermined the effective power of the central legislature and executive, and minimised the possibility of a really concerted national military policy. It was nothing short of miraculous that Washington was always able to hang on to the nucleus of a national army and prevent the whole struggle from collapsing completely. In the War of Independence above all one is compelled to recognise the importance of personal greatness and perseverance. Without Washington there would perhaps have been no army. And it is certain that without the Army there would have been nothing. Here one has to face a basic irony. The very lack of cohesion and a strong military-political apparatus that threatened the existence of the Army meant that the Army was of a particular importance in the struggle. For only it and the victories it might win could provide the concrete examples of national effort that would provoke the colonists into keeping up the struggle. Thus, while organisational factors hardly explain how the Americans managed to win militarily, they certainly reveal why it was absolutely essential to keep some kind of national armed force in existence at all times.

Obviously the question of the revolutionary party is not relevant to the Prussian example. The reforms in this case were pushed through from above and so the leadership was able to enlist the support of the existing administrative machinery to supply and organise the military effort. This leaves only the Chinese Revolution, and once more its paradigmatic nature is clear. For here too, despite the central importance of the correct handling of the ideological question, organisational factors were of significance. Just as in Russia, the Chinese Communists had a Party apparatus that was all powerful in the military and the civil spheres. Certainly, because the Chinese were engaged in the slow erosion of existing power, they had to pay more attention to the grass-roots demands of their rank-and-file. The commissars involved themselves much more with the ordinary problems of the soldiers and the supporting villagers than ever their Russian counterparts had done. Their legitimacy rested upon their revolutionary programme alone rather than upon their ability to exercise coercive state power. Even so it would be going too far to claim that the Chinese Communists completely eschewed the advantages of institutional hegemony in exchange for complete subservience to peasant demands. The purges of the Kiangsi period and the Rectification Campaign of 1942–4 show the extent to which Mao Tse-tung in particular realised that a disciplined Party was one vital prerequisite of the effective co-ordination of military and civil activities.

If organisational factors, rather than the exclusively ideological, are of such importance in explaining the military success of various revolutionary armies it might seem fair to ask why this book has laid so much stress upon the extent to which an army manages to harness the basic aspirations of the ordinary soldier. It has been shown in some cases that armies that failed, or could not afford, to do this were nevertheless victorious, whilst the only failure described in these pages is directly attributable to organisational weakness. Why then so much stress upon the notion of an authentic people's army? The answer is simply that military success does not always denote the triumph of the original revolutionary ideals. And I would contend that the more a revolutionary army has to adopt modes of organisation that do not give full play to popular attitudes and aspirations the more that revolution runs the risk of losing sight of its original vision and the dynamic that gave it birth. Military success bought at the price of a rigid emphasis upon regularisation and institutional efficiency can be a most ephemeral triumph in terms of the original conception of the aims of the revolution. The carnage of Drogheda, the futile heroics of Napoleon's *grognards*, the praetorianism of the Prussian officer-caste, perhaps even the revolutionary justice at Kronstadt, are all examples of idealistic radicalism gone sour, of 'mere mercenary soldiers' whose original political zeal has given way to the mindlessness of militarism and *étatisme*.

Notes

CHAPTER 2

1. C. Hill, 'James Mason and the End of the World' in *Puritanism and Revolution*, London, 1968, p. 310.
2. A. S. P. Woodhouse (ed.), *Puritanism and Liberty*, London, 1965, pp. 474–5.
3. See W. Lamont, *Godly Rule, Politics and Religion 1603–10*, for the clearest exposition of this transition.
4. M. Walzer, *The Revolution of the Saints*, London, 1966, p. 295.
5. *Ibid.*, p. 294.
6. *Ibid.*
7. Lamont, *op. cit.*, p. 97.
8. See, for example, M. Walzer, 'Puritanism as a Revolutionary Ideology' in *History and Society*, vol. 3, pp. 59–90.
9. Walzer, *Revolution of the Saints*, *op. cit.*, p. 285.
10. Woodhouse, *op. cit.*, p. 387.
11. C. Firth, *Cromwell's Army*, London, 1962, p. 313.
12. *Ibid.*, pp. 312–13.
13. G. Davies, 'The Parliamentary Army under the Earl of Essex' in *English Historical Review*, vol. 49, p. 53.
14. Firth, *op. cit.*, p. 325.
15. C. Hill, *God's Englishman: Oliver Cromwell and the English Revolution*, London, 1970, p. 77.
16. *Ibid.*, p. 78.
17. L. F. Solt, *Saints in Arms: Puritanism and Democracy in Cromwell's Army*, Stanford, 1959, pp. 77–8.
18. *Ibid.*, p. 77.
19. This section owes much to Chapter Eight, 'Politics and War', of Walzer's *Revolution of the Saints*, *op. cit.*, particularly pp. 268–74.
20. C. Hill, 'The Political Sermons of John Preston' in *Puritanism and Revolution*, *op. cit.*, pp. 247–8.
21. Walzer, *Revolution of the Saints*, *op. cit.*, p. 274.
22. *Ibid.*, p. 282.

23. Firth, *op. cit.*, p. 320.
24. Solt, *op. cit.*, p. 72.
25. *Ibid.*, p. 49.
26. See Firth, *op. cit.*, pp. 276–310.
27. Hill, *God's Englishman, op. cit.*, pp. 64–5.
28. *Ibid.*, pp. 66–7.
29. Woodhouse, *op. cit.*, p. 473.
30. *Ibid.*, p. 442.
31. L. Stone, 'The English Revolution' in R. Forster and J. P. Greene (eds), *Preconditions of Revolution in Early Modern Europe*, Baltimore, 1970, pp. 60–61.
32. Woodhouse, *op. cit.*, p. 390.
33. D. M. Wolfe (ed.), *Leveller Manifestoes of the Puritan Revolution*, New York, 1944, p. 326.
34. Woodhouse, *op. cit.*, p. 8.
35. *Ibid.*, p. 396.
36. For Gustavus Adolphus' armies, see M. Roberts, *Gustavus Adolphus: a History of Sweden 1611–32*, London, 1958, vol. 2, p. 218.
37. Firth, *op. cit.*, p. 318.
38. Wolfe, *op. cit.*, p. 243.
39. *Ibid.*, p. 373.
40. Solt, *op. cit.*, p. 22.
41. L. Hamilton (ed.), *Gerrard Winstanley: Selections from his Works*, London, 1944, pp. 169–73.
42. Lamont, *op. cit.*, p. 138.
43. Wolfe, *op. cit.*, p. 380.
44. *Ibid.*, pp. 380–81.
45. D. W. Petegorsky, *Left-wing Democracy in the English Civil War*, London, 1940, p. 100.
46. Wolfe, *op. cit.*, p. 245.
47. *Ibid.*, p. 244.
48. *Ibid.*, p. 362.
49. Firth, *op. cit.*, p. 318.

CHAPTER 3

1. C. Hill, 'The Norman Yoke' in *Puritanism and Revolution*, London, 1968, p. 70.
2. For a thoroughgoing analysis of the significance of anti-

British rhetoric, see B. Bailyn, *Pamphlets of the American Revolution*, New York, 1965 (particularly the long Introduction).

3. Twenty thousand mercenaries fought in America. They fought in nine battles and eleven engagements, and their losses amounted to 2,200 men. F. V. Greene, *The Revolutionary War of the United States*, London, 1911, p. 179.

4. For example the conduct of the militia from around Albany during Burgoyne's thrust from the North in 1777. Or the behaviour of the North Carolina militia in the Cowpens–Guildford Courthouse campaign of early 1781. Or the efforts of the New Jersey militia after Washington's victory at Trenton in January 1777. Or the raising of the men in the Watauga settlements in what is now Tennessee in September–October 1781.

5. G. E. Scheer and H. F. Rankin, *Rebels and Redcoats*, London, 1957, p. 111.

6. *Ibid.*

7. H. Commager and R. Morris, *The Spirit of '76*, New York, 1958, vol. 1, p. 420.

8. C. J. Stillé, *Major-General Anthony Wayne and the Pennsylvania Line*, Philadelphia, 1893, p. 122.

9. Scheer and Rankin, *op. cit.*, p. 349.

10. J. R. Pole, *The Revolution in America*, London, 1970, p. 66.

11. B. Mitchell, *Alexander Hamilton: Youth to Maturity, 1755–88*, New York, 1957, p. 174.

12. Scheer and Rankin, *op. cit.*, p. 432.

13. H. F. Rankin, *The American Revolution*, London, 1964, p. 292.

14. B. Davis, *The Cowpens–Guildford Courthouse Campaign*, Philadelphia, 1962, p. 56.

15. See particularly P. Miller, 'From the Covenant to the Revival' in J. W. Smith and A. L. Jamison, *Religion in American Life*, vol. 1, Princeton, 1961.

16. *Ibid.*, p. 333.

17. *Ibid.*, p. 335.

18. *Ibid.*, p. 338.

19. *Ibid.*, p. 333.

20. S. Hook (ed.), *The Essential Works of Thomas Paine*, New York, 1969, p. 37.
21. Scheer and Rankin, *op. cit.*, p. 428.
22. *Ibid.*
23. H. M. Ward, *The Department of War 1781–95*, Pittsburgh, 1972, p. 17.
24. E. Wright, *Fabric of Freedom 1763–1800*, London, 1960, p. 147.
25. E. F. Brown, *Joseph Hawley, Colonial Radical*, Columbia, 1931, p. 158.
26. Commager and Morris, *op. cit.*, p. 44.
27. *Ibid.*, p. 155.
28. *Ibid.*, pp. 152–3.
29. J. S. Littell, *Alexander Graydon, Memoirs of his own Time*, Philadelphia, 1846, pp. 137–8.
30. Commager and Morris, *op. cit.*, pp. 105–6.
31. *Ibid.*, p. 390.
32. *Ibid.*, p. 393.
33. *Ibid.*, p. 377.
34. *Ibid.*, p. 482.
35. *Ibid.*, p. 504.
36. Rankin, *op. cit.*, p. 280.
37. Greene, *op. cit.*, p. 293.
38. J. R. Western, 'The American and French Revolutions' in *The New Cambridge Modern History*, vol. 8, p. 195.
39. E. Robson, *The American Revolution 1763–83*, London, 1955, p. 161.
40. Hook, *op. cit.*, p. 105. Italics in the original.
41. Commager and Morris, *op. cit.*, p. 482.
42. *Ibid.*, p. 153.
43. *Ibid.*, p. 215.
44. *Ibid.*, p. 419.
45. Littell, *op. cit.*, p. 149.
46. Commager and Morris, *op. cit.*, p. 479.
47. *Ibid.*, p. 481.
48. M. F. Treacy, *Prelude to Yorktown*, Chapel Hill, 1963, p. 33.
49. Rankin, *op. cit.*, p. 101.
50. *Ibid.*, pp. 152–3.
51. Mitchell, *op. cit.*, p. 177.

52. Rankin, *op. cit.*, pp. 174–5.
53. Treacy, *op. cit.*, p. 212, n. 17.

CHAPTER 4

1. See R. Debray, *Revolution in the Revolution?*, London, 1968.
2. A. Saitta (ed.), *Babeuf, Le Tribun du Peuple 1794–6*, Paris, 1969, p. 207.
3. G. Rudé, *Revolutionary Europe 1783–1815*, London, 1964, p. 96.
4. J. Leverrier, *La Naissance de l'Armée Nationale 1789–94*, Paris, 1939, p. 38.
5. *Ibid.*, p. 77.
6. *Ibid.*, p. 57.
7. A. Soboul, *Les Soldats de l'An II*, Paris, 1959, p. 74.
8. *Ibid.*, p. 63.
9. Leverrier, *op. cit.*, p. 52.
10. G. Walter, *Histoire des Jacobins*, Paris, 1946, p. 66.
11. Leverrier, *op. cit.*, p. 155.
12. Soboul, *op. cit.*, p. 29.
13. Leverrier, *op. cit.*, p. 79.
14. *Ibid.*, p. 94.
15. *Ibid.*, p. 93.
16. *Ibid.*, p. 83.
17. S. F. Scott, 'The French Revolution and the Professionalisation of the French Officer Corps' in M. Janowitz and J. van Doorn (eds), *On Military Ideology*, Rotterdam, 1971, p. 27.
18. *Ibid.*, p. 33.
19. Soboul, *op. cit.*, p. 57.
20. Leverrier, *op. cit.*, p. 60.
21. Soboul, *op. cit.*, p. 55.
22. Leverrier, *op. cit.*, p. 62.
23. Soboul, *op. cit.*, p. 171.
24. Leverrier, *op. cit.*, p. 110.
25. S. F. Scott, 'The Regeneration of the Line Army during the French Revolution' in *Journal of Modern History*, September 1970, p. 329.
26. *Ibid.*, p. 308. He gives the following figures for the average strength per infantry regiment: 1786—1,155; 1787—1,130;

1788—1,104; 1789—1,068; 1790—909; 1791—1,051; 1792—1,409.

27. J. Godechot, *La Pensée Révolutionnaire 1780–99*, Paris, 1964, pp. 166–70.
28. Soboul, *op. cit.*, p. 113.
29. S. Lytle, 'Robespierre, Danton and the Levée en Masse' in *Journal of Modern History*, December, 1958, p. 327.
30. Leverrier, *op. cit.*, p. 123.
31. *Ibid.*, p. 124.
32. G. Lefebvre, *The French Revolution 1793–99*, London, 1964, p. 66.
33. See J. F. C. Fuller, *The Conduct of War 1789–1961*, London, 1962, pp. 26–41.
34. J. M. Thompson (ed.), *French Revolutionary Documents 1789–94*, Oxford 1948, p. 256.
35. Soboul, *op. cit.*, p. 200.
36. See, for example, R. R. Palmer, *Twelve Who Ruled*, Princeton, 1941, pp. 177–201.
37. M. Bouloiseau, *Le Comité de Salut Public*, Paris, 1968, p. 72.
38. Palmer, *op. cit.*, p. 183.

CHAPTER 5

1. C. de Grunwald, *Baron Stein*, London, 1936, p. 140.
2. G. A. Craig, *The Politics of the Prussian Army 1640–1945*, London, 1964, p. 37.
3. *Ibid.*, p. 41.
4. Grunwald, *op. cit.*, p. 108.
5. *Ibid.*
6. Craig, *op. cit.*, p. 40.
7. W. M. Simon, *The Failure of the Prussian Reform Movement 1807–19*, Cornell, 1955, p. 7.
8. Grunwald, *op. cit.*, p. 114.
9. For a detailed treatment of this question, see particularly K. Demeter, *The German Officer-Corps in Society and State 1650–1945*, London, 1965.
10. E. J. Hobsbawm, *The Age of Revolution 1789–1848*, London, 1962, p. 182.
11. Grunwald, *op. cit.*, p. 111.

12. Simon, *op. cit.*, p. 33.
13. *Ibid.*, p. 53.
14. *Ibid.*, p. 63.
15. G. Ritter, *The Sword and the Sceptre*, London, 1972, vol. 1, p. 51.
16. G. S. Ford, 'Boyen's Military Law' in *American Historical Review*, vol. 20, p. 533.
17. Craig, *op. cit.*, p. 23.
18. R. Parkinson, *Clausewitz*, London, 1970, p. 107.
19. W. O. Shanahan, *Prussian Military Reforms 1786–1813*, New York, 1945, p. 47.
20. *Ibid.*, p. 104.
21. *Ibid.*, p. 120.
22. Craig, *op. cit.*, p. 58.
23. Grunwald, *op. cit.*, p. 229.
24. Shanahan, *op. cit.*, p. 197.
25. *Ibid.*, p. 121.
26. *Ibid.*, p. 204.
27. Simon, *op. cit.*, p. 86.
28. Shanahan, *op. cit.*, p. 186.
29. Gomez de Arteche, cited in G. H. Lovell, *Napoleon and the Birth of Modern Spain*, New York, 1965, vol. 2, p. 717.
30. C. Petrie, *Wellington: a Reassessment*, London, 1958, pp. 73, 76–8.
31. R. A. Leonard, *A Short Guide to Clausewitz on War*, London, 1967, p. 175.
32. Parkinson, *op. cit.*, p. 135.
33. Simon, *op. cit.*, p. 170.
34. Shanahan, *op. cit.*, p. 187, n. 27.
35. Craig, *op. cit.*, p. 47.

CHAPTER 6

1. Between 1804 and 1814 some 2,400,000 men were conscripted into the Imperial armies 'of whom very few returned home before the fall of the regime'. R. Girardet, *La Société Militaire dans la France Contemporaine*, Paris, 1953, p. 15.
2. J. Bouillon, 'Les Démocrates et l'Armée aux Elections de 1849' in *L'Armée et la Seconde République*, Paris, 1955, p. 115.

3. C. Seignebos, *La Révolution de 1848 et le Second Empire*, Paris, 1921, p. 198.

4. *Ibid.*, pp. 203–4.

5. R. D. Challener, *The French Theory of the Nation in Arms*, New York, 1965, p. 143.

6. J. Desmarest, *Évolution de la France Contemporaine: la France de 1870*, Paris, 1970, p. 333.

7. *Ibid.*, pp. 354–5.

8. L. Thiriaux, *La Garde Nationale Mobile de 1870*, Brussels, 1909, pp. 21–2.

9. Challener, *op. cit.*, p. 24.

10. *Ibid.*, p. 27.

11. M. Howard, *The Franco-Prussian War*, London, 1967, p. 236.

12. J. Bruhat, *et. al.*, *La Commune de 1871* (second edition), Paris, 1970, p. 305.

13. *Ibid.*, p. 313.

14. *Ibid.*, p. 73.

15. Howard, *op. cit.*, p. 241.

16. Thiriaux, *op. cit.*, p. 157.

17. Howard, *op. cit.*, p. 242.

18. Thiriaux, *op. cit.*, p. 68.

19. Howard, *op. cit.*, p. 249.

20. *Ibid.*, p. 240.

21. Thiriaux, *op. cit.*, p. 59.

22. Howard, *op. cit.*, p. 252.

23. G. S. Mason, *The Paris Commune*, New York, 1930, p. 88.

24. F. Jellinek, *The Paris Commune of 1871*, London, 1937, p. 68.

25. Bruhat, *et. al.*, *op. cit.*, p. 83.

26. Mason, *op. cit.*, p. 115.

27. S. Edwards, *The Paris Commune 1871*, London, 1971, p. 127.

28. Bruhat, *et. al.*, *op. cit.*, p. 256.

29. A. Decouffle, *La Commune de Paris (1871): Révolution populaire et Pouvoir révolutionnaire*, Paris, 1969, p. 125.

30. *Ibid.*, p. 136.

31. *Ibid.*, p. 143.

32. *Ibid.*, p. 172.

33. *Ibid.*, p. 128.
34. *Ibid.*, p. 139.
35. *Ibid.*, p. 161.
36. Jellinek, *op. cit.*, p. 276.
37. Jellinek, *op. cit.*, p. 177.

CHAPTER 7

1. L. Trotsky, *Terrorism and Communism* (1920), Ann Arbor, 1969, p. 80.
2. E. H. Carr, *The Bolshevik Revolution 1917–23*, London, 1966, vol. 2, p. 37.
3. From figures in the Archives of the Provisional Government, Trotsky says that agrarian unrest was prevalent in 34 out of 624 counties in March, 174 in April, 236 in May, 280 in June and 235 in July. By autumn 482 were involved, 77 per cent of the whole of Russia and 91 per cent of the crucial western and central regions. L. Trotsky, *History of the Russian Revolution*, London, 1965, pp. 415 and 859.
4. *Ibid.*, p. 864.
5. *Ibid.*, pp. 868–9.
6. *Ibid.*, p. 877.
7. Carr, *op. cit.*, p. 42.
8. Only in two provinces was the average *per capita* increase more than half a *desyatin* (1 *des.* = 2·66 acres). And almost a half of the provinces showed an average *per capita* increase of less than 0·25 *des.* The increase generally ranged between 0·09 and 0·33 *des.* As regards levelling down, it is revealing to note that whilst in 1917 171,730 households (40·19 per cent) had sown up to 2 *des.* of crops, the figure for 1919 was 229,062 households (49·43 per cent). Correspondingly, the number of households sowing between 10 and 25 *des.* dropped from 20,610 to 7·149. T. Shanin, *The Awkward Class*, London, 1972, pp. 53 and 153.
9. Carr, *op. cit.*, p. 39.
10. L. Trotsky, *Écrits Militaires*, Paris, 1967, vol. 1, p. 59.
11. Trotsky, *Russian Revolution, op. cit.*, pp. 283–4.
12. Carr, *op. cit.*, p. 56.
13. *Ibid*, pp. 153–4.
14. Shanin, *op. cit.*, p. 147.

15. J. M. Meijer, 'Town and Country in the Civil War' in R. Pipes (ed.), *Revolutionary Russia*, London, 1968, p. 268 n.
16. *Ibid*, pp. 276–7.
17. Shanin, *op. cit.*, p. 147 n.
18. J. M. Meijer (ed.), *The Trotsky Papers*, The Hague, 1964, p. 410 n.
19. Meijer, 'Town and Country', *op. cit.*, p. 268.
20. *Trotsky Papers*, *op. cit.*, p. 221.
21. *Ibid.*, p. 309.
22. Trotsky, *Terrorism and Communism*, *op. cit.*, p. 115.
23. Maréchal Toukhatchevski, *Écrits sur la Guerre*, Paris, 1967, p. 177.
24. R. Luxembourg, *The Russian Revolution and Leninism and Marxism*, Ann Arbor, 1961, p. 46.
25. D. Footman, *The Civil War in Russia*, London, 1961, p. 135.
26. J. Erickson, 'The Origins of the Red Army' in Pipes, *op. cit.*, p. 233. This particular section relies heavily on Mr Erickson's detailed researches.
27. *Ibid.*, p. 242.
28. *Ibid.*, p. 249.
29. Carr, *op. cit.*, p. 59.
30. *Ibid.*, p. 153.
31. *Trotsky Papers*, *op. cit.*, p. 331.
32. L. Trotsky, *My Life*, New York, 1970, p. 437.
33. Trotsky, *Écrits Militaires*, *op. cit.*, pp. 160–61.
34. *Ibid.*, p. 223.
35. *Ibid.*, p. 37.
36. Erickson, *op. cit.*, p. 249.
37. Footman, *op. cit.*, pp. 144–5.
38. *Trotsky Papers*, *op. cit.*, p. 353.
39. J. Erickson, *The Soviet High Command*, London, 1962, p. 23.
40. *Trotsky Papers*, *op. cit.*, pp. 389–93.
41. *Ibid.*, p. 433.
42. *Ibid.*, p. 653.
43. Footman, *op. cit.*, pp. 73–4.
44. *Trotsky Papers*, *op. cit.*, p. 601.
45. Footman, *op. cit.*, p. 267.
46. *Ibid.*, p. 287.
47. *Ibid.*, pp. 144–5.

48. Erickson, 'Origins', *op. cit.*, p. 240.
49. See *Ibid.*, pp. 246–7.
50. *Ibid.*, p. 230.
51. Trotsky, *Écrits Militaires*, *op. cit.*, p. 35.
52. Bukharin and Preobrazhensky, *The ABC of Communism*, London, 1969, p. 267.
53. Toukhatchevski, *op. cit.*, p. 152.
54. Erickson, *High Command*, *op. cit.*, p. 33. Whilst between 1918 and 1920 the Soviet officer courses had produced only 39,914 new officers.
55. *Ibid.*, p. 46 n.
56. I. Deutscher, *The Prophet Armed* (*Trotsky 1879–1921*), London, 1963, p. 408.
57. *Trotsky Papers*, *op. cit.*, p. 107.
58. *Ibid.*, p. 205.
59. With regard to the influential role of the Imperial officers it is interesting to note that of the hundred authors of the Service Regulations of 1929, seventy-nine had been officers of the Imperial Army. R. Garthoff, *How Russia Wages War*, London, 1954, p. 21.
60. *Trotsky Papers*, *op. cit.*, p. 497.
61. Footman, *op. cit.*, p. 148.
62. *Trotsky Papers*, *op. cit.*, p. 797.
63. Carr, *op. cit.*, vol. 1, p. 175.
64. Trotsky, *Terrorism and Communism*, *op. cit.*, p. 307.
65. Trotsky, *My Life*, *op. cit.*, p. 411.
66. *Trotsky Papers*, *op. cit.*, p. 71.
67. *Ibid.*, p. 323.
68. Trotsky, *Écrits Militaires*, *op. cit.*, p. 307.
69. Trotsky, *My Life*, *op. cit.*, p. 430.
70. *Ibid.*, p. 400.
71. Footman, *op. cit.*, p. 152.
72. Erickson, *High Command*, *op. cit.*, p. 42.
73. *Trotsky Papers*, *op. cit.*, p. 79.
74. *Ibid.*, p. 117.
75. *Ibid.*, pp. 120–21.
76. *Ibid.*, p. 331.

CHAPTER 8

1. S. Swarup, *A Study of the Chinest Communist Movement*, Oxford, 1966, p. 80.
2. J. Guillermaz, *A History of the Chinese Communist Party 1921–49*, London, 1972, p. 83.
3. *Ibid.*, p. 137.
4. S. Schram, *Mao Tse-tung*, London, 1966, p. 140.
5. *Ibid.*, p. 135.
6. Guillermaz, *op. cit.*, p. 163.
7. *Ibid.*, p. 175.
8. Schram, *op. cit.*, p. 142.
9. F. F. Liu, *A Military History of Modern China*, Princeton, 1956, p. 19.
10. J. Gittings, 'The Chinese Army' in J. Gray (ed.), *Modern China's Search for a Political Form*, London, 1969, p. 194.
11. E. R. Wolf, *Peasant Wars of the Twentieth Century*, London, 1971, pp. 130–1.
12. Swarup, *op. cit.*, p. 57.
13. Mao Tse-tung, *Selected Works*, vol. I, Peking, 1964, pp. 23–4.
14. Guillermaz, *op. cit.*, p. 149.
15. Mao Tse-tung, *Selected Military Writings*, Peking, 1966, p. 13.
16. *Ibid.*, p. 21.
17. *Loc. cit.*
18. *Ibid.*, pp. 27–8.
19. E. Snow, *Red Star Over China*, New York, 1939, p. 159.
20. *Ibid.*, pp. 274 and 277.
21. *Ibid.*, p. 274.
22. *Selected Works*, vol. I, pp. 143–4.
23. *Selected Military Writings*, p. 139.
24. Swarup, *op. cit.*, p. 123.
25. Guillermaz, *op. cit.*, p. 170.
26. Swarup, *op. cit.*, pp. 129–30.
27. Guillermaz, *op. cit.*, pp. 211–12.
28. C. Johnson, *Peasant Nationalism and Communist Power*, Stanford, 1962, p. 12.
29. J. L. S. Girling, *People's War*, London, 1969, p. 94.
30. Guillermaz, *op. cit.*, p. 339.

31. Swarup, *op. cit.*, p. 127.
32. *Ibid.*, p. 134.
33. *Ibid.*, p. 163.
34. Wolf, *op. cit.*, pp. 148 and 149.
35. Guillermaz, *op. cit.*, p. 430.
36. J. Chen, *Mao and the Chinese Revolution*, London, 1965, p. 297.
37. *Selected Works*, vol. I, p. 106.
38. Snow, *op. cit.*, p. 158.
39. *Selected Works*, vol. I, p. 147.
40. *Selected Military Writings*, op. cit., p. 94.
41. *Ibid.*, pp. 229 and 261.
42. Johnson, *op. cit.*, pp. 53–4.
43. Chen, *op. cit.*, p. 254.
44. *Selected Works*, vol. I, p. 114.
45. *Selected Military Writings*, p. 141.
46. Guillermaz, *op. cit.*, p. 329.
47. S. Schram, *The Political Thought of Mao Tse-tung*, London, 1969, p. 290.
48. B. Compton (ed.), *Mao's China: Party Reform Documents 1942–44*, Seattle, 1952, p. 240.
49. *Ibid.*, pp. 167, 171 and 175.
50. Guillermaz, *op. cit.*, p. 211.

Bibliography

Alavi, H., 'Peasants and Revolution' in *The Socialist Register 1965*, Merlin Press, London.

Andrzejewski, S., *Military Organisation and Society*, Routledge and Kegan Paul, London, 1954.

Anon, Introduction to Tukhachevsky, *New Left Review*, No. 55, May–June 1965.

Apter, D. E. (ed.), *Ideology and Discontent*, The Free Press of Glencoe, New York, 1964.

Arendt, H., *On Revolution*, Faber and Faber, London, 1963.

Ashley, M., *The Greatness of Oliver Cromwell*, Macmillan, London, 1957.

Azema, J. P. and Winock, M., *Les Communards*, Editions du Seuil, Paris, 1970.

Bailyn, B., *Pamphlets of the American Revolution*, Belknap Press, Cambridge (Mass.), 1965.

Bass, R. D., *Swamp Fox: The Life and Campaigns of General Francis Marion*, Alvin Redman, London, 1960.

Belden, J., *China Shakes the World*, Victor Gollancz, London, 1950.

Bienen, H., *The Military Intervenes*, Russell Sage, New York, 1968.

Bill, A. H., *Valley Forge, the Making of an Army*, Harper Bros., New York, 1952.

Billias, G. A. (ed.), *George Washington's Generals*, William Morris, New York, 1964.

Boffa, G. (ed.), *Les Bolshéviques et la Révolution d'Octobre*, François Maspéro, Paris, 1964.

Bouchard, G., *Prieur de le Côte d'Or*, Clavreuil, Paris, 1946.

Bouloiseau, M., *Le Comité de Salut Public*, Presses Universitaires de France, Paris, 1968.

Brinton, C. C., *The Anatomy of Revolution*, Vintage Books, New York, 1952.

—— *The Jacobins*, Macmillan, New York, 1930.

Brown, E. F., *Joseph Hawley, Colonial Radical*, Columbia University Press, New York 1931.

Bruhat, J., Dautrey, J. and Tersen, E., *La Commune de 1871* (second edition), Editions Sociales, Paris, 1970.

Calvert, P., *Revolution*, Macmillan, London, 1970.

Carr, E. H., *The Bolshevik Revolution 1917–23*, 3 vols, Penguin Books, Harmondsworth, 1966.

—— *1917, Before and After*, Macmillan, London, 1969.

Cassou, J., *Saint-Just: Pages Choisis*, Editions du Point du Jour, Paris, 1947.

Challener, R. D., *The French Theory of the Nation in Arms*, Russell and Russell, New York, 1965.

Chalmin, P., *L'Officier Français de 1815 à 1870*, Marcel Rivière, Paris, 1957.

Charnay, J. P., *Société militaire et Suffrage politique en France depuis 1789*, Presses Universitaires de France, Paris, 1964.

Chassin, L. M., *The Communist Conquest of China*, Weidenfeld and Nicolson, London, 1966.

Chen, J., *Mao and the Chinese Revolution*, Oxford University Press, London, 1965.

—— *Yuan Shih-kai*, Allen and Unwin, London, 1961.

Chorley, K., *Armies and the Art of Revolution*, Faber and Faber, London, 1943.

Cobban, A., *A History of Modern France* (second edition), 3 vols, Penguin Books, Harmondsworth, 1968.

Commager, H. and Morris, R., *The Spirit of '76*, 2 vols, The Bobs-Merrill Company, New York, 1958.

Compton, B. (ed.), *Mao's China: Party Reform Documents 1942–44*, Washington University Press, Seattle, 1952.

Craig, G. A., *The Politics of the Prussian Army 1640–1945*, Oxford University Press, London, 1964.

Cunliffe, M., *George Washington, Man and Monument*, Collins, London, 1959.

Dautry, J., *La Révolution de 1848 en France*, Editions Hier et Aujourdhui, Paris, 1948.

Davies, G., 'The Parliamentary Armies under the Earl of Essex' in *English Historical Review*, vol. 49, 1934.

Davis, B., *The Cowpens–Guildford Courthouse Campaign*, J. B. Lippincott Company, Philadelphia, 1962.

Decouffle, A., *La Commune de Paris (1871): Révolution populaire et pouvoir révolutionnaire*, Editions Cujas, Paris, 1969.

Demeter, K., *The German Officer-Corps in Society and State 1650–1945*, Weidenfeld and Nicolson, London, 1965.

Desmarest, J., *Évolution de la France Contemporaine: la France de 1870*, Hachette, Paris, 1970.

Deutscher, I., *Trotsky 1879–1940*, Oxford University Press, London, 1971.

Dommanget, M., *Saint-Just*, Editions du Cercle, Paris, 1971.

Duveau, G., *1848*, Gallimard, Paris, 1965.

Earle E. M. (ed.), *Makers of Modern Strategy*, Atheneum, New York, 1966.

Eckstein, H. (ed.), *Internal War*, Free Press of Glencoe, New York, 1964.

Edwards, S., *The Paris Commune 1871*, Eyre and Spottiswoode, London, 1971.

Elliott-Bateman, M., *Defeat in the East*, Oxford University Press, London, 1967.

Erickson, E. J., *The Soviet High Command*, Macmillan, London, 1962.

Finer, S., *The Man on Horseback*, Pall Mall, London, 1962.

Firth, C., *Cromwell's Army*, Methuen, London, 1962.

Florinsky, M. T., *The End of the Russian Empire*, Collier Books, New York, 1971.

Footman, D., *The Civil War in Russia*, Faber, London, 1961.

Ford, G. S., 'Boyen's Military Law' in *American Historical Review*, vol. 20, 1915.

Forster, R. and Greene, J. P. (eds), *Preconditions for Revolution in Early Modern Europe*, Johns Hopkins Press, Baltimore, 1970.

Freeman, D. S., *Washington* (abridged version), Eyre and Spottiswoode, London, 1970.

Friedrich, C. J. (ed.), *Nomos VII: Revolution*, Atherton Press, New York, 1966.

Fuller, J. F. C., *The Conduct of War 1789–1961*, Eyre and Spottiswoode, London, 1962.

Garder, M., *A History of the Soviet Army*, Pall Mall, London, 1966.

Garthoff, R., *How Russia Makes War*, Allen and Unwin, London, 1954.

Gelder, S. (ed.), *The Chinese Communists*, Victor Gollancz, London, 1946.

Girardet, R., *La Société Militaire dans la France Contemporaine*, Plon, Paris, 1953.

Girling, J. L. S., *People's War*, Allen and Unwin, London, 1969.

Gittings, J., *The Role of the Chinese Army*, Oxford University Press, London, 1967.

Godechot, J., *La Pensée Révolutionnaire 1780–99*, Colin, Paris, 1969.

Görlitz, W., *The German General Staff*, Hollis and Carter, London, 1953.

Gottschalk, L. and Maddox, M., *Lafayette in the French Revolution*, University of Chicago Press, Chicago, 1969.

Gray, J. (ed.), *Modern China's Search for a Political Form*, Oxford University Press, London, 1969.

Greene, F. V., *The Revolutionary War of the United States*, John Murray, London, 1911.

Griffith, S., *The Chinese People's Liberation Army*, Weidenfeld and Nicolson, London, 1968.

Grunwald, C. De, *Baron Stein*, Jonathan Cape, London, 1936.

Guillermaz, J., *A History of the Chinese Communist Party, 1921–49*, Methuen, London, 1972.

Hamilton, L. (ed.), *Gerrard Winstanley: Selections from his Works*, Cressett Press, New York, 1944.

Harris, N., *Beliefs in Society: The Problem of Ideology*, C. A. Watts, London, 1968.

Hatch, L. C., *The Administration of the American Revolutionary Army*, Harvard University Press, New York, 1904.

Heilbrun, O., *Partisan Warfare*, Allen and Unwin, London, 1964.

Hill, C., *The Century of Revolution*, Sphere Books, London, 1970.

—— *God's Englishman: Oliver Cromwell and the English Revolution*, Weidenfeld and Nicolson, London, 1970.

—— *Puritanism and Revolution*, Panther Books, London, 1968.

—— *Society and Puritanism in Pre-revolutionary England*, Panther Books, London, 1969.

—— *Lenin and the Russian Revolution*, English Universities Press, London, 1968.

Hobsbawm, E. J., *Primitive Rebels*, Manchester University Press, Manchester, 1962.

—— *The Age of Revolution 1789–1848*, Weidenfeld and Nicolson, London, 1962.

Hook, S. (ed.), *The Essential Works of Thomas Paine*, Mentor Books, New York, 1969.

Hooker, R. J. (ed.), *The American Revolution: the Search for a Meaning*, J. Wiley and Sons, New York, 1970.

Howard, M., *The Franco-Prussian War*, Fontana Library, London, 1967.

—— (ed.), *The Theory and Practice of War*, Cassell, London, 1965.

—— (ed.), *Soldiers and Governments*, Eyre and Spottiswoode, London, 1957.

Howe, J. R. (ed.), *The Role of Ideology in the American Revolution*, Holt, Rinehart and Winston, New York, 1970.

Huntington, S., *The Soldier and the State: the Theory and Practice of Civil–Military Relations*, Harvard University Press, Harvard, 1957.

Isaacs, H., *The Tragedy of the Chinese Revolution*, Stanford University Press, Stanford, 1961.

Janowitz, M. and Van Doorn, J. (eds), *On Military Ideology*, Mouton, The Hague, 1966.

Jacobs, W. D., *Frunze, the Soviet Clausewitz*, Nijhoff, The Hague, 1969.

Jellinek, F., *The Paris Commune of 1871*, Victor Gollancz, London, 1937.

Johnson, C., *Peasant Nationalism and Communist Power*, Stanford University Press, Stanford, 1962.

Johnson, C., *Revolutionary Change*, University of London Press, London, 1968.

Katkov, G., *Russia 1917*, Fontana Library, London, 1969.
Kochan, L., *Russia in Revolution*, Weidenfeld and Nicolson, London, 1966.
Kumar, K., *Revolution*, Weidenfeld and Nicolson, London, 1971.

Lamont, W., *Godly Rule*, Macmillan, London, 1969.
Lefebvre, G., *Napoleon* (2 vols), Routledge and Kegan Paul, London, 1969.
—— *The Coming of the French Revolution*, Princeton University Press, Princeton, 1947.
—— *The French Revolution 1789–99* (2 vols), Routledge and Kegan Paul, London, 1964.
Leonard, E. G., *L'Armée et ses Problèmes au 18ème Siècle*, Plon, Paris, 1958.
Leonard, R. A. (ed.), *A Short Guide to Clausewitz on War*, Weidenfeld and Nicolson, London, 1967.
Leverrier, J., *La Naissance de l'Armée Nationale 1789–94*, Editions Sociales Internationales, Paris, 1939.
Liddell-Hart, B. (ed.), *The Russian Red Army*, Weidenfeld and Nicolson, London, 1956.
Littell, J. B. (ed.), *Alexander Graydon: Memoirs of his own Time*, Lindsay and Blakiston, Philadelphia, 1846.
Liu, F. F., *A Military History of Modern China*, Princeton University Press, Princeton, 1956.
Lovell, G. H., *Napoleon and the Birth of Modern Spain* (2 vols), New York University Press, New York, 1965.
Luxembourg, R., *The Russian Revolution and Leninism or Marxism*, University of Michigan Press, Ann Arbor, 1961.
Lytle, S., 'Robespierre, Danton and the Levée en Masse' in *Journal of Modern History*, vol. 30, 1958.

Mao Tse-tung, *Selected Military Writings*, Foreign Languages Press, Peking, 1966.
—— *Selected Works* (vols 1 and 2), Foreign Languages Press, Peking, 1964.

Marx, K., *The Civil War in France*, Progress Publishers, Moscow, 1968.

Mason, G. S., *The Paris Commune*, Macmillan, New York, 1930.

Meijer, J. M. (ed.), *The Trotsky Papers* (vol. 1), Mouton, The Hague, 1964.

Millis, W., *Arms and Men: a Study in American Military History*, Mentor Books, New York, 1958.

Mitchell, B., *Alexander Hamilton: Youth to Maturity 1755–88*, Macmillan, New York, 1957.

Moore, B., *Social Origins of Totalitarianism and Democracy*, Allen Lane, London, 1967.

O'Ballance, E., *The Red Army*, Faber and Faber, London, 1964.

Osanka, F. M. (ed.), *Modern Guerrilla Warfare*, The Free Press of Glencoe, New York, 1962.

Palmer, J. M., *General von Steuben*, Yale University Press, New Haven, 1937.

Palmer, R. R., *The Ages of Democratic Revolution* (vol. 1), Princeton University Press, Princeton, 1959.

—— *Twelve Who Ruled*, Princeton University Press, Princeton, 1941.

Paret, P., *Yorck and the Era of Prussian Reform*, Princeton University Press, Princeton, 1966.

Parkinson, R., *Clausewitz*, Wayland Publishers, London, 1970.

Peckham, H. H., *The War for Independence*, University of Chicago Press, Chicago, 1958.

Pernoud, G. and Plaissier, S., *The French Revolution*, Allen and Unwin, London, 1961.

Petegorsky, D. W., *Left-Wing Democracy in the English Civil War*, Victor Gollancz, London, 1940.

Petrie, C., *Wellington: a Reassessment*, Barrie, London, 1956.

Pipes, R. (ed.), *Revolutionary Russia*, Oxford University Press, London, 1968.

Pole, J. R., *The Revolution in America*, Macmillan, London, 1970.

Pomeroy, W. J., *Guerrilla and Counter-Guerrilla Warfare*, International Publishers, New York, 1964.

Pomeroy, W. J. (ed.), *Guerrilla Warfare and Marxism*, Lawrence and Wishart, London, 1970.

Preston, R. A., Werner, H. O. and Wise, S. F., *Men in Arms: a History of Warfare and its Interrelationships with Western Society*, Thames and Hudson, London, 1962.

Rankin, H., *The American Revolution*, Secker and Warburg, London, 1964.

Reed, J. F., *Campaign to Valley Forge*, University of Pennsylvania Press, Philadelphia, 1965.

Reinhard, M., *Le Grand Carnot* (2 vols), Hachette, Paris, 1950–52.

Ritter, G., *The Sword and the Sceptre: the Problem of Militarism in Germany* (2 vols), Allen Lane, London, 1972.

Roberts, M., *Gustavus Adolphus: a History of Sweden 1611–32* (2 vols), Longmans, London, 1958.

Robson, E., *The American Revolution 1763–83*, The Blatchworth Press, London, 1955.

Ropp, T., *War in the Modern World*, Collier Books, New York, 1962.

Rosinski, H., *The German Army*, Pall Mall Press, London, 1966.

Rudé, G., *Revolutionary Europe 1788–1815*, Fontana Library, London, 1966.

Scheer, G. E. and Rankin, H. (eds), *Rebels and Redcoats*, Mentor Books, New York, 1957.

Schram, S., *Mao Tse-tung*, Penguin Books, Harmondsworth, 1966.

—— *The Political Thought of Mao-Tse-tung*, Penguin Books, Harmondsworth, 1969.

Scott, S. F., 'The Regeneration of the Line Army during the French Revolution' in *Journal of Modern History*, 1970.

Serge, V., *Year One of the Russian Revolution*, Allen Lane, London, 1972.

Shanahan, W. O., *Prussian Military Reforms 1786–1813*, Columbia University Press, New York, 1945.

Shanin, T., *The Awkward Class*, Oxford University Press, London, 1972.

—— (ed.), *Peasants and Peasant Societies*, Penguin Books, Harmondsworth, 1971.

Shapiro, L. and Reddaway, P. (eds), *Lenin: a Reappraisal*, Pall Mall, London, 1967.

Shub, D., *Lenin*, Penguin Books, Harmondworth, 1969.

Simon, W. M., *The Failure of the Prussian Reform Movement 1807-19*, Cornell University Press, Cornell, 1955.

Smedley, A., *China Fights Back*, Victor Gollancz, London, 1938.

—— *The Great Road*, Calder, London, 1958.

Smith, J. W. and Jamison, A. L. (eds), *Religion in American Life* (vol. 1), Princeton University Press, Princeton, 1961.

Snow, E., *Red Star Over China*, Garden City Publishing Company, New York, 1939.

Soboul, A., *Les Soldats de l'An II*, Le Club du Livre Français, Paris, 1959.

Solt, L. F., *Saints in Arms: Puritanism and Democracy in Cromwell's Army*, Stanford University Press, Stanford, 1959.

Starkley, M. L., *A Little Rebellion*, Knopf, New York, 1955.

Stille, G. J., *Major-General Anthony Wayne and the Pennsylvania Line*, J. B. Lippincott, Philadelphia, 1893.

Swarup, S., *A Study of the Chinese Communist Movement*, Clarendon Press, Oxford, 1966.

Taber, R., *The War of the Flea: A Study of Guerrilla Warfare Theory and Practice*, Paladin Books, London, 1970.

Thiriaux, L., *La Garde Nationale Mobile de 1870*, Edition de l'Expansion Belge, Brussels, 1909.

Thompson, J. M. (ed.), *French Revolutionary Documents*, Basil Blackwell, Oxford, 1948.

Toukhatchevski, M., *Écrits sur la Guerre*, Plon, Paris, 1967.

Treacy, M. F., *Prelude to Yorktown*, University of North Carolina Press, Chapel Hill, 1963.

Trotsky, L., *Écrits Militaires* (vol. 1), L'Herne, Paris, 1967.

—— *History of the Russian Revolution*, Victor Gollancz, London, 1965.

—— *Military Writings*, Merit Books, New York, 1969.

—— *My Life*, Pathfinder Press, New York, 1970.

—— *Terrorism and Communism*, University of Michigan Press, Ann Arbor, 1969.

Various, *L'Armée et la Seconde République*, Bibliothèque de la Révolution de 1848, La Roche-Sur-Yon, 1955.

Vagts, A., *A History of Militarism: Civilian and Military*, Hollis and Carter, London, 1959.

Vigier, P., *La Seconde République*, Presses Universitaires Françaises, Paris, 1967.

Walter, G., *Histoire des Jacobins*, Aimery Somogy, Paris, 1946.

Walzer, M., 'Puritanism as a Revolutionary Ideology', *History and Theory*, vol. 3, 1964.

—— *The Revolution of the Saints: a Study in the Origins of Radical Politics*, Weidenfeld and Nicolson, London, 1966.

Watson, S. J., *Carnot*, Bodley Head, London, 1954.

Ward, H. M., *The Department of War 1781–95*, Pittsburgh University Press, Pittsburgh, 1962.

Whittemore, C. P., *A General of the Revolution: John Sullivan of New Hampshire*, Columbia University Press, New York, 1961.

Wilkinson, S., *The French Army Before Napoleon*, Clarendon Press, Oxford, 1915.

Williams, R. L., *The French Revolution of 1870–71*, Weidenfeld and Nicolson, London, 1969.

Wintringham, T. M., *People's War*, Penguin Books, Harmondsworth, 1942.

—— *Armies of Free Men*, G. Routledge and Sons, London, 1940.

Wolfe, D. M. (ed.), *Leveller Manifestoes of the Puritan Revolution*, Humanities Press, New York, 1967.

Wolf, E. R., *Peasant Wars of the Twentieth Century*, Faber and Faber, London, 1971.

Woodhouse, A. S. P. (ed.), *Puritanism and Liberty*, J. M. Dent and Sons, London, 1965.

Wright, E., *The Fabric of Freedom*, Macmillan, London, 1965.

Wright, M. C. (ed.), *China in Revolution: the First Phase 1900–13*, Yale University Press, Yale, 1968.

Wyndham, F. and King, D., *Trotsky: a Documentary*, Allen Lane, London, 1972.

Index

E4